Comprehensive Development of the Northeast

Window to India's Act East Policy

Comprehensive Development of the Northeast

Window to India's Act East Policy

Jitesh Khosla

(Established 1870)

The United Service Institution of India

New Delhi

Vij Books
New Delhi (India)

Published by

Vij Books
(An imprint of Vij Books India Pvt Ltd)

(Publishers, Distributors & Importers)
4836/24, Ansari Road
Delhi – 110 002
Phones: 91-11-43596460
Mob: 98110 94883
e-mail: contact@vijpublishing.com
web : www.vijbooks.in

First Published in India in 2023

ISBN: 978-81-19438-69-3 (HB)
ISBN: 978-81-19438-91-4 (PB)
ISBN: 978-81-19438-04-4 (Ebook)

Disclaimer

The Views expressed and suggestions made in the Book are solely of the author in his personal capacity and do not have any official endorsement. Attributability of the contents lies purely with the author.

Contents

Foreword

India's North East has long been buffeted by conflict arising from separatist insurgency, ethnic animosities and terrorism, posing a grave internal security challenge to the nation. For nearly seven decades, maintaining peace in this sensitive region has been a major remit of the Indian security forces. However, past experience has shown that a reactive strategy based solely on armed response, may temporarily blunt the impact of separatist or identity-based aspirations but is unlikely to bring lasting peace. Therefore, a more comprehensive response to the issues and problems of the North Eastern Region is felt necessary to complement the efforts of the security forces.

The Act East Policy is unique in that it removes the North Eastern Region from the periphery of the nation's attention and makes it centre-stage. It transforms a landlocked Region to a land connected geography linked to a rapidly growing part of Asia which is also a building block of the much-heralded Asian Century. In that sense, the North Eastern Region occupies a strategic space of great importance. It is not only a bridge to South East Asia but also a means of making India's comprehensive national power being asserted in this region in an environment of cooperation and mutual benefit. The requirement is to develop a comprehensive and wide perspective and to evaluate its strengths and shortcomings. This would help develop sound strategic options while bringing lasting peace to the NE Region itself. The possibility of a confluence of the Act East Policy and the comprehensive development of the North Eastern Region, it is felt, would definitely give a new impetus to India's strategic aims in the broader South Eastern Region and beyond.

While the Indian Security forces have steadfastly countered both internal security challenges as well as external aggression in the North East, the effort of the United Services Institution is to bring together diverse streams of experience to enable a multi-disciplinary response to national security issues. With this in view, The Assam Rifles Chair of Excellence was offered to Mr Jitesh Khosla, an Indian Administrative Service officer, former Chief

Secretary of Assam and a Distinguished Fellow of the Institute. Of particular value was Mr Khosla's exposure to counter-insurgency over several decades, his understanding of both national security and development issues and a first-hand experience of the changing politics of the region through a significant part of the long and difficult road of assimilation and nation-building in the region. The wide sweep of this work and joining together of various and diverse strands that would enable the North Eastern Region to measure up to its potential in delivering the promise of the Act East Policy is extremely useful. More than anything it helps to turn the narrative of the Region from conflict to economic development and thereby hope for the future.

The USI, draws upon a deep reservoir of experience in dealing with national security issues, with a large number of experienced and distinguished persons from the Armed Forces, the Administrative Services, the Foreign Service, Central and State Police forces contributing their ideas, experience and perspectives to develop a strategic outlook for the nation in respect of national security. It continues to encourage a search for strategic and tactical options in a fast-changing world. This study attempts to enable a better understanding of India's North East, with both its strengths as well as fault lines and is a part of the effort to build a sounder foundation for national security in that region.

Maj Gen BK Sharma, AVSM, SM (Retd)**
Director General
United Service Institution of India

Introduction

The North Eastern Region of India is unique in the sense that it brings together an interplay of imperatives for nation-building, internal security, national defence as well as considerable potential for economic and diplomatic engagement, with not only India's immediate neighbours in the East, but with the South Eastern Asian region as a whole. It lies practically separated from India, save for a narrow land corridor, surrounded by several independent nation-states yet provides a geographical and cultural bridge between India and the South East Asia Region.

The North Eastern Region today comprises of 8 states of the Indian Union extending over 262,184 sq. km and comprising approximately 8 percent of India's land area and with a population of 45,772,188 (2011 Census), about 3.8 percent of its population. Of these, seven - Assam, Arunachal Pradesh, Nagaland, Manipur Tripura Meghalaya and Mizoram (often referred to as the Seven Sisters)- are located to the east of Bangladesh and the eighth, Sikkim, north of West Bengal, just at the entry to the Region. Taken together, these states display incredible geographical, social and cultural diversity. Each of these states has also had a long and distinctive history of its own. Many of the peoples inhabiting these states and the past kingdoms that dotted the Region over most of the last two millennia have had deep contact with the Southeast Asian Region as well.

Even beyond the North Easter Region, India, both as a civilisational as well as a political entity, has had long cultural and trade links with Southeast Asian countries stretching back into history. Following its own independence from colonial rule in 1947, the modern Indian state played an active role in supporting the end of colonialism and the emergence of Asian regionalism. The decades immediately post-1947 also saw war and conflict in South East Asia as many Southeast Asian countries sought to shed off colonial dominance and struggled to establish their own political and governance systems.

Post-1947, India while being engaged in the complex process of nation-building that saw the emergence of a modern, constitutionally governed, democratic nation-state that saw the North Eastern Region gradually assimilating into it, also engaged positively with the South East Asian nations. International relations post WW-II were strongly influenced by the emergence of the Cold War between the two major power Blocs led by the USA and the Soviet Union, which resulted in conflicts in the Southeast Asian region as well, with one of them, the Viet Nam War, stretching over decades. Meanwhile, India saw wars of its own with Pakistan and China. During this period, the North Eastern Region continued to be afflicted with violent separatist movements and insurgency that necessitated search for solutions that would enable assimilation while accommodating the aspirations of its peoples. The conflict and violence in the North East have been gradually abating over the past few decades but have the capacity of erupting periodically. At the time of writing, the state of Manipur is in the grip of serious ethnic violence.

The 20th Century Cold War eventually ended in the early 1990s and the Southeast Region also became peaceful. Starting in the 1980s the Southeast Asian economies combined to form the ASEAN and grew rapidly. India as the second largest growing economy in Asia realised ASEAN's importance in terms of politics, economy, and diplomacy and in 1991 launched its "Look East" policy seeking a more active engagement in Southeast Asian affairs. Over the years, India's Look East Policy has evolved into a more active "Act East Policy. However, with rapid growth of the strength and size of its economy, China also actively pursued economic and geographical domination and influence in Southeast Asia. The worsening of relations between India and China post clashes in Eastern Ladakh after nearly two decades of peace and aggressive posturing by China in the South China Sea and vis-à-vis Taiwan has led to new rivalries and security concerns in the region. Meanwhile, the war in Ukraine has triggered new international alignments and apprehensions of a New Cold War. In this backdrop, the search for regional formations that could buffer international shocks has escalated, resulting in, among other initiatives, a broader Act East Approach, with a deeper engagement both with the SE Asian Region that is contiguous to India and beyond in the Indo-Pacific Region including countries further East such as Japan, Korea, Australia etc. The dynamic of engagement is quite different for the latter and is influenced by different geo-political imperatives.

Apart from regional groupings, in today's world, geo-political dominance of a nation-state is determined by its comprehensive national power i.e., the wide-ranging capability of a country to identify, pursue and realise its strategic objectives in the international arena through a combination of its economic strength, the nature of its economic relations with other countries, strategically determined foreign policy and diplomacy, internal cohesion and stability, efficiency and effectiveness of its governance models, Its soft power in terms of social and cultural influence; its ability to acquire and apply scientific knowledge and technology for its own and common international good, and of course, military strength and reach.

As for the North East, there remains the challenge of enabling a lasting peace that could be the basis of future prosperity. However, far too long has the narrative of the Region been defined by violence and conflict. Yet considering the progress, albeit slow and frequently disrupted, the process of assimilation has made over the past several decades, there is hope for the future. This work reflects upon and seeks to bring out how, despite all kinds of challenges, the North Eastern Region of India can be empowered to be a critical element of not only India's engagement with its immediate neighbourhood but also for projection of India's comprehensive national power in Asia's SE Region. This would be an important cornerstone for enabling India to ensure its relevance effectively in the emerging complexities affecting SE Asia and even beyond in the Asia-Pacific region.

Acknowledgements

This Study forms a part of the effort of the United Services Institution of India to bring together the complex interplay of various kinds of forces - political, economic, diplomatic, military and weave together multi-dimensional strands that are relevant to and can contribute to national security in the long term. However, the mandate of the Study is wider in that it seeks to position the North Eastern Region as a bridgehead to Southeast Asia and to look at and weave together strands that would make the Region an effective player in the engagement sought to be developed through the Act East Policy. In that sense, the Study builds upon the existing reservoirs of knowledge, available to openly anyone who would care to go through them, to build a common strategy that would not only build upon the engagement sought by India's Act East Policy but also positions India as a serious player in the Region by enabling a platform that allows for India's Comprehensive National Power being projected in South East Asia in a manner that is not hegemonistic or predatory but is mutually beneficial to all.

Therefore, first and foremost, it is relevant to acknowledge that this work is based on open-source material, which is immense, easily available in the public domain. Experts, researchers, journalists and authors have done sterling work in each individual domain affecting the North East. This of course begs the question as to why the Study. Given its diversity, developing a regional perspective for the North East is akin to traversing a limitless number of steep hills and deep valleys, one after another, each actually a storehouse of knowledge in its respective field. The need to put it all together in a cohesive and comprehensible whole, while highlighting the options for the future, establishes the raison d'etre for this work.

Unfortunately, the narrative of the North East has hitherto been that of conflict. Yet a multi -dimensional perspective can help us see the grand vista that is possible and can change this narrative to a more constructive and forward looking one. While this work does not claim discovery of hitherto undiscovered ground, it hopefully provides a perspective that would capture the many facets that would leverage the Region from being an economic laggard and a security problem to be the spearhead of a constructive engagement envisaged under the Act East Policy.

This is not a historical narrative, though it dwells briefly on the past of various populations of the North East. This is to get a greater insight into their identity and to trace the events since India's Independence in 1947 to understand the reason of the conflict and violence in the Region and the timeline of its assimilation into the modern Indian Nation State. This is also not a history of any particular force or formation but refers to various organisations- the Army, para-military forces like the Assam Rifles, Central Armed Police Forces such as the Border Security Force, The Central Reserve Police Force, the Sashastra Seema Bal etc. that provide the security architecture for the Northeastern Region.

The United Service Institution, founded in 1870, combines a wealth of experience of many serving and former members of the Army, Navy and Air Force comprising the Armed Forces of India. Special thanks are due to this Institution and to Major General B.K. Sharma, Director-General USI, who has strongly advocated and developed a multi-dimensional approach to national security issues, combining military, civil, social, economic aspects to find a lasting solution to the problems of the North East; to Major General Bhadauria for bringing together many officers of the armed forces, diplomats police officers and administrators who have served in the North East and South East Asia to share their experiences; to Dr. Roshan Khanijo for developing and implementing a multi-disciplinary program for the USI that has enriched the debate on a comprehensive approach to internal security problems.

The Study is supported by the Assam Rifles, through its Chair of Excellence in the United Services Institute. Assam Rifles, apart from being a guardian of the NER, has been intimately connected with the NER for the last two centuries and has seen every facet of its emergence as a part of independent India. Over time its perspective over the security issues has evolved and is more nuanced to the special circumstances of the North East. Due to its experience, though a paramilitary force, Assam Rifles can well be re-purposed to encourage the strengths of the Region and play a vital role in India's Act East Policy.

Special thanks are due to Lt. General S. Sangwan, AVSM, SM, former DG Assam Rifles and his successor, Lt. Gen P.C. Nair, AVSM, YSM, who not only supported this study whole heartedly but also participated in several discussions and presentations on the Study and provided invaluable insight and guidance into the realities of the North East. Special Thanks also to Mr J.N. Chaudhari IPS (retd.), former Director General of Police, Assam, to my many colleagues in the Indian Administrative Service and friends from the North East who provided many unique insights and many other police officers, diplomats and scholars who participated in the discussions on the subject of this Study.

PART - I

Chapter 1

Northeast India – Integration into Modern India

(The North Eastern Region of India, connected civilisationally both to the greater Indian sub-continent as well as SE Asia, but full of diversity with a long history of autonomous existence over the last two millennia, underwent a process of closer integration with the Indian Sub-continent and after 1947 became a part of the modern, independent, democratic Republic of India. The process of integration took place gradually and despite considerable success having been achieved, it is still a work-in progress. An understanding of its past and integration into the modern Indian State is in many ways fundamental in recognising its potential- and the underlying challenges- to act as bridge for India's Engagement East.)

For the better part of two millennia, the NE Region comprised of various kingdoms having suzerainty over territories now located in India's North East. The Region was also home to many autonomous tribal communities, both in its plains and in hill areas. The tribal societies living within the territories controlled by various North Eastern kingdoms owed allegiance to the respective kings but lived within their own social and cultural traditions. The kingdoms, while maintaining their independence and autonomy, had considerable religious and cultural affinity and interaction with the broader Indian sub-continental civilisation along with significant Tibeto-Burmese and SE Asian influences. In the ancient times (pre-12th Century AD), prominent amongst these were the Kingdoms of Kamarupa in Lower Assam, the Koch-Rajbanshi kingdoms of Cooch Bihar with their control over Dooars, that of Dimasa-Kacharis stretching over hill areas of Central Assam and Cachar. Similarly, in the South Eastern part of the Region, the chronicles of the Meitei kingdom of Manipur[1], known as Kangleipak since the 12th century, speak of succession of kings going back to the 1st century AD. The traditional history of the Kingdom of Tripura[2] (or Tippera), recorded in the *Rajmala Chronicles,* refers to nearly

200 kings[3]. In addition to monarchy, other governance systems, tribal or community based, also existed, such as in territories ruled by Jaintia and Khasi Chiefs, areas dominated by Buddhist priesthood in Bhutan and Dooars, tribal social systems in areas covering modern day Arunachal Pradesh, Nagaland and Mizoram. A multiplicity of kings and chieftains held sway in various parts of the North Eastern Region till the Tai-Ahoms[4], ethnic migrants from Northern Thailand, established their control over the Brahmaputra Valley in Assam in the 13th century with an unbroken rule of nearly six centuries.

While history of individual states and peoples of the Region is not the focus of this study, it is important to bear in mind the vigorous, and successful opposition by the North Eastern kingdoms to any attempt by the erstwhile ruling empires of the Indian Sub-Continent or South East Asia to subjugate them. The attempts to conquer the Ahom kingdom during the Mughal period constitute the most prominent example. Mughal Armies invaded the Ahom kingdom many times, to be beaten back each time, with the final battle of Saraighat in 1671 resulting in a decisive defeat of the invading Mughal forces. Even in pre-Ahom days, the Kingdom of Kamarupa (As areas falling in Western Assam were then known) and other successive kingdoms attracted the attention of the Turkish rulers of North India. Starting with Bakhtiyar Khilji, a series of expeditions were mounted from the then territories of Bengal (referred to in ancient Kamarup literature as the Land of Gaur) by different governors, all of them meeting fierce and prolonged resistance, with the invaders being pushed out each time. Similarly, Manipur's long history reveals the warlike and fiercely independent nature of the Kingdom, defending itself vigorously against any encroachment from the West or East alike.

The preservation of the unique identity of the peoples of the NE Region and their steadfast resistance to subjugation was also aided by the geography of the region - largely covered by dense forests interspersed with rivers, inaccessible hills and valleys. The arrival of the Tai Ahoms[5] into Eastern Assam in the 13th century and subsequent expansion of the Ahom kingdom was instrumental in bringing together various peoples inhabiting the Brahmaputra valley and surrounding hilly regions under one rule. Again, about two hundred years ago, British colonial expansion in the Indian sub-continent led to a radical change in the autonomous status of the North Eastern Kingdoms and societies. Centred around the British controlled territories of Eastern India this led to geographical and administrative integration of the North Eastern Region with colonial

4

India. A new dimension, assimilation, was acquired with the emergence of independent India.

The long process that determined the changes in India's North East was influenced at various times by turmoil in SE Asia caused by the expansionist policies of the then Myanmarese kings and the clash with British colonial administration in the Indian Sub-Continent, colonial rivalry and in SE Asia (then known as Indo-China), India's Freedom Struggle, the Second World War and finally Indian independence in 1947. However, the legacy based on geographically isolated, semi-autonomous identities of the people of the North East had a profound impact on the cultural, ethnic and linguistic assimilation with the modern Indian nation. This process, which continued well after Indian Independence, involved use of force by the Indian state, resulting in many military actions, negotiated settlements and agreements and compromises that influence events even today. All these events with deep geo-political ramifications resulted in eventual melding of a region of diverse tribal systems and ethnicities into the constitutionally ruled framework of independent India. However, the present geography of the region owes much to the events of the past couple of centuries, which, therefore merit a closer look.

The Clash of Empires

After the battles of Plassey (1757) and Buxar (1761), the East India Company was bestowed the *Diwani* (Revenue administration, taxation and land rights) of the territories covering the provinces of Bengal, Bihar and Odisha by the Mughal Emperor. The East India Company, however, went beyond the charters were given it by the Mughal Emperor and took practical territorial control of a vast area in covering the modern-day states of Bihar, Jharkhand, Bengal and Orissa in India and the whole of modern Bangladesh as the de facto sovereign. Eventually, it was faced with the imperative of securing its territories, which were proving valuable for its extractive operations and trade. In the process, the Company built up and expanded its army and undertook military campaigns to annex territories, and in the process, expanded eastwards.

Notably, as East India Company grew in power centred around Calcutta, there was also a revivalist effort in Myanmar. As early as the second half of the 16th century, the Taungoo dynasty (1510–1752) had unified Myanmar and founded the largest empire in the history of Southeast Asia. Over time it had disintegrated into smaller units. In the second half of the 18th century, the Konbaung dynasty (1752–1885) attempted to restore the

Taungoo glory, and went to war with its neighbours, seizing control of the Arakan Region, Manipur and finally, in 1817 the Ahom Kingdom itself. Soon after, they overcame the Kingdom of Cachar in the Barak Valley and pushed into Chittagong, thereby controlling most of the present-day North-Eastern Region. This brought them into direct confrontation with the British in India.

The threat to the East India Company controlled territories became acute as the clash between the two empires, British (through East India Company) and Myanmar became imminent[6]. The relations were hostile as Myanmar kings laid claim to several territories then under control of the East India Company. There were frequent skirmishes and raids from the East, mainly Myanmar, and from the tribes inhabiting the Indo-Myanmarese border region. The growing confrontation culminated in the Anglo-Burmese wars of the 19th Century[7].

Overall, the British colonial forces fought three wars with the Konbaung kingdom of Myanmar. The first Anglo-Burmese War 1824-26[8] resulted in the annexation of the areas in the Brahmaputra and Barak valleys, which had for some time, fallen under Myanmarese suzerainty, through the Treaty of Yandabo concluded in 1826. These included the Ahom Kingdom, the kingdoms of Cachar and Manipur and the Arakan region by the East India Company (in the name of the British Crown). Meanwhile, the rivalry between European colonial powers in Indo-China, particularly with French presence expanding in the Region, provided impetus for a further push by the British into Myanmar. Two more wars were fought with Burma, in 1852 and finally in 1885, when the last Myanmarese King was deposed and brought to India in captivity[9], and Myanmar (Burma) came under British control.

East India Company and the British Expansion in the East

Meanwhile, after the Treaty of Yandabo, the British continued their pressure eastwards and proceeded to annex various territories though a series of military actions and treaties. As early as 1809, the Kingdom of Tripura, due to its proximity to the Bengal Presidency and troubled by depredations from the East, had been made a British protectorate while continuing as a princely state. The Kingdom of Manipur, which had a long history of conflict with the Myanmarese kings, was also formally declared a British protectorate in 1824. It was eventually annexed much later after the Anglo-Manipuri war of 1891 without altering its character as a princely state. Khasi and Jaintia territories, ruled by autonomous tribal

6

chiefs were annexed in 1833 and 1835[10]. The Dooars, which is now known as the Bodoland Territorial Region and earlier governed by administrative mechanisms under the dual control of Bhutan and Ahom kingdoms, was taken over after 1826 with the continuation of the arrangement as it existed. Finally, following the Dooars Campaign in 1865, the British took complete possession of the Dooars and removed Bhutanese involvement altogether. The Naga Hills District was constituted under Assam in 1866 and gradually expanded by annexation of areas inhabited by Lotha, Ao, Sema, Konyak tribes. Later, under the Government of India Act 1919, it was constituted as a Special Excluded Area administered by the Governor of Assam. The present-day state of Mizoram, then referred to as Lushai (Lusei) Hills, was occupied after military expeditions of 1871-2 and 1889-90, undertaken in response to raids by Mizo tribes on Cachar areas. The Lushai Hill tracts were formally taken over by proclamation in 1895. The present-day Arunachal Pradesh initially formed as the North Eastern Frontier Tract after negotiations with tribal chiefs by the British in early 20th century, got its boundaries delimited as part of British Colonial possession after the Shimla Agreement of 1914. The British expansion into the Dooars brought them close to the Kingdom of Sikkim which had been founded by the Namgyal dynasty in the 17th century and had been ruled by Buddhist priest-kings known as the Chogyals. In 1890 Sikkim also became a princely state under the protection of British India.

Meanwhile, having obtained control of Assam and Cachar in 1826, the Colonial Government realised its economic potential and wasted no time in setting up arrangements for its security through the constitution of a special force - the Assam Rifles. In addition to providing protection to the then Bengal province, the Assam Rifles was charged with protection of British commercial interests in the Assam and Barak valleys. These interests centred largely around tea cultivation which began in Assam on a commercial basis through plantations, beginning in 1841. Soon, investment in tea plantations took place all over the Assam and Barak Valleys, Dooars and Darjeeling. As British owned tea plantations spread deep into Assam, the colonial Government at Calcutta felt the need for better administrative arrangements of the Region.

During the war of Indian independence in 1857, there was an effort to revive the Ahom kingdom. This was put down and the Ahom royal line was extinguished. In 1874 the Chief Commissionerate of Assam (eventually including the territories now constituting the states of Meghalaya, Nagaland and Mizoram) was set up with its capital at Shillong. Discovery of petroleum at the turn of the 19th century at Digboi, Assam made the province all the more valuable.

In 1905, Bengal was partitioned[11] and East Bengal was added to form the new Chief Commissioner's Province of Eastern Bengal and Assam. The new province, now placed under a Lt. Governor, had its capital at Dhaka. The Partition of Bengal was strongly protested in Bengal and Assam and was finally annulled. Subsequently, what was known as the Chief Commissioner's Province was reconstituted as the Assam Province, directly under British colonial rule, comprising most of the North East except Manipur and Tripura who were allowed to continue as princely states.

The Freedom Struggle and Integration

The Freedom Struggle against colonial rule that took place all over India was instrumental in imparting a common national idea to the diverse peoples of the entire Indian sub-continent. It also had stirrings in the North East. Its initial impact was felt in the widespread protest against the Partition of Bengal, attempting to create a new province of East Bengal and Assam. As the Freedom Struggle unfolded, democratic stirrings took place all over the Region, including in the princely states. Meanwhile colonial rule had united the Region through a common pattern of administration (with some special variations) with the rest of India. The mass mobilisation of people against the iniquity of colonial rule brought about aspirations for self-determination and commonality of a larger purpose with the rest of Indian Sub-continent. The Constituent Assembly set up to deliberate upon the constitutional framework of independent India and therefore included several members from the North East[12].

a) The Instrument of Accession and Abolition of Princely States

Under the British Colonial Rule, the numerous princely states[13] spread-out all-over India, were vassal states each under a local, indigenous or regional ruler in a Subsidiary Alliance with the British Raj. Distinct from the Directly Administered Territories, they retained their identity as kingdoms. However, the Doctrine of Paramountcy applied by the British Raj, whose economic and military power was unchallenged, allowed the government of British India to interfere in the internal affairs of princely states individually or collectively and issue edicts whenever it deemed necessary. At the time of Indian Independence, in addition to Directly Administered Territories, 565 princely states were officially recognised in the Indian subcontinent. While totally subject to British dominance, their status was acknowledged in various ways. The most important states had their own British Political Residencies which served as the de facto political power centres behind a façade of diplomacy.

The era of the princely states effectively ended with Indian independence in 1947; by 1950, almost all the kingdoms and principalities had been dissolved and had acceded to either India or Pakistan. In 1956, Through the States Reorganisation Act, 1956, the states in India, a part of the new federal structure established by the Constitution, were reorganised. This was done on linguistic basis, dissolving all previous territorial allegiances and wiping out all vestiges of kingdoms or principalities of old.

It is noteworthy that there were divergent opinions amongst various peoples and groups in the NE Region about joining the Indian Union. While Assam, which was a Directly Administered Territory (then also including Khasi, Jaintia, Garo, Naga and Mizo Hills areas) became a part of the Indian Union immediately, the princely state of Manipur, after retaining internal sovereignty in 1947, fully merged only in 1949. Tripura, acceded to the Indian Union but like Manipur, also fully merged in 1949. Both the princely states were initially constituted as Part C States[14]. North East Frontier Tracts, later named North East Frontier Agency and eventually Arunachal Pradesh remained for some years after independence, a special area administered by India through the Ministry of External Affairs.

Meanwhile in the Naga Hills, Naga National Council (NNC) was set up in 1946 under Angami Zapu Phizo's leadership, seeking separation of the Naga Hills region of Assam from the Indian Union with a view to forming an independent Naga State. After long deliberations, the NNC leaders and the then Governor of Assam, Sir Akbar Hydari, signed a Nine-Point Agreement which granted Nagas rights over their lands and legislative and executive powers. The period of Agreement was kept as ten years after which the Agreement could be extended or a new Agreement would be arrived at. Following this Agreement, the Naga Hills remained a part of Assam though the issue would be resurrected again on the eve of India's independence.

Integration into Independent India

b) The Tribal Regions

The Constituent Assembly of India was also faced with a demand for autonomous governance in the tribal regions of the North East. Afforded considerable autonomy under the Colonial Rule along with restricted access by outsiders, they expressed apprehensions about merger with the new Indian State. For peaceful accession of tribal population of the then Assam state, the right for self-governance in accordance with their traditions was proposed through special provisions in the Constitution. There was considerable debate over this proposal. Finally, as a compromise, the Fifth and Sixth Schedule were added to the Indian Constitution on 7 September 1949[15].

This Schedule made special provisions for the administration of tribal areas in the present-day north-eastern states of Assam, Tripura, Meghalaya, and Mizoram. Most laws passed by the legislative assemblies in these states do not apply to tribal areas; instead, these areas are governed by Autonomous Councils, which have wide-ranging powers to make laws on land, forest management, agriculture, village administration, and personal matters. Currently, there are ten regions under the Sixth Schedule spread across four north-eastern states. On 27 August 2020, the Arunachal Pradesh state legislative assembly unanimously passed a resolution to bring the entire state under the Sixth Schedule of the Indian Constitution.

Though controversial, the Sixth Schedule was a unique feature of the Constitution that eventually served to allay the apprehensions of many tribal societies in the North East. By giving them the means of protecting their customs and traditions as well as a measure of self-governance, it helped them integrate peacefully with the rest of the country. Over the course of time, it was also used to diffuse violent militant movements in Tripura and Assam.

Accession Negotiations

Post partition in 1947, while efforts were on to secure the accession of various princely states and territories to India (or Pakistan as the case might be), there was some degree of turmoil in the two princely states of the North East, Manipur and Tripura. On 11 August 1947, Maharaja Bodh Chandra Singh of Manipur signed an Instrument of Accession, joining India. Later, on 21 September 1949, he signed a Merger Agreement, merging the Kingdom into India, which led to it becoming a Part C State. This Accession and Merger was later disputed by some groups in Manipur as having been carried out under duress. Initially, bowing to public opinion in Manipur, the princely state of Manipur had proclaimed its own constitution[16], following which, elections were held in Manipur in June 1948 and the state became a constitutional monarchy. In the Legislative Assembly of Manipur there were sharp differences over the question of merger of Manipur with India. Finally, when the Maharaja signed a Merger Agreement in September 1949, it was claimed in some quarters that this was done without consulting the popularly elected Legislative Assembly of Manipur. This dispute combined with a strong sense of Meitei identity, later engendered a movement for Meitei revivalism, resulting in nearly 50 years of inter-ethnic violence and militant separatism in the state, with some insurgent groups demanding independence from India.

In Tripura, the last ruling King, Bir Bikram Kishore Deb Barman died in May 1947. His successor, Prince Kirit Bikram Kishore Deb Barman, was only eleven years old at the time. Accordingly, a Council of Regency was formed to run the administration under the presidency of the Queen, Kanchan Prava Devi, mother of prince Kirit Bikram Kishore Deb Barman. However, with the partition of the India, Tripura faced a great crisis, with major threat coming from the then East Pakistan. The Queen Mother dissolved the Council of Regency and became the sole Regent on 12 January 1948. More than a year later, on 9 September 1949, she signed the 'Tripura Merger Agreement'[18], and with effect from 15 October 1949[19] Tripura became part of the Indian Union.

Re-organisation Post Independence

With Indian independence in 1947, various kingdoms, chiefships and ethnicities inhabiting the sub-regions of the North East, presenting a wide diversity rooted in their unique respective histories and traditions stretching back over many centuries, merged into the Indian Union through a series of constitutional arrangements, compromises and agreements. Statehood, Nascent Political Aspirations and fault lines. However, the assimilation of local identities was not without its challenges and required frequent interventions by the Central Government and several re-organisations. As a means of recognising the Naga identity in the Indian framework the state of Nagaland was constituted on 1 December, 1963. Recognising the need for articulation of local political aspirations as a means of defusing separatism and insurgency, the erstwhile state of Assam was further reorganised in 1972 with constitution of Khasi, Jaintia and Garo Hills districts of Assam in a new State of Meghalaya. given full statehood in 1972. The Mizo and Lushai Hills were made into the new Union territory of Mizoram in 1972 which later gained statehood in 1986. The erstwhile princely states of Manipur and Tripura, initially constituted as Part C States (administered by a Chief Commissioner), made Union Territory in 1956, were accorded full statehood in 1972. At the same time NEFA was renamed Arunachal

Pradesh and made a Union Territory in 1972, and later in 1987, a full state of the Union.

Meanwhile, following Indian independence, Sikkim continued its protectorate status with the Union of India after 1947, and the Republic of India after 1950. In 1973, after a period of anti-royalist political turmoil in 1975, the Indian Army entered the Kingdom. A referendum was held in the state that led to the deposition of the monarchy and Sikkim joined India as its 22nd state.

With the political reorganisation of the North East, the States of Assam, Arunachal Pradesh, Nagaland, Mizoram, Meghalaya, Manipur and Tripura now comprising the North Eastern Region of India are constituted on lines similar to other states of the Indian Union but with some special provisions. Recognition of political aspirations of the people has also led to unleashing of equally strong economic aspirations which require policy, strategy and related investment focus to enable prosperity in the Region. However, political reorganisation notwithstanding, it has taken time for historical past and the linguistic, ethnic identities and tribal sub-nationalisms to be subsumed in the Indian State, something that still remains a work-in-process in many parts of the Region.

Building the Future and a New Engagement East

The process of assimilation and political integration of various constituents of the North East into the Constitutional framework of free India post-1947, however, was a long one and was neither dissent free or smooth. This process, which took place within a liberal, democratic India and within the framework of the Indian Constitution, was often beset by separatism, insurgency and terrorism. This required countering threats from extremist, separatist elements while continuing the dialogue for political solutions. Success was achieved in different parts of the North East through continued democratic engagement over time through a dialogue resulting in a series of arrangements and reorganisations and accords. While local identities remained strong, the resultant arrangements enabled disparate identities to participate fully as constituent units of the Union of India while articulating their social and cultural identities under the Constitution.

With the creation of new states and recognition of the right of the people to participate more directly in governance, different states of the North East, though geographically located in a contiguous region have embarked on political development trajectories that are specific to their local conditions and aspirations of the local population. While this may be considered as an imperative towards better local governance and economic development, it has also unleashed many conflicts and rivalries that have emerged from time to time. These will be dealt with in greater detail in subsequent chapters.

Comprehensive economic development of the NE Region will, therefore, need to find solutions to the lingering issues rooted in the diversity of the Region, the identities determining and guiding the political aspirations of the people and dynamics of the process by which the Region has been assimilated into the Indian Union. The process has been long, with many experiments and compromises along the way, yet successful. Gradually the organisation of political activity and governance has fallen into the constitutional patterns and brought unprecedented peace and economic development to the Region.

In the 21st century with growing diversity of economic activity, spread of education and distances shrunk through technology and far better and diverse means of communication, there is a strong impetus amongst the people to move away from conflict and violence and to enjoy the fruits of economic progress. Strategies have to be designed that not only speed up the physical, political, economic integration of the Region with the rest of the country but also for multi- dimensional economic growth of the Region. This would enable the Region to engage with the rest of the country as well as the South East Asia more meaningfully.

Notes to Chapter 1

1. The history of Manipur is chronicled in Puyas or Puwaris (stories about the forefathers), in the Meitei script. Manipur was known by different names at various periods in its history, such as, Tilli-Koktong, Poirei-Lam, Sanna-Leipak, Mitei-Leipak, Meitrabak or Manipur (present-day). Its capital was Kangla, Yumphal or Imphal (present-day). The Puwaris, record the events of each King who ruled Manipur until 1955 CE (a total of more than 108 kings). In 1824, the ruler of Manipur entered into a subsidiary alliance with the British Empire in India, which became responsible for Manipur's external defence. Manipur, however, remained internally self-governing, as a princely state.

2. The Kingdom of Tippera (or Twipra) was bounded by Burma in the East, the Padma River in the erstwhile Bengal province of colonial India in the West, Barak River in the North and Bay of Bengal in the South and included the modern-day state of Tripura, some areas falling in Barak valley (Assam) and modern Meghalaya, Comilla and Chittagong regions of Modern Bangladesh and some part of the Arakan region of Myanmar.

3. The former princely state of Tripura was ruled by Maharajas of Manikya dynasty. Rajmala Chronicles, the royal chronology of Tripura, records a total of 184 kings who ruled over Tripura before it merged with the Indian Union on 15 October 1949. It was an independent administrative unit under the Maharaja even during the British rule in India. Its independence after 1809 was, however, qualified. Tripura became a British Protectorate in 1809 and was subject to the recognition of the British as the paramount power of each successive ruler

4. The Ahoms or Tai-Ahoms were descendants of the Tai people who reached the Brahmaputra valley of Assam in 1228 when Sukaphaa, the leader of the Tai group with a few thousand followers entered Assam through its easternmost region and eventually established the Ahom kingdom at Charaideo, Sibsagar. Origins of Tai Ahoms could be traced to the Tai speaking people from the Guangxi region of China. They were forced to move from there in the 11th century after an uprising against Imperial China to Mong Mao region of South China and the Hukawng Valley in Myanmar.

5. Having settled in the Brahmaputra Valley, Ahoms gradually came to include not only the original Tai but also several Tibeto-Burman peoples they absorbed in Assam through a process of Ahomisation. The Ahoms also married liberally outside their own exogamous clans. Eventually the Ahom society itself came under direct Hindu influence. Suhungmung (r: 1497–1539), or Dihingia Raja I was the first Ahom king to adopt a Hindu title, Swarganarayana, and Ahom kings came to be known as the Swargadeo which is the Assamese translation of Ahom word Chao-Pha. Under Suhungmung,

the Ahom Kingdom expanded up to the Karatoya river (now in Bangladesh), the western boundary of the erstwhile Kamarupa Kingdom. By the 17th century, the Assamese had become the court language. The Ahom kingdom lasted nearly 600 years (1228–1826 CE), when after the Treaty of Yandabo it became a part of British India.

6. Concerned at the safety of their eastern possessions in India, the British sent several embassies to the Burmese emperor. However, these were of no avail as both sides failed to understand and communicate with each other. In 1824, the Burmese Governor of Ramree (a region located on the coast in Rakhine province of Burma) in a letter written to the British Governor General in Calcutta extended his claim to Ramu (part of Cox's Bazaar), Chittagong, Murshidabad and Dhaka, though it was not confirmed whether this was done on the directions or with approval of the Burmese King. Meanwhile several border incidents erupted into clashes, particularly in 1824, when the Burmese worsted the British units in Cachar and Jaintia regions, forcing the Raja of Cachar to flee and seek British protection. Similar clashes in Arakan resulted in the Anglo Burmese war formally breaking out on 5 March 1824.

7. Early in the war, Burmese forces were able to push back the British forces because the Burmese, who had been fighting in Manipur and Assam for over a decade were battle hardened and more familiar with the terrain. In May, Burmese forces defeated British troops at the Battle of Ramu and Gadawpalin, and went on to capture Cox's Bazar. The Burmese success, of course, caused extreme panic in Chittagong and in Calcutta. However Burmese forces did not march on to Chittagong, which was actually lightly held. Had they taken Chittagong, the Calcutta, the capital city and headquarters of the British East India Company would have been gravely threatened.

8. The British retaliated by launching a sea-borne invasion of Burma. The Burmese rulers and their army regarded sea as their natural defence and were totally unprepared for this. They also had no idea of what it meant to fight a well-equipped, European armada armed with a large number of cannon and a well-trained army. The expedition sailed up the Irrawaddy to Rangoon and completely destroyed Burmese forces, albeit after a heroic defence by the Royal Burmese army led by their famous general Maha Bundula who was eventually killed in action.

9. After the Third Anglo Burmese war of 1885 the last Myanmarese King was deposed and brought to India in captivity, where he finally died and the imperial Konbaung dynasty came to an end. The Anglo Burmese wars of the 19th century brought Burma under the rule of British as a province of British India. This dispensation remained in force till 1937 when Burma, still under British control was separated from India. Burma which became independent in 1948 later adopted its ancient name, Myanmar.

10. The Khasis first came in contact with the British in 1823, after the latter captured Assam. The area inhabited by the Khasi people became a part of the then Assam Province after the "Khasi Hill States" (which numbered about 25 Chiefdoms) entered into a subsidiary alliance with the British. This region is located in the present-day state of Meghalaya. The Khasi people are related to the Mon-Khmer people of Southeast Asia.

11. The Partition of Bengal was done in 1905 to form a new province with a population of 31 million by uniting Assam, which had been a part of the province until 1874, with 15 districts of East Bengal. The capital was Dacca (now Dhaka, Bangladesh. This act of partition brought the Bengal province to the brink of open rebellion. Agitation against the partition included mass meetings, rural unrest, and a swadeshi (native) movement to boycott the import of British goods. The partition was carried through despite the agitation, which sparked off an underground terrorist movement. In 1911, the year that the capital was shifted from Calcutta (now Kolkata) to Delhi, east and west Bengal were reunited by an imperial decree announced by the then King-Emperor of colonial India at the Delhi Durbar. Assam again became a chief commissionership, while Bihar and Orissa were separated to form a new province.

12. The then composite state of pre-1947 Assam was represented by a substantial contingent comprising Nibaran Chandra Laskar, Dharanidhar Basumatari, Gopinath Bardoloi, J. J. M. Nichols-Roy, Kuladhar Chaliha, Rohini Kumar Chaudhury, Muhammad Saadulla, Abdur Rouf etc. The princely states of Manipur and Tripura were represented by Girija Shanker Guha, the revenue minister of Tripura, (apparently not to the liking of the then Maharaja of Manipur who wanted a separate representative for Manipur).

13. Many of these such as Hyderabad of the Nizams, Mysore and Travancore in the South, Jammu and Kashmir in the Himalayas, and Indore in Central India were larger than many nation states of the world. The most prominent among those – roughly a quarter of the total – had the status of a "salute state", one whose ruler was entitled to a set number of gun salutes on ceremonial occasions.

14. Part C states included both the former chief commissioners' provinces and some princely states, and each was governed by a chief commissioner appointed by the President of India. The ten Part C states so categorised after India's independence in 1947 were Ajmer, Bhopal, Bilaspur, Coorg, Delhi, Himachal Pradesh, Cutch, Manipur, Tripura, and Vindhya Pradesh. All these states, apart from Manipur and Tripura, were absorbed into the Re-organised states of the Union, formed on linguistic lines, in 1956. Manipur and Tripura became Union Territories and later full-fledged states.

15. In order to protect the interests of Scheduled Tribes with regard to land and other social issues, various provisions have been enshrined in the Fifth

Schedule and the Sixth Schedule of the Constitution. The Fifth Schedule under Article 244(1) of Constitution defines "Scheduled Areas" as such areas as the President may by order declare to be Scheduled Areas after consultation with the Governor of that State. The Sixth Schedule under Article 244 (2) of the Constitution relates to those areas in the States of Assam, Meghalaya, Tripura and Mizoram which are declared as "tribal areas" and provides for District or Regional Autonomous Councils for such areas. These councils have wide ranging legislative, judicial and executive powers.

16. Manipur State Constitution Act 1947

17. The Manipur Merger Agreement, 1949

18. Some royalist elements in Tripura claimed that the Queen Regent had 'questionable legitimacy' after the unilateral dissolution of the Council of Regency.

19. The Tripura Merger Agreement, under which Tripura became part of the Indian Union, was signed on 9 September 1949 and took effect from 15 October 1949.

Chapter 2

War, Insurgency and Unrest: A Turbulent Journey into the Present

(The NER was exposed to War from external aggression several times. It was also exposed to long drawn internal conflict resulting from separatist insurgencies in different parts of the region. Efforts made to resolve conflicts post 1947 had a significant impact on its political reorganisation and eventually aided the integration of the region with the rest of India). While the Indian State has been able to largely overcome conflict and over the last seven decades and achieve a significant degree of integration of diverse identities, this background has shaped the perspective on national security making it an important factor in any strategy for the future.)

For a better part of a century, the identity of the NE Region was also forged on the battlefield and through several long-drawn militant insurgencies. Ever since India's independence in 1947, in addition to being a theatre of War in three different conflicts involving foreign aggression, different parts of the North East have faced internal conflict that posed a significant threat to national security. This has resulted in a long, and often intense, military engagement in the region. The almost continued deployment of Indian security forces was accompanied by political accommodation by successive governments at the Centre. This led to political solutions that enabled disaffected populations, separatist and extremist groups and local identities a share in political power and governance. This process spanning over half a century, punctuated with various accords and agreements with insurgent groups and disaffected populations, has today resulted in the political map of the present-day North East. While incorporating political institutions of the modern India republic, the fault lines of identity inspired sub nationalism remain. It is therefore relevant to understand the environment of conflict that has shaped the political, social and ethnic discourse of the region.

20th Century Wars and the Northeast

WWII

While the colonial expansion of the 19th Century had resulted in a series of localised wars and military actions, the early 20th Century was relatively peaceful for the region. However, as the world became engulfed in the Second World War, India's North East became one of the bloodiest theatres of War following Japanese expansion in the SE Asia. Japanese armies over-ran Burma[1] (now Myanmar) and launched a campaign to invade India through Naga Hills and Manipur. During occupation of Burma by the Japanese, several British Indian Army formations continued to strike deep into occupied territory. However, as Japanese armies approached the borders of British India, some of the fiercest and bloodiest battles of the War were fought around Kohima and Imphal.[2] The British Indian Armies, comprising both British and Indian regiments with Indian troops drawn from various parts of India constituting the bulk of the defending army, eventually beat back the invading force after long drawn-out battles with heavy loss of life on both sides[3]. Eventually, the invading Japanese armies were totally destroyed and retreated with heavy losses.[4] Subsequently Northeast was the launching pad when the Allied forces counterattacked to take back control of Burma.

The Allied war effort and mobilisation in the region, however, resulted in its constituents being drawn together in one geographically interconnected entity with establishment of many army encampments, dozens of airfields, development of critical roads and railheads, movement of troops across the region and busy operation of supply lines stretching across the Bengal and Assam provinces of the then undivided India right up to the Burma border.[5] While the WW II served to integrate the NE Region geographically, fierce fighting with the invading Japanese forces all along the Burma front brought recognition of the region as a part of India, to be subsequently strongly defended against invasion and external aggression.

The New Republic, Partition and External Aggression

Barely had the wounds of the Second World War begun to heal when the North East suffered the trauma of Partition in 1947, which left it geographically isolated with its traditional approach routes from other parts of India cut off. East Pakistan emerged as a hostile area, practically isolating the region from the main body of India except through a narrow corridor along the Himalayas. Following the Partition migration of populations and communal/ethnic conflict also took place in the East though not at the same scale as compared to the violent upheavals in the western part of the sub-continent[6]. Though the Nehru-Liaqat Pact of 1951[7] served to douse flames in the East, the potential for conflict remained, which surfaced much later.

As various constituent entities of the region came to terms with the cessation of British Sovereignty and the emergence of the modern democratic Republic of India, local ethnic and linguistic identities and sub-nationalisms came to the fore as the new India Republic set about the task of nation building. Shortly after independence, a militant insurgent movement engulfed Naga Hills, foreshadowing the times to come. Politically linguistic issues accompanying Reorganization of States agitated Assam as it asserted its distinct identity based on the Assamese language as the basis of statehood.

The Wars of 1962 and 1971

War resulting from external aggression remained a predominating feature even after independence, highlighting the sensitivity of the region in terms of national security. The region became a theatre of War again twice- In 1962 and 1971. The 1962 war with China, which has engulfed most of the present Arunachal Pradesh in the eastern sector, has been well documented. It highlighted, among other things, the vulnerabilities of the North Eastern border and demanding nature of War in the high Himalayas. It also highlighted the need for infrastructure to enable supplies for the potential war effort along the entire 1129 km long border with China. In fact, the external national security threat along this border has persisted till today, with an unsettled border with and recurrent claims over Indian Territory by China.

The War for the Liberation of Bangladesh, fought in 1971, followed a long period of repression and genocide in the erstwhile East Pakistan which sent millions of refugees from that country largely into Assam and Tripura[8]. They were given shelter and humanitarian aid in these states.

The swift and successful offensive launched by the Indian Army for the liberation of Bangladesh highlighted the militarily strategic geography of the region. After the War, many refugees went back to what was now Bangladesh. Many however stayed back, resulting in continuing ethnic and linguistic tensions in the region.

The Conflict Within - Insurgency

While external wars raged the region witnessed serious armed insurgent outbreaks, sometimes aided and abetted across porous international borders. It is relevant to briefly dwell upon some of these conflicts as they have shaped the polity of the region ever since independence. Most such conflicts, currently quiescent, cast their shadow over the imperative for national security.

While linguistic and communal fault lines remained, the reorganisation of the North Eastern Region with the creation of several Hill States such as Meghalaya, Nagaland, Mizoram, Arunachal Pradesh also recognised ethnicity as the basis of the political identity. Over a period of time conflicts have been caused and fuelled by a combination of inter-ethnic/inter-tribal/ linguistic/communal differences as also rising local political aspirations. To understand the region, it is also essential to be aware of the conflicts of the recent past as well as their resolution. What follows is by no means a history of the North East but a brief overview of the conflict in the Region post India's independence.

Nagaland

The insurgency in Nagaland is also known as the "mother of all insurgencies "in the North East. Starting immediately with India's independence it has lasted over half a century. While the level of militant violence has gone down, the separatist impulse has not yet been fully put to rest.

Ever since the assumption of control in 1866, the Colonial Administration had restricted access to Naga Hills. The entire area was placed under Inner Line Regulation in 1873, with very few outsiders, other than missionaries, colonial administrators and military personnel being allowed in. However, some Nagas were venturing out as a part of the colonial armies. In 1918, some Nagas who had served in the Great War (WW I) in the French Labour Corps set up the Naga Club. In 1929 the Club submitted a Memorandum to the Simon Commission seeking a separate independent status for the Naga people. Later the Government of India Act of 1935 termed predominantly Naga inhabited areas as "Excluded Area".

In 1946, as it became clear that the British were withdrawing from India, the Naga National Council (NNC) was formed, led by Angami Zapu Phizo, who sought independence of Naga dominated areas from the British. However, after protracted negotiations with Mr Akbar Hydari, Governor of Assam, representing the Interim Indian Government prior to full independence, a Nine Point Agreement was signed in 1946 with the NNC which provided guarantees to the Nagas to protect their society and culture. Among other things, the Agreement provided a 10-year period after which NNC would be consulted on whether the Agreement would be extended or a new agreement arrived at[9].

However, the movement for an independent Nagaland assumed militant-separatist colour and did not wait for the completion of the 10-year period. The Phizo led NNC, rejected the 9-Point Agreement and declared Nagaland an independent state on 14 August, 1947. While the Central Government continued its transition of power from colonial to independent India, the NNC pressed the demand for an "independent" Nagaland after calling for a referendum[10] in Naga inhabited areas on the issue. The first General Election organised in the country in 1952 was boycotted in Nagaland.

The demand for a sovereign Nagaland was rejected by the Indian Government and efforts intensified to deal with the insurgency which soon assumed a violent form with attacks on police stations and disruption of road and rail links. In 1953, the Assam government imposed the Assam Maintenance of Public Order (Autonomous District) Act in the Naga Hills and intensified police action against the insurgents. However, the situation worsened and the Government of Assam enacted the Assam Disturbed Areas Act, 1955, providing a legal framework for intervention by paramilitary forces and the armed state police to combat insurgency. Soon after, on 23 March, 1956 NNC claimed to have formed a parallel independent government, the Naga Federal Government (NFG), followed by the establishment of a militant organisation named the Naga Federal Army (NFA). In 1958, seeing that the level of armed disturbance in the area was going beyond capacity of the state government to control, the Central Government enacted the Armed Forces (Assam and Manipur) Special Powers Act, 1958 (initially promulgated as an Ordinance). Later in 1958 itself, the name of this Act was changed to the Armed Forces (Special Powers) Act (AFSPA), which has remained in force till today.

Eventually, after a decade long conflict, in July 1960, a Sixteen-Point Agreement[11] was signed with the Naga People's Convention. It was agreed to separate Naga territories from the state of Assam and constitute them as a state named Nagaland. The Agreement also contained special provisions to protect the local culture, customs and practices. On 1 December, 1963, Nagaland was formally constituted as a state of the Union by adding the Tuensang Tract (at the time a part of NEFA), to the Naga Hills of Assam. Efforts were made to bring an end to militancy permanently in Naga Hills and a ceasefire agreement was also signed. However, the NNC/NFG/NFA continued to indulge in violence and by 1967 the Ceasefire Agreement broke down, leading to fresh counter-insurgency operations.

After several years of violent confrontation, on 11 November, 1975, the Government of India and the then NNC and NFG leaders signed the Shillong Accord[12] which signalled the formal acceptance by most of the Naga separatists to join the constitutional framework of India. However, a group of about 140 members led by Thuingaleng Muivah, who were at that time in China, refused to accept the Shillong Accord, and in 1980 formed the National Socialist Council of Nagalim. Muivah also had the support of other Naga leaders namely Isaac Chisi Swu and S. S. Khaplang. Later, in 1988 after intra tribal clashes the NSCN split into factions led by Isaac Swu & Muivah (IM) and the faction led by S. S. Khaplang, NSCN (K).

The leader of the NNC, Angami Zapu Phizo died in London in 1991 and the NNC declined in influence. NSCN (IM) now came to be seen as the major Naga insurgent group. A dialogue with NSCN leaders was restarted in the 1990s, with several meetings with Indian Government representatives including with the Prime Ministers and other senior Ministers. These meetings took place outside India in locations such as Paris, Bangkok, Geneva, Zurich etc. The Government of India signed a ceasefire agreement with NSCN (IM) on 25 July, 1997, which came into effect on 1 August, 1997 and has since been in force with periodic extensions. Following the ceasefire, nearly 100 rounds of talks between the two sides have been held subsequently spanning nearly two decades. NSCN (K) however, abrogated the ceasefire agreement and continued militant activities including attacks on Indian security forces

As the dialogue between the movement leaders and the Government of India continued, governance institutions provided under the Indian Constitution gradually took root in Nagaland. Regular elections took place in the state, ushering in successive elected governments and administration on a pattern prevailing in the rest of the country. While elected government took charge in the state, the dialogue with the Naga Underground faction leaders also continued. The Underground separatist factions also split from time to time with some factions favouring talks and a negotiated settlement. With time further factions of NSCN emerged of which NSCN (Reformation) was the most significant as it eschewed militancy and sought to negotiate with the Government. Yet the extremist element remained, bolstered with armed cadres and support from across the international border.

Another feature of the militancy in Nagaland has been border clashes with Assam over several disputed areas, some of them so violent that neutral central forces were required to be interposed between the two sides along the contentious areas. Several boundary Commissions were appointed to resolve the dispute but to no avail. Eventually, the Assam government filed a case in the Supreme Court of India in 1989 for resolving the border dispute which is still in progress. Recently efforts have been made to resolve the issues at a political level.

Amidst all these developments, aspirations for Naga sovereignty continued in the shape of a broader demand for a "Greater Nagalim" [13] comprising "all contiguous Naga-inhabited areas", along with Nagaland. These include several districts of Assam, Arunachal and Manipur, as also a large tract of Myanmar. The aspirational "Greater Nagalim" claims about 1,20,000 sq km, while the present state of Nagaland consists of 16,527 sq. km. To some extent this development is traced to the formation of NSCN(IM), which unlike the erstwhile NNC, was led by leaders from territories outside the State of Nagaland. The concept has found greater favour with the Naga Underground factions who continue to be influential. Thus, despite ongoing dialogue with the Central Government, the elected Nagaland Assembly has endorsed the 'Greater Nagalim' demand as many as five times and the last as recently as on 27 July, 2015. While NSCN (IM) is no longer insisting upon greater Nagalim given up its demand for Greater Nagaland but not so NSCN (Khaplang) faction who continues to resort to violence and was probably involved in the attack on the Indian Army in Manipur in June 2015[14].

In 2015 a Framework Agreement was signed between the Government of India and the NSCN (I-M). However, both sides-maintained secrecy about the contents of the Agreement. In November 2017, with a view to making the process more inclusive, Naga National Political Groups (NNPGs) were also brought on board the peace process by the Indian Government. Over time the Framework Agreement has landed into controversy with both the Government of India and NSCN (IM) interpreting the framework of sovereignty implied in it differently. The Framework Agreement is also viewed with great concern by the neighbouring states of Arunachal Pradesh, Assam and Manipur, each of which has sizable Naga populated areas. The differences have also arisen between NSCN (IM) with leaders drawn from Naga regions of Manipur and NNPGs, whose members are primarily from Nagaland.

Meanwhile the breakaway faction NSCN (K) abrogated the ceasefire entered into with Naga Underground in 1997. It continued its violent activities, staging ambushes and exchanging fire with the security forces, sometimes in collaboration with other North East Militants. It has continued to oppose any accord with Indian Authorities. In view of its militant policies, it has been declared a terrorist organisation and banned by the Government of India.

The situation in Nagaland therefore continues to be ambivalent. On the one hand the ceasefire agreement holds with the political process in Nagaland being determined by constitutionally provided arrangements, with elections being held and popular governments being regularly sworn in at regular intervals. At another level, however, the extremist factions comprising a large number of heavily armed cadres constitute what has come to be known as the Naga Underground. Meanwhile some Naga factions refuse to acknowledge the ceasefire and resort to violent attacks on the security forces The armed "Naga Underground" continues its fundraising activities through "contributions" from the general public, obtained voluntarily or otherwise[15]. It also lends its support periodically to other militant groups in the region by supplying arms and providing sanctuary. During the peak period of insurgency, Naga separatists moved freely from India to Myanmar across the border and thence to China, where they got considerable support in terms of arms and funds. Their links in these countries remain. As a result, security forces are obliged to maintain a close look at the situation in the state which sees periodic outbursts of militant violence and sometimes leads to unfortunate incidents arising through mistaken identity or wrong information.

Mizoram

1960s saw emergence of armed insurgency in Mizoram, which lasted over two decades. While Mizo-dominated areas (Lushai Hills) in India were initially a part of the Mizo Hills district of the erstwhile Assam state, various Mizo organisations, including the Mizo Union, raised the demand for a separate state for the Mizos. In 1959, the Mizo populated areas of Assam were engulfed in a severe famine. Assam Government's inadequate handling of the situation angered many amongst the Mizos. The proclamation of Assamese as the official language of the state in 1960, rehabilitation of the Chakma refugees from East Pakistan in the Mizo Hills District further stoked ethnic anxieties.

The growing discontent ultimately resulted in a secessionist movement led by Mizo National Front (MNF), an organisation that had evolved out of a famine relief team. While the Mizo Union's demand was limited to a separate state for the Mizos within India, the MNF aimed at separating from the Indian Union altogether and establishing a sovereign nation. On 1 March 1966, the Mizo National Front (MNF) made a declaration of independence, and launched coordinated attacks on the Government offices and security forces in different parts of the Mizo Hills district. On 2 March 1966, the Government of Assam responded by invoking the Assam Disturbed Areas Act, 1955 and the Armed Forces (Special Powers) Act, 1958, proclaiming the entire Mizo Hills district as "disturbed".

Meanwhile the Assam Rifles HQ and outposts located in the district came under heavy attack and were isolated. The situation was bad enough to warrant calling in of the Indian Air Force (IAF). However, the efforts of IAF to assist the besieged AR camp were resisted by heavy fire by the insurgents. Eventually on 4 March 1966, the IAF jet fighters strafed the MNF targets in Aizawl to suppress rebel activity[16]. However, it took an extensive military operation, coordinated by the HQ of Eastern command itself, to quell the uprising. Finally, by 25 March, the Indian Army, supported by Assam Rifles, recaptured all the places seized by the MNF and forced the rebels to retreat into the jungles. Following this, the MNA headquarters, originally located in Aizawl, moved multiple times, finally taking shelter in the Chittagong Hill Tracts in (then) East Pakistan. The Mizo National Front was eventually outlawed in 1967. Meanwhile, the MNF insurgents moved into the thick jungles[17] covering most of Mizo Hills or merged with the local population and continued to carry out armed attacks against the security forces.

Insurgency in Mizoram inflicted great hardship on the people as the insurgents resorted to guerrilla warfare to launch attacks on the patrols of the security forces, the non-combatant villagers, comprising vast majority of the population, suffered from both sides. For some time, the local population was also forced to shift from their traditional villages under the so-called "Grouping Policy" [18]. This was done to deny local support to militants. As insurgency continued, the need for creating space for political negotiations was felt by both sides. While the Government was keen on restoring peace and order in the area and disengaging the army, the Mizo Union also blamed MNF for violent insurgency and creating trouble for the people. In August 1968, the Government of India offered amnesty to the insurgents, which resulted in the surrender of 1524 MNF members. This was followed by more amnesty offers during 1969–70 and ending of the hated "grouping policy". The dialogue with various Mizo groups, including the MNF was initiated. The North Eastern Areas Reorganisation Act 1971, (which came into force in 1972) provided for Mizo Hills District being separated from Assam and constituted as a Union Territory. The Act also opened the gate for entry of the MNF into mainstream politics.

Counter-insurgency operations however, continued over the next few years, although the intensity diminished over time. At the same time a dialogue for long lasting peace in the area between the Government of India and various Mizo factions led by MNF also continued. Finally, in 1986 the Mizoram Peace Accord, which was an official agreement between the Government of India and the Mizo National Front (MNF) to end insurgency and violence in Mizoram, was signed. Following the Accord, the Union Territory of Mizoram was constituted as a full-fledged state of the Union with Aizawl as its capital. MNF, in return, decided to give up its secessionist demand and the use of violence.

Mizoram is peaceful today and is one of the progressive states of the North East with high literacy rates. However ethnic tensions remain with antipathy towards outsiders from the adjoining Barak Valley of Assam as well as tribal groups, such as Hmars, from other parts of the North East. Like Nagaland, Mizoram also has border disputes with the State of Assam which boil over into bloody clashes periodically, the latest being in 2021 itself. Being located on the border with Myanmar, Mizoram is also subject to influx from across the border resulting from repressive measures by the Myanmarese army. Meanwhile the days of famine and militancy as well as the military response that followed remains ingrained in the collective memory of the Mizos till date.

Assam

Migration into the Region resulted in serious disruption in Assam the largest of North Eastern states. Immigration into Assam in particular stoked apprehensions regarding survival of local cultures and loss of political control and has sparked off mass agitation which lasted nearly a decade and even led to insurgency.

Migration into Assam from neighbouring Bengal was initially encouraged by the colonial administration as it sought to bring more and more areas under cultivation, either for food grains or for tea plantations. Subsequent waves of migrants were caused by the Partition, the War for liberation of Bangladesh and the internal conflicts in that country in the early years of its formation.

During late 1970s, Assam, the largest of the North Eastern states with population nearly three fourths of that of the entire region, saw the beginning of a widespread Anti Foreigners Agitation in the state. Time to time efforts were made to deal with the issue. However, dissatisfaction with the solutions attempted (including political solutions) amongst some sections of the population led to a violent separatist movement which continued over the next two decades.

The origins of the agitation in Assam lay in the growing apprehensions amongst the local population of being outnumbered and eventually losing both their cultural identity as well as the political control of the State due to a heavy influx of migrants from the erstwhile East Pakistan (Bangladesh after 1971). The reorganisation of Assam in 1972 not only saw its geographical area shrink considerably but was seen as a political compromise with local identities who presented the threat of militant separatism. There was an equally strong assertion of the Assamese identity and culture. Beginning with the by-elections in the Mangaldai parliamentary constituency in 1978, there was a strident demand for a scrutiny of the electoral rolls which were suspected to contain names of a large number of illegal immigrants.

Soon this demand turned into a long-drawn Anti Foreigners Agitation involving large sections of the population and led prominently by students. The demand for rectification of state -wide electoral rolls and detection and deportation of illegal immigrants grew strong. Efforts to hold elections in 1983 without a consensus on the agitators' demands led to violent opposition which soon turned to widespread ethnic violence in different parts of the state leading to arson and killings, turning into massacres notably at Nellie, Mangaldai and Silapathar. The 1983 elections also unleashed a militant reaction which eventually morphed into a widespread insurgent/ separatist movement spanning the 1980s and 90s.

Meanwhile talks with the Agitation leaders continued and led to the historic Assam Accord in 1985. The Accord provided a framework for segregation of migrants into Assam with 1971 being the cut-off date. In addition, the Accord provided for investment in several infrastructure projects in Assam along with safeguards for Assamese culture. Notably it led to formation of a state level political party, the Asom Gana Parishad (AGP), which went on to win elections, rule the state for a full term of 5 years and restored peace to some extent. However even this political development failed to curb violent extremism. Many extremist elements did not accept the Accord. A violent extremist-terrorist movement emerged in Assam., led by the United Liberation Front of Assam (ULFA) that continued during most of the 1980s and early 1990s. in fact extremist violence reached such levels that in November 1990 the state Government was dismissed, President's rule imposed and the Army called in. Army immediately carried out a series of operations starting with Operation Bajrang, destroying ULFA camps and seizing their arms and ammunition[19]. Fresh elections were held leading to AGP losing its majority to the Congress Party. The new Government adopted a conciliatory note and granted general amnesty to ULFA detainees. ULFA, however regrouped and started its militant activities again[20]. In September 1991, fresh army action, namely Operation Rhino, was launched under which several more ULFA camps were raided and destroyed. Under pressure from the Indian Army, ULFA along with some other smaller militant organisations (such as NDFB, BLT, KLO and even some members of NSCN) sympathetic to it shifted their bases to Bhutan. Their heavily armed presence led to many apprehensions in that country. On 15 December 2003, the Royal Bhutan Army attacked several militant camps in Bhutan in a major operation named Operation All Clear[21] and inflicted heavy casualties on the militants.

After the military action in India and Bhutan the extremist movement in Assam suffered a setback with its cadres fleeing to largely to Myanmar and Bangladesh. ULFA itself split into Pro- and Anti-Talks factions. With the change in Government in Bangladesh, the support provided to Assam extremists was stopped. Most were forced to leave Bangladesh and some prominent ones were arrested and extradited to India. While the Pro-Talks faction came over ground and entered into dialogue with the Government of India, the anti-talks faction relocated to Myanmar continued its militancy and tied up with NSCN(K) and some extremist Bodo groups

Meanwhile, opposition to presence of illegal migrants in Assam lingered on. One reason was the dissatisfaction with the Illegal Migrants Tribunals Act 1983. This Act, while seeking to establish tribunals for detection and deportation of illegal migrants was seen as being ineffective as, unlike the Foreigners Act 1945, it placed the burden of proving the illegal status of a migrant on the accuser. The Act was challenged in the Supreme Court of India and was eventually set aside in 2006. Legal action to detect and deport the foreigners, however continued before the Supreme Court of India. Eventually in 2013, the Supreme Court of India directed the updating and recompilation of the National Register of Citizens, initially compiled in 1951 to identify and then detect and deport illegal immigrants. A comprehensive revision of the National Register of Citizens was carried out in the state and was completed under the supervision of the Supreme Court. The exercise left many people dissatisfied. On the one hand the exercise left out 1.9 million persons whose citizenship could not be categorically ascertained. On the other hand, criticism was voiced in some quarters over the allegedly no-comprehensive nature of the exercise. The Central Government established Foreigners Tribunals to verify the claims of the population whose status as citizen was alleged to be doubtful and enacted the Citizenship Amendment Act in an attempt to address the status of some of the persons left out. Dissatisfaction prevails in many quarters in the state over both the measures and even two decades into the 21st Century, the problem lingers on. However, with all that, Assam has witnessed political stability with regular elections and popularly elected governments serving out their regular tenures.

Apart from the broader immigration and linguistic division between Assamese and Bengali speaking population, Assam is a communally sensitive state with a sizable Muslim minority and home to many ethnic groups and tribes with inter-tribal rivalries and animosities breaking out in violence from time to time. The conflict so inherent feeds into armed violence not only between population groups but also against the State. Of these, the most serious was the movement by the Bodo tribals of Assam for a separate Bodoland State.

Assam - Bodo Militancy

The Bodos are an ethno-linguistic community native to the Brahmaputra Valley in Assam state of India. Belonging to Indo-Tibetan stock, they are regarded as original inhabitants of Assam. In the mid-1980s, Bodo politicians, alleging discrimination against Bodos, started a campaign for the creation of Bodoland. While majority of the Bodos envisaged Bodoland as an autonomous territory or state within India, a small section demanded complete sovereignty. In 1986, Bodo Security Force (BdSF), an armed group comprising of Bodo militants was formed that carried out several violent attacks against non-Bodo civilians. They also attacked the Assam Police Battalion headquarters at Choraikhola in Kokrajhar district and made off with a large quantity of weapons and ammunition.

In a pattern similar to Assam where the Anti Foreigners Agitation was led by the All-Assam Students Union, the Bodoland movement soon came to be led by the All-Bodo Students Union (ABSU) and Bodo Peoples' Action Committee (BPAC). In 1993, these two groups signed the Bodo Accord with Indian government, agreeing to the formation of Bodoland Autonomous Council within Assam. BdSF, however, opposed this Accord.

The territories of the BAC also remained under dispute. In 1994, the BdSF, who was renamed National Democratic Front of Bodoland (NDFB). The NDFB then launched an ethnic cleansing campaign, attacking people from non-Bodo communities in the disputed villages. During the 1996 Assam Legislative Assembly elections, NDFB attacks resulted in hundreds of Santhal, Munda and Oraon Adivasi inhabitants of territories claimed under Bodoland being killed. Several thousand were displaced. In response, the Adivasis formed the Adivasi Cobra Force, their own militant group.

In the mid-1990s, NDFB also faced a rival within the Bodo community, in the form of Bodo Liberation Tigers Force (BLTF). The BLTF had evolved from an older militant group called the Bodo Volunteer Force. It considered NDFB's secessionist agenda unrealistic and unattainable, and focused on establishment of an autonomous Bodo territory within India. After 1996, the two groups clashed violently for supremacy. BLTF allied with Bengali Tiger Force to protect Bengalis from NDFB attacks, and also supported Indian security forces against NDFB. The conflicts between Christian-dominated NDFB and the BLTF, majority non-Christian, polarised the Bodoland movement along religious lines. In 2003, BLTF surrendered *en masse* in return for the establishment of the Bodoland Territorial Council, while the NDFB went underground.

Following the surrender of BLTF and on culmination of talks with them, a Memorandum of Settlement was signed on 10 February 2003 between the Government of India, the Government of Assam and Bodo Liberation Tigers. In pursuance of this Memorandum, the Bodoland Territorial Council was constituted under the Sixth Schedule to the Constitution of India in 2003 itself. The Constitution of this Council under the Sixth Schedule was aimed at providing a certain degree of autonomous self-governance to fulfil economic, educational and linguistic aspirations, preservation of land-rights, socio-cultural and ethnic identity of the Bodos and to speed up the economic development of the BTC area through earmarked central Government funds.

Meanwhile, NDFB had established several camps for their armed cadres on the Bhutan side of the Bhutan-Assam border. During 2003-2004, the Royal Bhutan Army destroyed these camps as part of its Operation All Clear. After this, the NDFB also decided to go for ceasefire and talks to resolve the issue in 2004. This resulted in a ceasefire agreement between NDFB and the Government on 25 May 2005. However, certain factions of NDFB continued militancy.

31

Over time, NDFB split into Pro-Talks and Anti-Talks Factions. NDFB(P), the pro-talks factions led by B Sungthagra supported peace talks with the government while NDFB(R), led by Ranjan Daimary, refused to give up militancy. In 2008, a bomb explosion took place in Guwahati resulting in death and injury to large number of people. The NDFB (Anti Talks) faction led by Ranjan Daimary was held responsible for this outrage. In December 2008, the NDFB(P) indicated its plans to indirectly or directly participate the Lok Sabha elections. In 2012, I. K. Songbijit, the chief of the NDFB(R) faction's "Bodoland Army", announced the formation of a nine-member "interim national council", resulting in a further split in the Anti-Talks faction. NDFB(S), the faction led by Songbijit, is still continuing with militant approach.

During the period 2012-14, several attacks took place on non-Bodo people living in BTC areas or which were attributed to the NDFB(S). There were clashes between different communities with large scale arson and killing. Many thousands were uprooted from their villages and forced to take shelter in heavily guarded camps. Eventually, the Government of India launched Operation All Out to eliminate the NDFB(S) militants and deployed as many as 9,000 soldiers of the Indian Army and the Central Reserve Police Force for the purpose. As a result, peace was restored in the Bodo territories and thousands of people who had fled their homes out of fear were able to return.

Recently after yet another accord in 2020 the BTC was named the Bodo Territorial Region with further enhancement of autonomy and clarity on some of the villages to be included/excluded[22].

Manipur

Though the Kingdom of Manipur merged with the Indian Union on 15 October 1949, many amongst the Meiteis who wanted to revive Manipur's former glory resented the merger. The insurgency in the neighbouring Nagaland and according of statehood to Nagaland was seen as Manipur's claims being ignored. 1964 saw the formation of the United National Liberation Front (UNLF), a separatist organisation having the objective of establishing an independent Manipur. Eventually, Manipur was given statehood in 1972, but this failed to assuage the separatist elements and Manipur was afflicted by a very violent insurgent movement aimed at Meitei revivalism. Between 1977 and 1980, many more armed insurgent groups were formed such as the People's Liberation Army of Manipur (PLA), the People's Revolutionary Party of Kangleipak (PREPAK) and the Kangleipak

Communist Party (KCP). On 8 September 1980, Manipur was declared a disturbed area, when the Indian Government imposed the Armed Forces (Special Powers) Act, 1958 on the region, which currently remains in force.

The emergence of National Socialist Council of Nagaland (NSCN) and its advocacy of the United Nagalim, which included several areas falling within the Manipur state, led to ethnic tensions between Manipuris and Nagas. Violence by the Naga groups spilled over into Manipur, with several clashes between the NSCN-IM and the Khaplang faction of National Socialist Council of Nagaland (NSCN-K) being reported from the hill districts of the State. Presence of heavily armed Nagas in Manipur led to friction with other tribal groups with violent ethnic clashes between the Nagas and Kukis erupting in 1993. Consequently, a number of other tribal groups such as Kukis, Paite, Vaiphei, Pangals and Hmars also established their own militant groups. The rise of tribal militias was responsible for ethnic violence that took between Nagas and Kukis during most of the 1990s.

A report of the State Home department in May 2005 indicated that 'as many as 12,650 cadres of different insurgent outfits with 8830 weapons are actively operating in the State'. Meanwhile the incidents arising from use of force while exercising powers under the AFSPA resulted in the State witnessing an unprecedented civic protest which continued for a long time.

Eventually several militant groups such as the Kangleipak Communist Party (KCP), Kanglei Yawol Kanna Lup (KYKL), People's Revolutionary Party of Kangleipak (PREPAK), People's Revolutionary Party of Kangleipak-Pro (PREPAK-Pro), Revolutionary People's Front (RPF). United National Liberation Front (UNLF), United People's Party of Kangleipak (UPPK) have come together as the CorCOM -a short name for Coordination Committee. CorCom is on the extremist organisations list of the Government of India, and is responsible for many bombings.

Manipur witnessed a series of protests starting in July 2015, following demands for the implementation of the Inner Line Permit (ILP)[23] system in the State. The protesters demanded that the government introduce the ILP bill in the State Assembly[24]. The Inner Line Permit (ILP) is an official travel document issued by the Government of India to grant inward travel of any person, including Indian citizens into a protected area for a limited period. Currently, the Inner Line Permit is operational in Arunachal Pradesh, Mizoram and Nagaland. The legal framework for imposition of the ILP regime is provided in the Bengal Eastern Frontier Regulation, 1873 and the conditions and restrictions vary from state to state.

The Kuki population of Manipur is wary of the motives of the ILP campaign[25]. The apprehension has recently been heightened by the fact that some within the Meitei community have called the Kukis' foreigners. The Kukis are a population group that is akin to Mizos of Mizoram and Chins inhabiting Indo-Myanmar Border, sharing common ancestry with both. They are however an indigenous group in Manipur now. There are apprehensions amongst the Kukis that Meiteis could use the ILP to advance their stand of Kukis being foreigners. This also seems to be an important reason why many within the Kuki community do not support the ILP or the Meiteis' demand for tribal status.

The Manipur state assembly passed three bills to give more rights to indigenous groups. This was followed by counter protests by the Kukis and Nagas to withdraw the bills resulting in violence and deaths. The tribal groups claim that the new bills, would allow Meiteis to buy land in the hill districts of Manipur where the Nagas and Kukis live. Further they argue that these bills were passed without consulting them. This has led to a tense situation till now.

The porous border with Myanmar and presence of people from same ethnic group on both sides enables sanctuary and weapons supplies to militants. On 4 June, 2015, 18 Indian Army jawans were killed and several others were injured when suspected militants ambushed their convoy in Manipur's Chandel district. In response, the Indian Army, in one of its biggest covert missions sent troops into Myanmar to strike at two militant camps located across the border and, according to official estimates, killed over 20 suspected militants.

During 2023 friction between the Meities and Kukis and other tribal groups boiled over into long drawn and bloody ethnic clashes following a ruling of the High Court directing the Government to accord tribal status to Meities, an order interpreted by Kukis as being detrimental to their traditional land rights and benefits. Despite heavy presence of security forces, Meitei-Kuki clashes have continued with virtual breakdown of law-and-order machinery and significant loss of life on both sides. As of date, Manipur remains on the boil. The conflict also threatens to spill over beyond Manipur as Mizoram has come out in support of the Kuki population, with groups of former militants giving calls for Meiteis living in Mizoram to leave that state.

Tripura

Tripura's demography underwent a major change as a result of migration from former East Bengal and subsequently from Bangladesh. Indigenous Tripuris, mostly tribals, were outnumbered and pushed to the hills. Gradually politics and administration in the state became dominated by the Bengali-speaking immigrants. This resulted in resurgence of Tripuri, nativist nationalism. Eventually it led to insurgency on ethnic lines as a Tribal versus Immigrant conflict.

The first militant outfit to form was Tripura National Volunteers (TNV). It was active until 1988. However, most prominent ones were National Liberation Front of Tripura (NLFT) and All Tripura Tiger Force (ATTF). NLFT wanted to establish an independent Tripura and ATTF wanted to finalise the Tripura merger agreement. However, all of them wished to remove immigrants who had entered Tripura after 1950 despite of their ideological differences.

Eventually The Tripura Tribal Areas Autonomous District Council (TTAADC) Act 1979 was passed by the Indian parliament setting up the autonomous district council to empower the Indigenous people of Tripura to govern themselves and also to protect and preserve their culture, customs, and traditions. It finally came into effect from 1 April 1985 covering about 68% of the total area. The number of Scheduled Tribes of the state who reside in the TTAADC area is 87.55% of the total Indigenous population of Tripura.

These groups received the major blow when their leaders were all arrested in their hideout camps in Bangladesh. From the end of 2020, A resurgence has occurred led by the NLFT with incidents of kidnapping workers and killing of a trader marking the emergence of insurgency in the state again.

Conflict over Inter State Boundaries

The formation of new states also left some issues of inter-state boundaries unresolved. As new states were carved out of Assam the traditional access to populations on either side came to be at a variance with the newly drawn state boundaries. The tribal/ ethnic assertion of statehood has led to demands for incorporation of ethnically related population pockets located in other states. While boundary disputes exist between other states of India as well, ethnic identity has led to a peculiar set of boundary disputes between NE States which occasionally results in armed conflict, sometimes with the participation of armed police on one or both sides.

Clashes have taken place along Assam- Nagaland border[26] periodically since mid-1960s till 2014, with those in 1979, 1985 and 2014 being particularly bloody, with a large number of people killed and several thousands being forced to flee their villages and take shelter in relief camps. At Chungajan, on 5 January, 1979, armed Nagas attacked Assamese villages bordering Nagaland killing 55 Assamese and burning hundreds of dwellings. Sporadic clashes carried on before exploding again on 4 June, 1985, at Merapani in the Doyang reserve forest in Jorhat. That time, Nagas, accompanied by their state's armed police, left 40 Assamese policemen dead and 90 others, including police personnel, injured. Assam claims that 878 sq. km of its land in the disputed, and encroached, reserve forests of Jorhat and Sibsagar districts, has been occupied illegally by people from Nagaland whereas the Nagas view this area as their own territory[27]. The Central Government had earlier constituted two commissions[28], the Sundaram Commission (1971) and the Shastri Commission (1985), to settle the Assam-Nagaland border dispute. However, the recommendations of these Commissions were not accepted by the State Governments concerned. Eventually neutral central forces had to be stationed along the contentious area along the Assam-Nagaland border as neither of the population groups trusted the police forces of the other state. The Assam government filed a case in the Supreme Court in 1988 for resolving the border dispute which is still under consideration.

There is simmering tensions along Assam's border with other states as well[29], such as Meghalaya and Mizoram. More recently, in 2021 clashes erupted between police personnel from Assam and Mizoram along Assam Assam-Mizoram border over some disputed territory, leaving six Assam policemen dead. A tract of forest land of about 1300 sq Km is claimed by Mizoram as its own (following the 1875 notification under the East Bengal Frontier Regulation of 1873, which described the Inner Line Reserved Forest) should be the basis for delineating the border while Assam asserts it lies within the boundaries of Assam as defined post the North-Eastern Areas (Reorganisation) Act, 1971, which in turn was based on the 1933 notification of the Lushai Hills Inner Line.

Of late effort has been made to settle boundary disputes through political dialogue and negotiations. Some success has been achieved in respect of a few disputed villages along the Assam -Meghalaya and Assam -Arunachal border. While both Nagaland and Mizoram have shown some interest in a politically negotiated settlement, it remains to be seen whether these efforts are sustainable given the turn of political complexion in the negotiating states.

The Legacy of Conflict – A Reality Check for the Present

Internal security in the NER has always been a critical area requiring continuous attention. It has been a complex milieu of conflict- both inter se and against the State- terrorism, insurgency, mass protests and agitations.

The political developments in the North East since independence have also unleashed many conflicts and rivalries from time to time. The internal conflict in the NE has religious-communal, linguistic and ethnic dimensions with clashes and conflicts take place along these fault lines. In many cases such tensions turn into resentment against the State and turn into violent movements, leading to the creation of terrorist/ insurgent groups and organisations.

The North Eastern region has a significant bearing on the national security environment due to the un-demarcated border with China and its location surrounded by China, Bangladesh, Myanmar and Bhutan and Nepal (Sikkim, though geographically separate, has also been tagged to the North East). The situation is further compounded by the current unrest in Myanmar. Therefore, Indian Military presence in the North East is likely to continue in the region for any foreseeable length of time.

The journey towards peace and stability, however has been quite turbulent and has been punctuated by periodic out bursts of violence. The militant-secessionist fringe, though underground or exiled and isolated, still exists. So do identity-based fault lines. Some significant issues of the past, such as Naga demands for sovereignty and detection and deportation of foreigners from Assam are still to reach a closure. The challenge of enabling resettlement of surrendered militants still remains.

The background of insurgency and unrest ensure that the state and central police and paramilitary forces, combining as internal security forces are also likely to retain a significant presence along with the presence of the Indian Army and other para-military forces, to maintain regional peace and security. The imperative of dealing with external and internal security threats have also led to a huge investment in infrastructure, which is well adapted to economic use. However, the challenge is to ensure that the turbulent past of the NE Region does not become a constraint for its future development. As institutions of participative governance take root and grow in the region, the infrastructure for transport, communications and various business activities is expanded and modernised, the environment for economic development would continue to be strengthened.

Yet it is prudent to keep in mind the past while devising new strategies for the future. The extensive presence of the Indian Security Forces in the region is not going to be reduced anytime soon. This effort will have to be sustained so that strategies for economic growth may be worked out and implemented. Only then can the natural advantage of the NER as a bridge to SE Asia be leveraged through the Act East Policy.

Notes to Chapter 2

1. The Japanese, having over-run Burma through rapid advances in 1942, sought to extend their domination to India. For this they planned to attack Manipur as this was the launching pad for Brigadier Wingate's "Chindit" operations behind Japanese lines and later on was being prepared as the assembly point for Allied forces for a counter-attack into Burma. In March 1944, the Japanese 15th Army began a two-pronged advance against India's north-east frontier. One part of the attacking force was to capture the British supply bases on the Imphal Plain while the second was to attack Kohima and push towards the railhead at Dimapur through Kohima, and thereafter possibly move on to the Assam plains.

2. The battle for Kohima has been referred to by authors such as Martin Dougherty and Jonathan Ritter as the "Stalingrad of the East". Military historian Robert Lyman said that the battle of Kohima and Imphal "changed the course of the Second World War in Asia... For the first time the Japanese were defeated in a battle and they never recovered from it". In 2013, a poll conducted by the British National Army Museum voted the Battles of Kohima and Imphal as "Britain's Greatest Battles".

3. The Japanese Offensive started on 30 March 1944. Between 5 April and 18 April, Kohima saw some of the bitterest close-quarter fighting of the War. Kohima had a 2,500 strong garrison. Faced by 15,000 Japanese, the British-Indian troops held on to a defensive perimeter centred on Garrison Hill. In one sector, only the width of the tennis court separated the two sides. Meanwhile the siege of Imphal, which also started on 30 March, continued till the end of May by which time the Japanese had suffered extremely heavy casualties and were no longer able to continue their military operations in the Imphal sector.

4. The Japanese 15th Army, 85,000-strong, eventually lost 53,000 dead and missing, a 62% fatality rate. The British/Indian forces sustained 12,500 casualties at Imphal, while the fighting at Kohima cost them another 4,000 casualties. (Ref National Army Museum). According to Robert Lyman, the Japanese combat force that crossed the Chindwin River was about 65,000 men and suffered 53,000 casualties, an unprecedented percentage of 81 %.

5. In fact, lines of supply were extended even beyond colonial India. NER was not only the launching pad for the Burma Counteroffensive but also for providing military aid to Nationalist Chinese forces resisting Japanese invasion. This was done through many airfields located in Assam and the famous Burma Road stretching from Ledo in Assam to Kunming in South China, through Northern Burma.

6. Migration continued, primarily from East Pakistan to India, right up to the liberation of Bangladesh in 1971, both on an ongoing basis and with spikes

during periods of particular communal unrest such as the 1964 East Pakistan riots and the 1965 India-Pakistan War, when it is estimated that 600,000 refugees left for India.

7.   The Nehru-Liaquat (or the Delhi Pact) was a bilateral treaty signed in New Delhi by the Prime Minister of India Jawahar Lal Nehru and the Prime Minister of Pakistan Liaquat Ali Khan on 8 April, 1950. The treaty sought to put an end to attacks on minorities on either side after the Partition of India by guaranteeing their rights. The imperative to avoid another war between India and Pakistan, soon after the 1948 war in Kashmir most likely weighed on the two sides. As per the treaty, refugees were allowed to return to dispose of their property, abducted women and looted property were to be returned, forced conversions were de-recognised and minority rights were confirmed.

8.   It is estimated that around 10 million refugees from the then East Pakistan entered India during the early months of the Bangladesh Liberation War 1971 due to atrocities committed by the Pakistani army on the local population. Of these approx. 1.5 million may have stayed back after Bangladesh became independent.

9.   Eventually, clause 9 of the 9-Point Agreement of 1946 was to prove contentious as both sides interpreted it differently. The Indian Government accepted post-Agreement dispensation only under the Indian Constitution while the Naga side interpreted it to mean an arrangement providing them full sovereignty.

10.   This "referendum" was allegedly carried out in a restrictive manner, leading to it being disregarded by the Government of India as also many amongst the Nagas.

11.   The Agreement provided for constituting the territories that were heretofore known as the Naga Hills-Tuensang Area under the Naga Hills-Tuensang Area Act, 1957, as a State within the Indian to be known as Nagaland. The Agreement also stipulated that the Nagaland shall be under the Ministry of External Affairs of the Government of India: The 16 Point Agreement between the Government of India and the Naga People's Convention, 26 July 1960.

12.   As per the Accord: "The representatives of the underground organisations conveyed their decision, of their own volition, to accept, without condition, the Constitution of India. It was agreed that the arms, now underground, would be brought out and deposited at appointed places. Details for giving effect of this agreement will be worked out between them and representatives of the Government, the security forces, and members of the Liaison Committee."

13.   The aspirational "Greater Nagalim" claims about 1,20,000 sq. km, while the present state of Nagaland consists of 16,527 sq. km.

14. In 2015, NSCN-K became affiliated with a new organisation named the United Liberation Front of Western South East Asia (UNLFW), formed as a united front of Northeast Indian militant groups. In 2015 NSCN(K) unilaterally abrogated the ceasefire agreement signed by it in 2001 and carried out several attacks on security forces, including the 2015 Manipur ambush (Tangel District), in which 18 soldiers of the Indian Army were killed and 15 were wounded. The militant group later claimed that the attack was a joint operation by it with other Manipuri insurgent groups namely the Kanglei Yawol Kanna Lup and Kangleipak Communist Party. In 2018, NSCN (K), now led by Khango Konyak, revoked its 2015 decision of abrogation of ceasefire.

15. NSCN denies any extortion though there are reports of the" Naga Underground" which includes armed cadres of NSCN, taking a tax from the government employees living in areas dominated by them and also a fixed tax for houses, shops and commercial establishments operating in such areas. These levies are considered legitimate by the "Underground" factions.

16. The day of the airstrikes, the only instance of IAF carrying out a combat airstrike in Indian territory, is still observed by the people as Zoram Ni ("Zoram Day").

17. The insurgent militancy was sharp and intense and brought the security forces face to face with jungle warfare. Feeling the need to train the soldiers in fighting with the rebels in this mode, the Counterinsurgency and Jungle Warfare School was also set up at Vairangte in 1967.

18. Starting in January 1967, the Government resorted to involuntary displacement of people under the so-called "grouping policy" under which nearly 80% of the rural population was forcibly shifted from their villages and resettled along the highways. The new settlements were kept under the control of the security forces. This resulted in farms and houses in earlier villages being destroyed leading to collapse of farm output and near-famine conditions.

19. Operation Bajrang took place on the night of 27 November 1990, in the forest of Lakhipathar (in Tinsukia district) where the ULFA had their Central Headquarter (CHQ) and General Headquarter (GHQ) and in the forests of Charaipung (in Sivasagar district). The ULFA leadership however got wind of the proposed operation and fled the camps before the operation was started. The army captured the camps at Lakhipathar and Charaipung after a few gunfights and disposing of the land mines planted by the fleeing extremists. During the operation, 15 activists (including sympathisers and civilians) were killed, 1208 weapons and a large amount of cash (about Rs 5.0 Cr.) seized. Over 2000 suspected militants were arrested. (India Today). Operation Bajrang denied these forest areas for further insurgent operations and also uncovered mass graves of persons who had been killed by ULFA during their reign of terror in the area. During the operation, the ULFA-LTTE link was

also exposed as the landmines found in Lakhipathar were similar to those used by LTTE during that period.

20. Between November 1990 and March 1991, the ULFA reportedly killed 97 people including Assam Pradesh Congress(I) Committee's General Secretary Manabendra Sarma. (India Today)

21. The Royal Bhutan Army (RBA) destroyed 30 ULFA camps, confiscated 500 AK 47/56 assault rifles and a huge quantity of other weapons including rocket launchers, mortars and communication equipment, along with more than 100,000 rounds of ammunition and an anti-aircraft gun. About 120 militants were killed. ULFA's central command headquarters located at Phukatong in Samdrup Jongkhar were seized along with capture of several senior ULFA commanders. As a result, large numbers of rebels fled to Bangladesh or surrendered to Indian forces across the border. The captured rebels and civilians along with seized weapons and ammunition were handed over to the Government of India by the RBA along with five top ranking militants, including KLO vice-chairman Harshabardhan Barman, who were transferred to Tezpur, India.

22. As per the 2020 Agreement, the Bodoland Territorial region (BTR) also got the right to be represented at national level sports and cultural events. The Agreement also made the Bodo language with Devnagri script an associate official language of Assam.

23. The ILP concept comes from the colonial era. Under the Bengal Eastern Frontier Regulation Act, 1873, the British framed regulations restricting the entry and regulating the stay of outsiders in designated areas along the North East border of colonial India. In doing so the British were mindful of the tribal ethos of the areas in question and their acquisition by the empire by military force. The colonial administration, while taking these areas under their protection, did not wish to create trouble for itself by treading on the sensitivities of local tribes with regard to influx of "outsiders" from the rest of India. The ILP was therefore designed to prevent "British subjects" (Indians) from entering these regions in an unregulated manner. In 1950, the Indian government recognised the need to address local concerns about protecting the interests of the indigenous people and in addition to the Sixth Schedule, continued with the ILP system by replacing "British subjects" with "Citizen of India".

24. The latest application of the ILP regime was in Manipur in 2019, where it was imposed on the demand of the State Government.

25. The Kuki population of Manipur is wary of the motives of the ILP campaign. The apprehension has recently been heightened by the fact that some within the Meitei community have called the Kukis' foreigners. Though the Kukis are an indigenous group in Manipur, there are some who fear that the Meiteis

could use the ILP to advance their stand of Kukis being foreigners. This also seems to be an important reason why many within the Kuki community do not support the ILP or the Meiteis' demand for tribal status.

26. The State of Nagaland Act, 1962 defined its borders based on the 1925 notification. The government of the newly formed state of Nagaland, however, did not accept the boundary delineation and demanded that Nagaland should comprise all areas which according to the Nagas, were part of the Naga territory in 1866, but which were excluded by establishment of the Inner Line Regulation of 1873

27. Assam and Nagaland share a 434-kilometre border along which about 66,000 hectares of land are disputed constituting the Disputed Areas Belt (DAB). This is divided into six sectors -- A, B, C, D, E and F. which fall in Sivasagar, Golaghat, Jorhat and Karbi Anglong districts of Assam. The DAB, officially, is forest land (Forest Reserves or reserved forests) and includes parts of Diphu, South Nambor Doyang, Rengma, Doyang and some other Reserve Forests covering approx. 12880 sq Km of area. However, these reserved forests barely exist as most of the DAB has been converted to agricultural land with encroachments being encouraged from both sides-Assam and Nagaland- even though an official status quo is in place. As all occupation is informal, there are frequent disputes between squatter groups which periodically escalate into serious inter-ethnic clashes. In 1979 the CRPF, along with Assam Rifles, was deployed into the DAB as a "neutral" force. Following the 1985 Merapani incident the entire DAB was put under the CRPF. Later after 2014, the SSB was also inducted.

28. Sundaram Commission (1971) Shastri Commission (1985). JK Pillai Commission 1997 Supreme Court mandated Variava / Tarun Chatterjee Local Commission (2006); Mediators Sriram Panchoo and Niranjan Bhatt (2010)

29. The State of Assam filed Original Suit No. 2/1988 before Hon'ble Supreme Court for identification of boundary and resolving of border disputes with Nagaland and for granting permanent Injunction restraining the State of Nagaland from encroaching the areas within the constitutional boundary of Assam and to declare that state of Assam as rightful owner of all the encroached areas and direct the state of Nagaland to hand over peaceful possession of those areas. In 1995, the Assam government withdrew the suit only to renew it in 1998. The matter is now in the trial stage before the Hon'ble Supreme Court of India.

In the aftermath of the violent clashes of 2014, the Assam government moved the Supreme Court again. Eventually, In September 2020, , the governments of the two states held a high-level meeting towards settling the border dispute. However, the issue escalated soon after as Assam accused Nagaland of setting up a police camp inside Dissoi Valley Reserve Forest and countered by deploying armed Assam police in the area. The situation was brought under control but the orders of the apex court are still awaited.

(For details refer to   State Making and the Suspension of Law in India's Northeast- The Place of Exception in the Assam-Nagaland Border Dispute; Suykens, Bert; Also see Inter-state Border Disputes in Northeast India- Das, Pushpita, Research Fellow, Manohar Parrikar Institute for Defence Studies and Analyses, New Delhi)

Chapter 3.

NER Today: Assimilation Despite Conflict

(The political and administrative integration of India's North Eastern Region in the modern Indian State is an enduring phenomenon. This Chapter examines the factors that made it so, enabling the next phase of economic development to be ushered in and preparing the region as a base for further engagement East.)

Given the diversity of the North East, transformation to a new uniform national identity has been a process fraught with conflicts arising from various factors such as local identities and loyalties, sub–nationalistic, separatist impulses, lack of economic development etc. and is yet a work-in-process. Though the journey has been turbulent and fraught with conflict and pain, the Indian State has been able to assimilate the constituents of the NE Region with considerable success.

Today, in terms of political, geographical and administrative institutions, the North Eastern Region is fully integrated into the Indian Union. The entire region is politically subdivided into eight States of the Union, with seven of these lying east of the Siliguri Corridor. Each State has its governance structure derived from the Constitution of India, comprising of the executive, legislative and judicial organs of the state identical to the rest of the country. Political power is held based on the State Elections for the respective State Legislative Assemblies and conducted under the supervision of the Election Commission of India. Each State has its legislature to enact laws as per the State or the Concurrent List of the Constitution. Each State also elects its members to both houses of the National Parliament, on the basis of General Elections to the National Parliament also conducted under the supervision of the Election Commission. Each state also has its administrative, criminal administration system and police machinery to deal with civil administration, policing and law and order requirements. Each state has districts, subdivision, blocks, police stations etc on a pattern common to the country as a whole. The Indian judicial system has been extended into the region with High Courts established at Guwahati, Shillong, Imphal, Agartala and Gangtok with Benches at Itanagar, Kohima and Aizawl. Each state has district and subordinate courts based on a common pattern but is also empowered to implement Tribal laws and traditions in certain areas.

Before a reality check on the situation, as it prevails in the NE today, it is worthwhile taking a look at the policies and instrumentalities that have, over the last seven decades or so, marked the process of assimilation and nation-building in the region.

Constitutional Democracy

After independence, India opted for a liberal, democratic polity, determined by an elaborate, written Constitution that not only safeguarded basic fundamental rights of its citizens but also established a democratic, federal system of Government based on universal suffrage, with apportionment of rights and duties between the Central Government and the constituent states. The Constitution provides a framework that was flexible enough to accommodate aspirations of a large diversity of peoples while providing protection to tribal cultures and socially disadvantaged sections of the population.

This framework, set India on a trajectory that was quite different from that followed in most other nations in Asia. This was a tough journey considering that in Asia, many regimes established immediately after independence, initially democratic, were toppled by military coups soon after. While China, a major Asian country came under single party communist rule, some other countries such as Korea and Vietnam became victims of violent proxy conflicts resulting from the Cold War and like North Korea, Cambodia and Viet Nam ended up with authoritarian regimes. Where the choice was for democracy, the democratic system did not last long, lapsing into military rule (many West Asian countries, Pakistan, Indonesia, Myanmar and eventually even Thailand). Many of these countries faced ethno-linguistic-religious conflict that resulted in the country breaking apart (Pakistan, with the formation of Bangladesh) or separatist tendencies which have not died down despite brutal repression over several decades. Many Asian countries ended up with military regimes along with internal and external conflicts unleashed on the retreat of colonialism, which continue till today in even more virulent form. In many countries there are zones or regions where the writ of the national government does not run.

The liberal democratic constitutional framework envisaged by the Founding Fathers of India, however, survived and thrived in India and became the bedrock of nation building, enabling the diversity of the sub-continent to be subsumed in shared values. As in other parts of the country, in the North eastern region it provided the platform for political negotiation, flexibility and accommodation to assimilate diverse viewpoints without threatening local identities and cultures. Over a period of time, the understanding amongst the disaffected peoples of the North East found that the constitutional framework did not threaten their identity or political aspirations paved the way for negotiation, compromise and accommodation. Sustainable peace in the North East is, in fact, incumbent upon the continued commitment of the Indian State and its peoples to the principles enshrined in the Constitution. A political agenda built upon majoritarian dominance is likely to spark off reactions amongst various minority ethnic groups interspersed all over the North East. It would be well to build upon the successes of the past through inclusive democracy.

Military intervention- A Means to an End

In the 1950s, post the devastation of the Partition, as various provinces of colonial India transitioned to their new identity as federating states of the independent Union of India, the Indian Nation State was engaged in the gigantic task of nation building amidst its immense diversity. As the Centre and the States, comprising the federal structure envisaged in the Constitution assumed their functions, the Nation faced many new challenges. These also included repeated external aggression as well as internal disturbances. The resources of the new Indian State in terms of administrative coverage and policing, as indeed its military, were quite limited, more so in the far-flung areas of the North East. The connectivity with- and within the NE Region- was very poor as the traditional routes connecting the region to the rest of India were lost in Partition. The remoteness from the governance centres provided an environment of assertion of identity, leading to secessionism. It also provided advantage to armed insurgents/militants in terms of inaccessible operating bases, freedom from surveillance, little opposition by ill-equipped local police force, limited in numbers and reach, and sanctuaries across the border when needed. As a result, it was often possible for them to outgun local police and intimidate local population.

The induction of paramilitary forces in the 1950s, and later the Indian Army to address the challenge to internal security gradually addressed this asymmetry. It is now known that at various times insurgency and militancy

47

in the North East had support across international borders, particularly from Pakistan and China. However, it soon became clear that motley insurgent groups could not withstand resolute action by the Indian Armed Forces and also while external powers may support the militants through training and supply of arms and ammunition, none would intervene on their behalf to enable their secessionist goals. As this reality dawned on the militants, it encouraged them to consider the option of negotiated settlements more seriously. The other factor was the hardship caused to the people, caught in the crossfire between the militants and the security forces. This also brought about pressure on the militants to cease their activities.

The Armed Forces Special Powers Act, 1958 (AFSPA) has come in for a fair share of criticism. It would, however, be well to remember that AFSPA was a special response to an extreme situation involving violence perpetrated by heavily armed militants. Significantly, the use of the Indian Armed Forces was always a means to the achieve the objective of restoring participative democracy and not of perpetual oppression or marginalisation of populations or groups. The Indian security forces, therefore, operated with the over-arching objective of restoring law and order to enable the normal functioning of the democratic, constitutional institutions in the areas affected by insurgency. Therefore, the pressure exerted by the Armed Forces resulted in progressive movement towards the eventual holding of elections and the functioning of Constitutional governance rather than the creation of special areas or zones ruled under extraordinary powers outside the purview of the Constitution. The response involving armed force, operated under active governance feedback and was always sought to be calibrated to the situation, with pull-backs to prevent it from being disproportionate or excessive. This is not to say that there were no excesses at any time. There have been instances of excessive application of force due to wrong intelligence, mistaken identity or even rogue elements in the security forces. There were indeed cases where the deployment and action by armed forces resulted in great difficulties and harassment of the local population. However, gradually the oversight by the elected governments, courts, media and civil society led to such situations being brought to light and eventually reduced. The security forces have also developed their internal discipline mechanisms to curb such occurrences. The positive impact of this policy was borne out as many state governments in the North East requested continuation of the AFSPA in certain areas while the erstwhile militants gradually abandoned militancy and re-joined the national mainstream.

Further, as the connectivity and law and order infrastructure in the region improved, the nature of response by the security forces also changed. Local police forces were strengthened with more personnel, better reach, logistics and equipment. More Central Armed Police Forces (CRPF, BSF) etc were inducted and established their permanent Regional headquarters, bases and supply lines, making for rapid deployment. While the Army remained as a backup to be used in extreme situations, the variety of Central Police Forces deployed also acquired understanding of the local terrain and the people and learnt to respond in a more measured way. In addition, new administrative instruments, such as the Civil-Military Unified Command were developed to ensure coordination and provide feedback both to the State and Central Governments as well as to the security forces. As connectivity improved so did the security infrastructure. Over the last decade, Army deployment on Internal Security duties has reduced over the years, leading to Army concentrating more on external threats across national borders.

In this back-drop, over nearly seven decades, many hard-core militants gave up the resort to arms and chose to participate in the Indian democracy, through negotiated peace. This acceptance of political solutions within the Indian Constitution would have been unlikely in the absence of resolute action by the Indian Army over the decades. However, while on the one hand it is important to inculcate a sense of security amongst various ethnic groups constituting minority population in some states, it is imperative that the Security forces continue to build a more nuanced, intelligence based and well-crafted response involving use of minimum necessary force in dealing with such confrontations.

Open Door Policy for Negotiation and Dialogue:

The process of weaning away the general public and militants of the NER from extremist /separatist ideologies has been facilitated by the ability of the Indian State to maintain openness towards dialogue with anyone willing to talk peace. The policy was guided by the perception that militants/insurgents were really Indian citizens led astray, who had the right to return as long as they gave up their ideology of separatism and violence. Therefore, the door always remained open to welcome back any of the elements that had, at different times adopted militancy and armed struggle to achieve their separatist aims.

The means adopted were opening doors to talks between the militant leaders and the Indian state, patiently persevering with the dialogue and eventually leading to mutual understandings expressed through various talks, ceasefire agreements and peace accords. In many cases the talks were long drawn and had their ups and downs. As people and administrations tired of the long-drawn conflict there was also a genuine desire to restore peace. Throughout this process, calls were made to militants to lay down arms. These calls were responded to on several occasions, resulting in agreements for Suspension of Operations and surrenders by armed militants. Dialogues with specific insurgent groups and separatist movements were continued despite political changes in the Central and State Governments and led to several Accords, that were sometimes accompanied by territorial reorganisations, granting of administrative autonomy under the Constitution in certain areas, dropping of legal action against the militant/insurgents, according them freedom to form political parties or groups with the same rights as others.

This political accommodation and power sharing resulted in erstwhile separatists joining the political process by contesting elections and even winning them, forming governments and sharing political power at all levels. This process, going through several iterations over the past half century or so has come to stabilise itself in the region. However, the political option can also be derailed if political power is seen and used as a path way to majoritarian patronage. To wean away the people from militancy and separatism and to prevent their return to such thinking in the future, it is essential that age-old ethnic identity base animosities are not resurrected.

Political Reorganisation and Statehood

Ever since India's Independence, the NE Region has been reorganised several times with creation of new states and administrative units to recognise local political aspirations and to provide for self – governance under the Constitution[1]. The first such measure came with the statehood for Nagaland in 1963 on the basis of the 16 Point Agreement of 1960. This was followed by the North Eastern Areas (Reorganisation) Act 1971 which came into force in 1972and resulted in the creation of a new, separate state of Meghalaya by carving out Khasi, Garo and Jaintia Hills districts from the erstwhile state of Assam. The areas falling under the North East Frontier Agency (NEFA), as also the Mizo Hills district of Assam, were both separated from Assam and constituted as the Union Territories of Arunachal Pradesh and Mizoram respectively. Manipur and Tripura, who were Union Territories till that time, were constituted as full- fledged states. In addition, there were several Accords and Agreements that paved the way for return of Agitation leaders or separatists to the political mainstream[2].

The Assam Accord of 1985, while not reorganising any territory, opened the door for political participation by the leaders of the Anti-Foreigners Agitation which had continued over the last several years. In 1986, following the Mizo Accord, Mizoram was accorded full statehood. Finally in 1987, Arunachal Pradesh was given full statehood. This re-organisation assuaged the political exclusion felt by many population groups in the North East but also laid the seed of the perception that boundaries of identity and governance must coincide- a perception that will have to be dealt with sensitively in the future.

The Sixth Schedule and Self Governance

The Fifth and Sixth Schedule[3] of the Constitution were devised keeping in view the diversities of tribes and ethnicities in various regions and to provide self-governing institutions to the tribes that inhabited certain contiguous areas but were not numerous enough to form viable states. Of these the Sixth Schedule applied specifically to the tribal areas of Assam in the North East. Initially it was applied to a number of districts in the then composite state of Assam such as Khasi and Jaintia, Garo, Karbi Anglong, North Cachar Hills, Areas falling under NEFA, Naga Hills and Mizo Hills Districts etc.

The Sixth Schedule was resorted to for addressing aggressive sub-nationalisms and averting ethnic bloodshed in areas where constitution of a state was not warranted but the conflict tended to assume shape of separatist terrorism if left unchecked. Two instances of application of this framework could be seen in Tripura and Assam. The Tripura Tribal Areas Autonomous District Council (TTAADC) Act 1979 was passed by the Indian Parliament in response to movements launched by the Indigenous people of Tripura. The Act came into force on 15 January 1982 and the provisions of the Sixth Schedule were applied to the TTADC by the 49th Constitution (Amendment) Act, 1984, coming into effect on 1 April 1985. The Sixth Schedule was again in play in Bodoland with an Accord in 2003 leading to the formation of the Bodoland Territorial Council under the Sixth Schedule, covering 8970 Sq. Km of area with four clearly demarcated districts and enhanced powers covering land management and almost all the development activities for the territory. Through another accord in 2020, the BTC was named the Bodo Territorial Region along with resolution of its boundaries, some parts of which had been disputed till then.

Over a period of time, the resort to Sixth Schedule in both cases served to address local ethnicity-based aspirations without causing further fragmentation of the states concerned. In Tripura the energetic implementation of the TTADC Act yielded almost immediate peace dividend while in Bodoland, it took nearly three decades to resolve the conflict, probably due to the degree of mobilisation and militarisation of Bodo insurgents. There are issues about the implementation of development schemes and management of public institutions in Sixth Schedule areas, but resort to this constitutional provision did enable a peace dividend. Its future success will depend upon the manner in which District Councils set up in such areas go about meeting the aspirations of the people.

Investing in Economic Development and Security Infrastructure

North Eastern Council (NEC) was constituted as a statutory advisory body under the North Eastern Council Act 1971[4] and came into being on 7 November 1972 with its headquarters at Shillong. The eight States of Northeast India viz. Arunachal Pradesh, Assam, Manipur, Meghalaya, Mizoram, Nagaland, Tripura and Sikkim, are members of the council, with their respective Chief Ministers and Governors representing them. Sikkim was added to the council in the year 2002. The Council functions under the Ministry of Development of North Eastern Region (DONER) of the Government of India.

The Council was initially set up as an advisory body but since 2002 has functioned as a regional planning body.[5] Funded largely by the Central Government, it has demonstrated considerable achievements, mostly in setting up institutions of regional character in education, medicine, science and capacity building. The Council has also taken up major highway and bridge building projects and funds several engineering and medical colleges. In addition to development related activities, the NEC was also empowered to monitor the internal security situation in the North East.[6]

A big push for development of infrastructure in the North East was given with the setting up of M/DoNER in 2001 making it responsible for the matters relating to the planning, execution and monitoring of development schemes and Infrastructural projects in the NE region. As per the Ministry's charter It acts as a facilitator between the Central Ministries/ Departments and the State Governments of the North Eastern Region in the economic development including removal of infrastructural bottlenecks, provision of basic minimum services, creating an environment for private investment and to removing impediments to lasting peace and security in the North Eastern Region.

The development push given in the North Eastern States over the past quarter century has resulted in significant improvement in rail, road and air connectivity and overall economic development of the region. While much remains to be done this aspect primarily holds out hope through a wider and more intense engagement with South East Asia through the Region-a promise that could well be fulfilled by the Act East Policy.

NER Today

The resolute action by the Indian State to preserve the integrity of its territories and borders, the continuous pressure exerted by the Indian security forces, combining the Army, paramilitary and Central armed police forces, as also the vastly improved state police forces have persuaded most of the militants of the North East to bid farewell to arms and return to the mainstream. The secessionist movements of the past have also splintered with the bulk of their followers giving up militancy and returning to peaceful life. However, some hard-core extremist organisations and militant elements still remain. While being a minority, many of these have been forced to retreat to remote areas of the region or across the border to Myanmar.

Yet the shadow of the past remains over the region. The legacy and memories of the armed insurgency, the hardships and loss of life and opportunity suffered by the people still rankle the public mind. The dispensation of justice and redressal through judicial oversight over actions by the security forces often ends up being "too little, too late". The same shadow persists in the form of large numbers of erstwhile militants struggling to rehabilitate themselves, of continued existence of large quantities of arms still to be seized or surrendered, of ultra extremists regrouping outside India's borders, of continued assertions of communal, linguistic, ethnic identity and the fault lines so caused, of support by foreign powers hostile to India ever willing to fish in troubled waters.

Another risk factor lies in politics of inclusive development becoming politics of identity-based patronage. In such a case, investment for development could turn into distribution of benefits that, given the complex ethnic, communal, linguistic composition of the North East could come to be viewed as a zero-sum situation by various population groups. This would stoke conflict rather than defuse it. The solution to the persistent problems of the North East, such as the recent conflict in Manipur, lies through fair and impartial governance and a continuous re-assertion of Constitutional values, strengthening inclusive democratic institutions and expediting judicial action at various levels.

The road to sustainable peace and development in the NER, therefore, depends essentially on deriving the right lessons from the past and devising the strategies based on democratic constitutionalism and continuous negotiation and political accommodation. Of course, State effort has to be backed by effective and nuanced use of the elaborate security structure already in place in the region. It would, however, be well to realise that military solutions cannot be durable in situations engendered by perceived iniquities amongst various ethnicities in terms of access and opportunity. It is critical that focus is maintained on economic development of the region with beneficial impact on employment and incomes enabling people of the region to share in prosperity based on trust and cooperation. Only then can the NER be an effective means of projecting India's Act East Policy.

Notes to Chapter 3

1. Legislation for Reorganisation of the North Eastern Region

   i) State of Nagaland Act, 1962.

   ii) The North-Eastern Areas (Reorganisation) Act, 1971 (came into Force in 1972)

   iii) The State of Mizoram Act 1986

   iv) The State Of Arunachal Pradesh Act, 1986

2. Agreements and Accords

   Nagaland

   i) The 9-Point Agreement, June 1947; between the then Governor of Assam, Sir Akbar Hydari and the representatives of the Naga National Council at Kohima for a duration of ten years.

   ii) The 16 Point Agreement between the Government of India and the Naga People's Convention, 1960.

   iii) The Shillong Agreement between the Government of India and the Underground Nagas, Shillong, 11 November 1975.

   iv) The Naga Framework Agreement, 2015; signed between the NSCN (IM) and Union Ministry of Home Affairs (MHA); (Secret Agreement, Details not yet declassified).

   Assam

   v) The Assam Accord, 1985, was a Memorandum of Settlement (MoS) signed between representatives of the Government of India and the leaders of the Anti-Foreigners Agitation in Assam.

   Mizoram

   vi) The Mizoram Peace Accord, 1986; an official agreement between the Government of India and the Mizo National Front (MNF) to end insurgency and violence in Mizoram.

3. The Sixth Schedule to the Constitution of India was applicable to the Tribal areas of the North East.

4. The North Eastern Council Act, 1971.

5. The provisions of the North Eastern Council Act, 1971 lay down the regional character of this body which was entrusted with regional planning. As per the Act (Section 4) the Council shall –

(1) function as a regional planning body for the north-eastern area.

(2) While formulating the regional plans for the north-eastern area, the Council shall give priority to schemes and projects which will benefit two or more States: Provided that in case or Sikkim, the Council shall formulate specific projects and schemes for that State including the review of implementation of such projects and schemes.

(3) The Council shall—

(a) review, from time to time, the implementation of the projects and schemes included in the regional plan and recommend measures for effecting co-ordination among the Governments of the States concerned in the matter of implementation of such projects and schemes;

(b) where a project or scheme is intended to benefit two or more States, recommend the manner in which, —

(i) such project or scheme may be executed or implemented and managed or maintained; or

(ii) the benefits therefrom may be shared; or

(iii) the expenditure thereon may be incurred;

(c) recommend to the Government of the State concerned or to the Central Government the undertaking of necessary surveys and investigation of projects in any State represented in the Council to facilitate consideration of the feasibility of including new projects in the regional plan

6. NEC was also entrusted with duties to monitor internal security. As per Section 4(4), "The Council shall review from time to time the measures taken by the States represented in the Council for the maintenance of security and public order therein and recommend to the Governments of the States concerned further measures necessary in this regard."

Chapter 4

North Eastern Region: A Potentially Compatible Bridge to South East Asia

Over the last two millennia, India's NE Region, in addition to being culturally, ethnically and economically connected with the Indian sub-continent, has also been linked to SE Asia. Migrations across the SE Region brought SE Asian population groups into the North East. Ahoms, a tribe originally hailing from Northern Thailand migrated into Assam in the 13th century and established the Ahom Kingdom that lasted nearly 600 years, dominating most of the Region. Tribes from Cambodia are believed to have migrated northwards and eventually settled in the Khasi Hills region of the present-day Meghalaya. The conflict and engagement of the Ahom Kingdom with the then Kingdom of Burma (now Myanmar) in early 19th century was to have most significant impact of all. Between 1808 and 1826 the Burmese armies invaded the Ahom kingdom, defeated the Ahoms and occupied their capital at Sibsagar. This occupation, which brought Burmese presence right next to the then Bengal province, the most prized possession of East India Company headquartered at Calcutta, eventually led to military intervention by Company. In fact, the proclivity of the Burmese to launch raids along Bengal's Eastern borders, apart from being disliked by the border kingdoms e.g. Tripura and Manipur, had long been a matter of concern to Calcutta, leading them to take both the kingdoms under their protection in the early 19th century.

The occupation of Assam by the Burmese, though violent, resulted in intermingling between the peoples of two regions with Assamese culture being carried back to Burma once the Burmese retreated after the Anglo-Burmese war. Naga tribes inhabiting the Naga Hills region of India (later Nagaland) also peopled areas in Northern Burma as did Karen, Kachin and Singhpho tribes of Burma in Eastern Assam. For many centuries the Eastern trade route to China passed through Myanmar via Mandalay and on to Kunming in Yunnan. The erstwhile kingdoms of Manipur and

Tripura not only interacted closely with Bengal from pre-Mughal times but also thrived on trade with Burma and with other regions beyond. Over time, they also participated in riverine and coastal trade through Dhaka and Chittagong.

While ancient Indian kingdoms on the Eastern Coast, such as Odisha encouraged sea trade which had a major coastal component. In addition to links across the seas, the great Indian cultural imprint on SE Asian Countries passed equally through the land mass of the North Eastern Kingdoms, which stood as bridge between the Indian Subcontinent and SE Asia. Eventually, through coastal trade or through the land mass, Indian culture and languages, including the legends of Ramayana and Mahabharata, were carried to Thailand, Cambodia, Malaysia and Indonesia, to be reflected through many temples and shrines. (The ancient capital of the kingdom of Siam was named Sri Ayutthya).

The cultural interaction and imprint continued into SE Asia with the spread of Buddhism into Burma, Laos, Thailand and beyond. Later, Islam, though introduced to Sumatra in the 7th century by Arab traders was effectively brought to Malaysia by Indian Muslim traders in the 12th century AD. When Sultan Mudzafar Shah I (12th century) of Kedah (Hindu name Phra Ong Mahawangsa), became the first ruler to be known to convert to Islam after being introduced to it by Indian traders. As a result of the Indian connection, Islam was adopted by the coastal trading ports people of Malaysia and Indonesia, through peaceful contact and absorption rather than violent conquest. The linkages of religion and culture, art and commerce, language and literature, which evolved over a long period of time following such contacts, still endure in both India as well as Southeast Asia.

The engagement with SE Asia, however, took a different form during the colonial period. A large number of Indians went to work wherever the British went, particularly to Burma, Malaya, Singapore. Initially, they went as soldiers of the colonial military machine but were soon followed by others as indentured labour, clerical workers, traders and suppliers, money lenders etc. Soon Indian presence grew in other territories as well such as Indonesia and the Philippines. Such presence, however, was seen as a part of colonial dominance and was not liked by the local people. The direction of trade also changed as the colonial powers e.g. Britain, France, and Netherlands concentrated more on extractive exploitation across South and South East Asia. All these created prejudices and antagonisms towards people of Indian origin as South East Asian Countries emerged from colonial rule. How such antagonisms and suspicions gradually turned into mutual respect and friendship is not only a story of long historical engagement but also of assimilation of the Indian diaspora and contributions by Indian professionals to economies of those countries, of a policy peaceful and positive engagement by India in the post-independence era, which, all combined, laid the foundation of India's soft power in the SE Region.

India, Post-Colonial World and SE Asia

The decades post World War II saw colonialism being dismantled all over the world with many new countries emerging in Asia and Africa. This was also the era of the Cold War between the Western World and the Soviet Bloc comprising two competing economic and political ideologies. In addition to the Korean war, South East Asia saw violent struggles for independence in Indonesia, Malaysia and a long period of war of freedom and unification that lasted nearly three decades in Viet Nam.

During the first few decades post-1947, India sought to rebuild its economy after nearly two centuries of exploitative colonial rule, in the backdrop of devastation wreaked by the Second World War, struggles and conflict accompanying the dismantling of colonial empires, regional conflicts arising from intense cold war rivalry. This called for bold choices and radical departures from the long-established colonial policies. For instance, as part of the British Colonial Empire, Indians troops constituted a major part of the colonial armies that were deployed to suppress struggles for independence and self- determination in many SE Asian countries well into the 1940s. Independent India, however, immediately withdrew such elements of the British Indian army inherited by it and resolutely and consistently supported the dismantling of the Colonial order while expressing solidarity with the newly emerging post-colonial states.

Immediately after independence, India launched this policy by calling the Conference on Asian Relations in New Delhi in 1947, bringing together leaders of 29 countries to express solidarity with the freedom struggles in other parts of Asia and foster cooperation amongst Asian people. This initiative continued in many international fora, notably the Bandung Conference in Indonesia, followed by the 12th session of ECAFE in Bangalore in 1956. Soon India emerged as a key international player campaigning against colonialism and giving voice to the newly emergent, post-colonial nations in Asia and Africa. India also distanced herself from the two Cold War power Blocs and as a founding member of the Non-Aligned Movement, became a prominent voice speaking for the interests of the "Third World". This also drew the attention and support of the new independent nations of the SE Region. This approach endured through the difficult decades during which India faced wars from external aggression (1962-71); imperilled food security due to drought and famine of 1960s; international pressures resulting from the Cold War as well as violent insurgency within. This continuing commitment provided the foundation of a more focused engagement later.

After the end of the Viet Nam War in mid-1970s and the resultant demilitarisation, the SE Asian region entered into a period of economic growth which, in a couple of decades was nothing less than spectacular. This resulted in some SE Nations being branded as the Asian Tigers and compelled the world to take notice. Eventually, even the financial crises of 1997-98 and 2007-08 also failed to halt their march

Meanwhile, with some early initiatives in the 1980s, India also sought to modernise and by 1991, following a serious balance of payments crisis, opened up its economy with dismantling of various kinds of controls and internal barriers to trade. During the same period, bringing a greater focus to the engagement with SE Asia, India formally articulated its Look East policy, which substantially encompassed better trade relations with SE Asia and an increasing engagement with Japan and South Korea. However, India's engagement with the Asia Pacific economies of Japan and Korea took a different shape with opening up of the Indian manufacturing for investment by private companies from these countries. The focus with SE Asia, on the other hand, was on building and developing the institutional structure for trade, which got added impetus through The Act East Policy.

ASEAN

In 1947, considering the devastation of WWII in Asia the United Nations set up the Economic Commission for Asia and the Far East (ECAFE) in Shanghai, China, to assist in post-war economic reconstruction. Two years later, in January 1949, it moved to its present-day headquarters in Bangkok. In 1974, ECAFE evolved into the Economic and Social Commission on Asia and Pacific (ESCAP). Earlier, on 31 July 1961 a Group called the Association of Southeast Asia (ASA), consisting of Thailand, the Philippines, and the Federation of Malaya, was set up. ASEAN itself was created on 8 August 1967, when the foreign ministers of five countries: Indonesia, Malaysia, the Philippines, Singapore, and Thailand, signed the ASEAN Declaration. In the Declaration, the aims and purposes of ASEAN were stated as being to accelerate economic growth, social progress, and cultural development in the region, to promote regional peace, collaboration and mutual assistance on matters of common interest, to provide assistance to each other in the form of training and research facilities, to collaborate for better utilisation of agriculture and industry to raise the living standards of the people, to promote Southeast Asian studies and to maintain close, beneficial co-operation with existing international organisations with similar aims and purposes. The Secretariat of ASEAN was located at Jakarta, Indonesia. The end of the Vietnam War and later the Cold War allowed ASEAN countries to exercise greater political independence in the region, and in the 1990s ASEAN emerged as a leading voice on regional trade and security issues.

Look East-Act East Policy and the Importance of Own Neighbourhood

After articulation of the Look East Policy, in 1991, India undertook an elaborate multi-pronged engagement with ASEAN and became a Sectoral Dialogue Partner in 1992 and a Full Dialogue Partner in 1996. Trade talks were initiated with ASEAN and eventually the ASEAN India Free Trade Agreement 2004-2009 was signed. Meanwhile, on 15 December 2008, ASEAN member states launch a Charter, signed earlier in November 2007, which turned ASEAN into a legal entity and aimed to create a single free-trade area for the region encompassing 500 million people. President of Indonesia Susilo Bambang Yudhoyono stated: "This is a momentous development when ASEAN is consolidating, integrating, and transforming itself into a community. It is achieved while ASEAN seeks a more vigorous role in Asian and global affairs at a time when the international system is experiencing a seismic shift". Referring to climate change and economic upheaval, he concluded: "Southeast Asia is no longer the bitterly divided, war-torn region it was in the 1960s and 1970s".

India's engagement with ASEAN continued with the Indo-ASEAN Summit in 2012 where dialogue was initiated on investment and trade in Services. In 2014, with a view to speeding up the engagement India renamed its Look East Policy as the Act East Policy. The ASEAN India Agreement on Investment and the ASEAN India Agreement on Trade in Services were both finalised and signed in 2015

The other emerging trend in SE Asia is the growing dominance of China. Over last three decades it has become the largest trading partner and investor in ASEAN. However, Chinese trade and investment has been quite asymmetrical in China's favour, raising concerns about China's economic dominance over the region. This conflict has been intensified with China's expansion and territorial claims in the South China Sea and beyond with maritime disputes with Indonesia and Philippines. The emerging US-China rivalry has also added another layer of anxiety and uncertainty in the region.

Cultural Contiguity East

The economic emergence of the ASEAN Region as an economically prosperous region with considerable trade, productive and consumption potential has focused attention of the world on the different nation-states. It is no longer possible for the world to group all the peoples and countries together as "Indo-China", divided into areas dominated by erstwhile colonial powers. As SE Asian nation-states play a greater role in the world, the people inhabiting these countries also seek a better understanding of their culture and history. This has, interestingly, thrown up many cultural and ethnic links and commonalities between peoples of the ASEAN countries and India.

The SE Asian Region, while being home to a diversity of peoples and cultures, is geographically contiguous to and shares a common past with India. A significant part of this inter- change is through the land mass of the North Eastern India. In fact, it is possible to regard the Indian North East as a confluence of Indic, Tibetan and several SE Asian cultures. This intermingling has been enabled by periodic migrations as detailed in the earlier part of this chapter and the ebb and flow of the kingdoms and empires, which made for peaceful co-existence between many peoples and ethnic groups of the region. It is to be seen as to what extent these historical trade and cultural links can reinforce friendly relations amongst peoples and economic cooperation and interdependence. Very often cultural memories outlast political divisions and can serve as a comforting yet strong basis for peaceful economic relations.

South East Asia: The Emerging Challenges – and Opportunities

India's engagement with the region, through stretching long back into history, faces new challenges today, not least due to the increasing hegemonistic designs of China over the region. In the past decade, several developments have taken place that challenge the carefully calibrated Act East engagement of India.

The Belt and Road Initiative

China's Belt and Road Initiative (BRI), sometimes referred to as the New Silk Road, is one of the most ambitious infrastructure projects ever conceived. Launched in 2013, a vast collection of development and investment initiatives were planned by China that would stretch from East Asia to Europe, aimed at significantly expanding China's economic and political influence. The plan has two components: the overland Silk Road Economic Belt and the Maritime Silk Road. The two were collectively referred to first as the One Belt, One Road (OBOR) initiative but eventually became the Belt and Road Initiative (BRI).

Over land, the BRI agenda envisages creating a vast network of railways, energy pipelines, highways, and streamlined border crossings, special economic zones etc. both westward—through Central Asia across former Soviet republics—and southward, to Pakistan and Southeast Asia. The sea-based plans for the 21st Century Maritime Silk Road were unveiled at the 2013 summit of the ASEAN in Indonesia. To accommodate expanding maritime trade traffic, China declared that it would invest in port development along the Indian Ocean, from Southeast Asia all the way to East Africa and parts of Europe.

The Belt and Road Initiative has been viewed with concern in some countries, including India, and has also stoked opposition in some host countries. BRI projects are built using low-interest loans extended by China as opposed to aid grants. Some BRI investments have involved opaque bidding processes and required the use of Chinese firms. As a result, contractors have inflated costs, leading to cancelled projects and political backlash. Centre for Global Development notes that eight BRI countries are vulnerable to debt crises. CFR's Belt and Road Tracker shows overall debt to China has soared since 2013, surpassing 20 percent of GDP in some BRI host countries.

India has been opposed to BRI on account of the China Pakistan Economic Corridor (CPEC) Project taken up under BRI and running through disputed territories in Pakistan Occupied Kashmir. India has, therefore, not joined the BRI and has tried to convince countries that the BRI is a plan to dominate Asia, warning of what some analysts have called a "String of Pearls" geo-economic strategy. Considering the economic crisis faced by some BRI recipient countries in the recent past it has warned against the BRI strategy whereby where by unsustainable debt burdens created under BRI compel its Indian Ocean neighbours to cede territorial rights to China enabling it to seize control of regional choke points. This has also influenced India's China policy, which till recent past was based on normalisation of ties and growing trade relations with China. India was also a founding member of China's Asian Infrastructure Investment Bank (AIIB), and both Indian and Chinese leaders had supported closer diplomatic ties. However, now India- China ties already destabilised by BRI, have taken a turn for the worse after the confrontation in the Himalayas in 2020 when India was in the grip of a pandemic.

Internationally, while Central Asian countries have welcomed BRI (possibly as a counterpoise to Russian influence), the United States and other Western countries believe that China is likely to militarise the BRI. This is also a matter of concern for India. Increasing Chinese presence, including naval presence, in the Indian Ocean, in the backdrop of the confrontation in the Himalayas, has radically altered security perceptions in India. In an article entitled "The Coming Post-COVID Anarchy", published in Foreign Affairs on 6 May, former Australian prime minister Kevin Rudd maintains that a decision in Beijing to militarise the BRI would increasingly raise the risk of proxy wars.

The Clash in the Himalayas and the QUAD

The relations between India and China took a nosedive in June 2020 when Indian and Chinese soldiers clashed in the Himalayas in Eastern Ladakh resulting in 20 Indian and an unknown number of Chinese soldiers being killed in a violent clash. The clash took place between border patrols of the two countries without use of firearms through hand-to-hand fighting. These patrols had long been operating along the un-demarcated international border in Eastern Ladakh on the basis of agreements and standard operating procedures developed over the last 20 years. Chinese troops, in a major alteration of the status quo, aggressively advanced into some new positions along the Line of Actual Control, which was resisted by the Indian side, leading to the clash. Since then, many talks have taken place to enable disengagement and de-escalation on the disputed border with restoration of status quo ante, but have been futile. The Chinese have refused to restore the status quo in Ladakh. Consequently, Indian and Chinese armies are face to face with more than 100,000 soldiers of both armies deployed in the high Himalayas.

However, India has stood firm in opposition to Chinese posture and in addition to bolstering its military presence has insisted on restoration of *status quo ante*. India has also banned use of some Chinese goods and

Chinese-origin digital apps and telecom technology. But India's limited economic leverage over China has rendered these measures relatively ineffective. The standoff has radically altered not only the security situation for India but also the international relations in the region. India is now more open to cooperation with the US who has, of late, viewed India as a counterweight to a China-dominated Asia and has sought to knit together its strategic relationships in the region via the 2017 Indo-Pacific Strategy. Consequently, in addition to increasing defence partnership with the US, India is also an active member of the QUAD which brings together navies of US, Japan Australia and India. In addition, India is now a major partner in the emerging Indo -Pacific partnership being forged under the leadership of the US along with several Western nations.

The other direct effect has been of concerns in India about the increasing economic and military presence of China in the SE and East Asian Region, which are now being viewed as an attempt to create Chinese hegemony in the region, threatening economic and territorial security of not only India but also the ASEAN countries- a perspective that is bolstered by the recent events in the South China Sea.

Regional Comprehensive Economic Partnership

On 15 November, 2020, 15 Asia-Pacific nations, representing nearly a third of the world's gross domestic product, signed The Regional Comprehensive Economic Partnership (RCEP), a free trade agreement creating the world's largest trading bloc and also marking a significant achievement for China as it seeks economic supremacy in the Asia-Pacific region.

RCEP was envisaged as a way to bolster trading ties among nations across Asia-Pacific and promote trade and economic growth in the region. Initially, it included the 10 member countries of the Association of Southeast Asian Nations (ASEAN) and five Asia-Pacific countries with whom ASEAN had existing FTAs, namely: Australia, China, Japan, New Zealand and South Korea. India had also planned to join the deal but pulled out in November 2019.

While not as comprehensive as the earlier envisaged Comprehensive and Progressive Agreement for Trans-Pacific Partnership (CPTPP) which was abandoned after the then US administration under President Trump pulled USA out of the proposed partnership (though there have been attempts to revive it under the Biden Administration), RCEP is intended to lower or eliminate tariffs on a broad range of goods and services and establish rules on such things as investment, competition, and intellectual property, including digital copyright. Unlike the CPTPP, RCEP does not include provisions on labour and environmental standards.

RCEP represents growing predominance of China and a new set of conditions determining economic relations in SE Asia and the Pacific Region. While India has currently chosen to stay out, it has a standing invitation to join at a time of its choosing later. It remains to be seen how this new arrangement affects India's Act East policy.

South China Sea

One of the world's busiest waterways, the South China Sea is subject to several overlapping territorial disputes involving China, Vietnam, the Philippines, Taiwan, Malaysia, and Brunei who all have conflicting territorial claims over the sea, based on various historical and geographic accounts.

The South China Sea is a very important commercial waterway connecting Asia with Europe and Africa, and its seabed is rich with natural resources. One-third of global shipping, or a total of US$3.37 trillion of international trade, passes through the South China Sea. The sea is also believed to contain significant natural resources, such as natural gas and oil and accounts for 10 percent of the world's fisheries, making it a critical food source for millions of people.

China claims more than 80 percent of the South China Sea, while Vietnam claims sovereignty over the Paracel Islands and the Spratly Islands. Other nations like Philippines, Taiwan, Malaysia, and Brunei also have claims over their territorial waters and several associated geographical features and islands dotting the sea. With oil being discovered beneath the South China Sea waters, the claims have become all the more strident, with China moving in militarily to making most of the South China Sea its own territory. Consequently, apart from alarming the smaller SE Asian claimants, the conflict has recently emerged as a flashpoint in China-U.S. relations in Asia.

In 2002, the Association of Southeast Asian Nations (ASEAN) and China came together to sign the Declaration on the Conduct of Parties in the South China Sea. The Declaration sought to establish a framework for the eventual negotiation of a Code of Conduct for the South China Sea. The parties promised "to exercise self-restraint in the conduct of activities that would complicate or escalate disputes and affect peace and stability". China, however, has shrugged of the 2002 Agreement and has put forward a "nine-dash line" map. This line moves around the South China Sea edges and encompasses all of the sea's territorial features and the vast majority (nearly 80%) of its waters. Besides China has militarised a number of islands in the sea and has adopted threatening posture towards even the right of peaceful passage by merchant marine of other nations.

On 22 January 2013, the Philippines filed an arbitration case against China, under the auspices of the U.N. Convention on the Law of the Sea (UNCLOS) with claims centring around maritime law issues. In 2016, the tribunal largely ruled in favour of the Philippines, concluding that China's claim regarding its nine-dash line was invalid. China, however, has rejected the Tribunals award. Its threatening posture is perceived as being obstructive to free passage of international commerce and seriously detrimental to freedom of navigation on the high seas.

While the smaller ASEAN countries do not have the wherewithal to challenge China, the loss of sovereignty over territorial waters regarded by them as their own is of concern to them. The South China Sea, due to its geographical position astride the Straits of Malacca, is also emerging as a flashpoint between US and China. Concerned at China's aggressive posturing, U.S. Navy has started patrolling the South China Sea. US has also rallied Australia, Japan and India, to form the QUAD, initially a platform for joint exercises by the navies of these countries but now extending to other cooperation as well. As the confrontation grows tense, the security situation in the region becomes more and more sensitive, with position of the smaller ASIAN nations being very fragile as they are trapped between two giants.

Myanmar

Meanwhile, recent events in Myanmar resulting from pro-democracy protests, known locally as the Spring Revolution which began in early 2021, have thrown the up new challenges for international relations in the SE Asia. These protests began in opposition to the coup d'état on 1 February, staged by Min Aung Hlaing, the commander-in-chief of the country's armed forces, the Tatmadaw. The protesters mostly employed peaceful and nonviolent forms of protest including civil disobedience, labour strikes, a military boycott campaign, public processions against the takeover etc.

Myanmar has substantively remained under military rule ever since 1962, when Gen. Ne Win seized power following a coup. While the reforms of 2011 followed by elections in Myanmar ushered in a civilian presence, overarching military dominance remained. The 2021 Myanmar coup d'état began on the morning of 1 February 2021, a day before the Parliament of Myanmar was due to swear in the members elected in the November 2020 general election. The democratically elected members of Myanmar's ruling party, the National League for Democracy (NLD), were deposed by Myanmar's military. This was accompanied by Declaration of a year-long state of emergency and vesting of power in Commander-in-Chief of Defence Services Min Aung Hlaing and setting up of a State Administrative Council. President Win Myint and State Counsellor Aung San Suu Kyi were detained, along with ministers and their deputies and members of Parliament.

The coup took place amid the COVID-19 pandemic. Myanmar was struggling with one of the most severe outbreaks in Southeast Asia, owing to its poor health infrastructure and ongoing internal conflict. The country's economy had also been greatly affected by the pandemic, shrinking by 5 percent during 2020.

Following the coup, several political parties, including the Shan Nationalities League for Democracy (SNLD), the Democratic Party for a New Society (DPNS), the Karen National Party, and Asho Chin National Party, announced they had rejected the military's offer to participate in the State Administration Council.

In response to the growing protest movement, the military leaders of the coup initially responded by internet and social media blackouts, repression of the press and TV media, arrests and criminal prosecution of the protesters. However, the protests grew and soon the military resorted to violent use of force to suppress the protests. As of 16 May 2021, at least 796 protesters and bystanders, of which at least 44 were children, have been killed by military or police forces and at least 3,778 people detained. The protests, however, see no sign of ending.

The response of Myanmar's neighbours has differed. China sees no merit in democracy and has come out in support of the Military Junta, but now seriously risks antagonising the Myanmar's public at large who have shown hostility towards Chinese investments and presence in Myanmar. India has taken a cautious stand and maintained silence but would require considerable diplomatic tight-rope walking while dealing with the Military Junta. Other neighbours, notably Thailand, itself de facto ruled by a military Junta has stayed aloof. While the U.S., EU and U.K. have imposed sanctions on top military brass and some Army-linked businesses, ASEAN has remained silent, treating the events in Myanmar as being that country's internal affair. The meeting of ASEAN leaders and Foreign Ministers held in April 2021 included Myanmar's military regime and has drawn widespread criticism from activists, human rights groups and protesters on this account.

The internal situation in Myanmar, despite military rule of more than half a century, has had a long history of conflict. The northern regions of the country have been prone to insurgency since the 1950s and have long provided shelter and arms to militants on the Indian side as well. The control of the Myanmar Government over these regions has always been tenuous. In recent times, the ethno-religious conflict within Myanmar (2017) led to nearly 7,00,000 Rohingyas fleeing to Bangladesh. As the situation in that country continues to be chaotic, 20 or so armed groups that have battled the Government for decades have become active again, seizing some military outposts and looting weapons. The Myanmar army has bombed them, with collateral damage to civilian population. The decades long conflict with the Karen National Liberation Army has already resulted in several refugee camps along Thailand border. In some cases, the Myanmarese militants have come together to form new groups such as the Arakan Liberation Army. In addition to selling arms and weapons to militants in various countries, guerrilla conclaves in Myanmar also produce heroin and are world's biggest suppliers of methamphetamines.

The consequences for India are therefore serious. Apart from the growing influence of China on the Myanmar Military Junta, the connectivity of the Indian land mass with SE Asia is seriously jeopardised. Some important infrastructure projects such as the Trilateral highway connecting Thailand, Myanmar and India and the Kaladan Multi-modal transportation project are adversely affected. On a broader scale the ability of ASEAN to function as a homogeneous economic bloc is impaired as the deteriorating situation in Myanmar threatens all neighbours with spreading militancy, drugs, illegal arms, refugees and economic disruption.

COVID 19

Overshadowing all international and domestic affairs since the beginning of 2020 is the pandemic caused by COVID-19. This disease has been caused by a new coronavirus called SARS-CoV-2, with first mass infections occurring in Wuhan, in the People's Republic of China. As it spread globally from Wuhan, the World Health Organization declared the outbreak a Public Health Emergency of International Concern on 30 January 2020, and a pandemic on 11 March 2020. Globally, since its outbreak, as of

July 2023, there have been 767,726,861 confirmed cases of COVID-19, including 6,948,764 deaths, reported to WHO. India itself reported 44,994,351 confirmed cases and 531,908 deaths. Experts, however, agree that these numbers could be a gross under-estimation due to deficiencies in public health outreach and difficulties in confirmation and validation of infections as the cause of death in many countries. Eventually, in 2023, the pandemic appears to have lost its virulence as the Covid strains mutated in to less harmful viruses. However, while it raged, the pandemic caused a major disruption of the world economy, seriously jeopardising world trade and the WTO based international trade order. Many countries, in grappling with the pandemic, armed themselves with special powers and imposed restrictive public policy regimes, curtaining the freedoms available to its citizens. In fact, as the world emerges from the shadow of the pandemic and economic activity revives the international order has been marked by a diminution of liberal order and globalisation, replaced by growing nationalism and authoritarianism.

The economic impact of the pandemic on India's economy, already showing a declining GDP growth rate by 2019-20 was severe. India's GDP growth turned negative during 2020-21, registering a growth rate of (-) 8%. As the pandemic raged on in India during 2021-22 as well, the projections of recovery could not materialise. With the decline in the first wave and discovery of vaccines against COVID, India, with its renowned pharma industry, had started supplying vaccines to many parts of the world including SE Asia. However, with the intense second wave, and inability to meet domestic demand, India was compelled to stop the export of vaccines. However, the Indian Pharma industry eventually rose to the occasion by not only enabling vaccination of its 1.35 Bn population but by also restarting exports of vaccines to other countries. Combined with the economic disruption, impact of the pandemic on India has seriously jeopardised its credibility as a source of global public goods- in this case for healthcare. Post-COVID, the world has changed significantly. Restoring India's credibility post-pandemic is a significant challenge to be addressed by its Act East Policy.

Supply Chain Resilience Initiative

One fallout of the growing belligerence of China and the pandemic is that in April 2021, Australia, India and Japan launched the Supply Chain Resilience Initiative (SCRI) in Indo-Pacific. First conceived last year, the SCRI is the product of the supply-chain disruption caused by Covid-19, which served as a wake-up call exposing states' excessive dependence on

China for critical products such as food and pharmaceuticals. Furthermore, growing tensions between the Chinese and "like-minded" Indo-Pacific partners such as the United States, exacerbated by Beijing's aggressive military and diplomatic tactics, only made risk diversification by moving value chains away from China a more urgent goal.

In this context, the Indo-Pacific centred SCRI has been conceived as a mechanism aimed at enhancing economic and political security by challenging China's dominance in trade and Beijing's growing clout from its more robust foreign policy, particularly its ambitious Belt and Road Initiative (BRI).

Building India's Comprehensive power and projecting it through various means in the South East Asian Region requires not only addressing the challenges within but also carefully navigating the international geo-political situation in the region. Therefore, the Act East Policy will necessarily require both and internal as well as external dimension-obviously not an easy task.

Chapter 5

Looking Ahead- Foundations for the Economy of the Future

Recalibrating the Basics

The states constituting the North Eastern Region have all established political governance and administrative systems on a pattern provided for by the Indian Constitution. The enthusiastic participation of the people in elections at all levels and smooth changes of power are harbingers of stability. While the last two decades have seen decreasing trend in militancy in the region various sporadic conflicts still beset the region. However, for the region to be a bridge to SE Asia it must come up to the level of the SE Asian countries and prepare for the economy of the future. Many foundational factors need to come together to leverage economic growth. It is, therefore, worthwhile recalling and reviewing some of the core issues and challenges in the light of contemporary realities. Of all the factors that need to come together to push economy of a region forward, there are none so critical as the four basics of Good Governance, Human capital, Capacity Building and Infrastructure. A look at some of the core issues reveals that there are several challenges that will need to be addressed to leverage the region into a high-growth path in the future.

Internal and External Security

Security is the primary requirement for any geography or jurisdiction seeking economic growth. In the North Eastern region, the significant presence of the security forces and resolute action against militancy, insurgency and terrorism have yielded good results in restoring peace to the region. The task, however, is not yet over.

The region has been an important theatre of war twice after India's independence- in 1962 and 1971. The threat from the Northern borders is an ever present one as the Border with China is still undelimited. The external military threat takes many shapes, morphing into Hybrid or Grey Warfare depending upon the relations between India and her neighbours. Similarly, past experience has shown that internal political and social trends in Bangladesh can also have a serious impact on the security situation in the North East. On the Eastern border the fallout of the Rohingya crisis and current unrest due to pro-democracy protests in Myanmar has already led to revival of armed groups and "armies" that the Govt. of Myanmar can do little about. The fact that some of them are ethnically connected to populations of Indian side of the border makes the situation volatile for India as well.

Internally, taking into account the legacy of conflict generated during the process of integration of the North Eastern peoples, with their strong sense of identity magnified by past grievances, the possibility of disaffection amongst some elements in the region is an ongoing phenomenon. This is further compounded by easy availability of arms and ammunition from across the borders. Given the location of the NER, surrounded as it is by several foreign countries, the possibilities of the internal dynamics and unrest in those countries spilling over into the North East is an ever-present possibility. The existence of several state jurisdictions poses coordination problems for law enforcement, anti-terrorist and anti-insurgent action. In addition, the anxieties and fears generated by in-migration combined with the distrust and fear of the "outsider" tend to keep the region on the boil.

The challenge is therefore for the security forces, comprising of the Indian Army, the Paramilitary and Central and State Police forces to keep vigil over various fronts and dimensions. They also have to take into account the local sensitivities and nuance their response suitable while overcoming jurisdictional boundaries and divisions. All this to ensure that normal civic life can function in the region with freedom of movement and safety. All state agencies have to coordinate their actions and responses to that end.

Governance

Governance is the combination of structures and institutions, laws and rules that allow the public choices to be articulated in a generally acceptable and peaceful manner. Good governance must not only ensure safeguard safety and security of the individual but also provide human development support and build harmony in the community at large. It must also establish and honour institutions that enforce and enable various kinds of rights to be defended with peaceful dispute resolution. Reduction of conflict, which often results from collapse of governance institutions, lowers risks and costs of doing business, improves economic efficiency and encourages investment.

North East Region comprises of eight states including Sikkim. With the exception of Assam and Tripura, other states are small and sparsely populated. Due to geographical isolation, poor infrastructure and general lack of investment in the past (a situation that is being remedied but will take time to show results), they do not have the volume of economic activity to raise resources to meet their revenue and developmental needs. As such NE States depend heavily upon federal assistance to meet their governance, administrative, social, developmental and policing expenditures.

The reconstitution of the region with creation of several separate states has also created multiple jurisdictions. As a result, there is diversity of land and property ownership laws, business support and industrial policies, criminal justice administration and civil policing. The availability of skilled manpower and existence of business related regulatory and legal institutional structure is also uneven. As a result, problems of coordination abound.

The political development of North Eastern states has also been diverse. Many states were constituted to give representation to ethnic and tribal identities. This has resulted in multiplicity of special laws and jurisdictions. Paradoxically, opening up of the region has heightened local anxieties with demands for Inner Line Permits being raised in several states. There is pervasive antipathy to non-locals combined with fear of exploitation by them as also resentment against any Government benefits being extended to them.

Internally, within each of the states, their troubled past also casts its shadow on the present as many erstwhile militants, having come overground, are yet to fully surrender their arms and weapons. They are also yet to be resettled economically and reintegrated with the society. Thus, while insurgency has gone down, ethnic conflict, criminal activity and local law and order problems persist.

To attain a sustainable and reasonably high economic growth trajectory, governance institutions in the North East have to be efficient, in tune with technological and social changes, responsive to economic environment while encouraging trust. This would enable the public- and businesses – to innovate, work and grow peacefully. Administration and Civil policing have to be modernised along with operation of an effective and just criminal administration system. The movement of people, goods and services across state borders has to be seamless and efficient.

Most business and commerce related laws fall in the jurisdiction of the Central Government but the local state governments have a significant role in ensuring their smooth operation. As the North Eastern Region grows economically and begins to connect with neighbouring countries, imperatives of international trade and commerce have also to be kept in sight. This however requires capacity building in local administrations to enable them to support expansion of business activity.

The Human Capital

Human capital is an intangible asset that is a combination of talent, ability, education, health and well-being, capacity building and an open social and economic environment that enables diverse talents to flourish. It contributes immensely to diversity of economic activity, innovation and adaptation to change and to quality and levels of production. What is necessary are the conditions that allow human capital to develop and prosper through entrepreneurship. In today's knowledge-based environment with human capabilities leveraged through Information technology and communications, there is a strong relationship between human capital and economic growth. While human capital can be enhanced through education and capacity building, it can also depreciate in a restrictive or oppressive system that inhibits innovation, through long periods of unemployment or through inability to keep up with technology and innovation.

The interesting aspect of the North Eastern Region is the amazing range of talent of its people in all walks of life. It has a sizable young population, high levels of literacy and college education. Young people from the North East are acquiring ever increasing levels of education and making their mark in several spheres of activity in India and abroad. The challenge is therefore to leverage the capacities of this population group for the development of the North East itself.

The focus of governance must be on building human capital by affording access to education at all levels and efficient health services. The approach to education has to be diversified to accommodate talent diversity and enable multiplicity of vocations. Human development takes place best in open systems with multiple opportunities for mental growth and engagement.

In addition to providing the wherewithal, the incentive for human growth has also to be provided. The governance imperative has to shift to economic growth in all the NE states. Diversity of economic opportunity is the surest way of positive engagement of the energies of the people and to wean them away from violence and conflict. The economy must grow to absorb the diverse and rich talents of the local population and to give it opportunity to grow. Such opportunities grow manifold with increasing trade and commerce Every such opportunity would create many more for others to step in and contribute.

One of the features of the ASEAN economic miracle has been the considerable growth of its human capital. To enable the human capital in the NE Region to take the challenge of interacting with the region on terms of equality it must be enhanced through facilities for education and public health, wide ranging medical services, orderly and efficient urban development, tourism and trade.

Capacity Building

Capacity building improves the abilities of the entities and individuals functioning in an economy and helps application of knowledge, resources, and solutions successfully developed elsewhere to community issues. It also fosters a sense of ownership and empowerment encourages people to find better solutions to local problems and issues themselves. Strengthened confidence, skills and knowledge that increases with capacity building is by itself a valuable resource.

The disparity between SE Asia and India's North East must be dispelled to enable entrepreneurs from the region to offer economically viable options to markets in SE Asia. Capacity building, however, cannot take place overnight and requires considerable effort over a long period of time and investments in terms of financial support, building up the required institutions, involvement of experts and handholding of trainees as they venture into new areas and start using their new knowledge and skills. It must be accompanied by an ecosystem that rewards acquisition of such skills.

While capacity building must enable modern industrial production systems to be operated in the NE itself, it must also focus on new-age areas of digital technology and imaging, knowledge outsourcing, wellness, adventure, nature and ethnic tourism and hospitality, educational attainments, medical treatment, music and entertainment. It must enable building up of both soft and hard skills.

Infrastructure

All states and geographies, rural and urban have economic, demographic, fiscal and environmental requirements that need modern, efficient and reliable infrastructure. It helps in establishing durable supply chains and connects households and production systems across rural and urban areas. This enables well-functioning, accessible markets for various types of goods and services and provides opportunities for employment, healthcare and education.

The Challenge

Over the last two decades there has been considerable investment in conventional infrastructure such as highways, bridges, main line railways, airports etc. The development has largely been through Federal funding in terms of building linkages between the NE Region and the rest of the country. While there has been development of some important nodes, the development has been uneven with the hill states still short of necessary infrastructure. For the future, local infrastructure requirements have to be identified and met including intra-regional and local connectivity. For instance, while mega projects have been taken up to generate and electricity outside the region, there is a need to invest in modern and efficient local transmission and distribution systems for all states. Road development has to go beyond national highways to cover rural, and especially border areas.

There is a need to expand the envelope of infrastructure further to develop waterways and rail grids, in addition to roads, linking economically important hubs in India, Bangladesh, Nepal and Myanmar. These grids must include logistics hubs with multi modal connectivity linking roads, waterways and railways. As urbanisation grows in the North East and cities develop, there would be increasing demand for properly planned urban areas and business centres, with water and electricity supply and sanitation and waste disposal. In addition to transport requirements, for the NER to develop as a services hub, telecom and high-speed digital connectivity infrastructure would also be necessary. The requirement for reliable infrastructure in the NER, therefore, spans roads and bridges, telecommunication systems, broadband networks, railways, energy generation, transmission and distribution, public transportation, well designed urban areas and cities, buildings and parks, hospitals and educational facilities at all levels.

Speed of implementation of infrastructure projects is a critical element in enabling utility of infrastructure at a reasonable cost. So far implementation of infrastructural projects in the NER have faced inordinate delays and cost overruns. There also has to be an expansion of policy options to finance infrastructure of the quality being implemented across most of SE Asia. To enable sustained investment and maintain quality, user charges would need to be levied while a stable regulatory regime would enble long term private investment. All these aspects would require major policy and implementational changes.

The Future

To meet the challenges so that all the above aspects provide strong foundation for economic growth, a re-orientation of the mindset to promote economic activity, policy changes that support business and private enterprise and implementation push that uses technology, reduces arbitrary power of the bureaucracy, eliminates controls and bottlenecks and prioritise economic growth will be required to be adopted consciously. The economic development strategy will also need to focus on both intra-regional as well as extra regional linkages. The regional grids of roads and railways with trade and customs facilitation, of electricity with adequate transmission, interchange and settlements need to connect to all the states within the region as well as neighbouring countries. The strategy adopted must also recognize local strengths and vulnerabilities and has to be multi-dimensional. Eventually the combination of Good Governance, Human capital, Capacity Building and Infrastructure would not only enable local development but also leverage the position of India's North east as an important trading hub for SE Asia. In subsequent chapters we shall see what is possible and how it can be achieved.

PART - II

Chapter 6

Leveraging Local Strengths

(North Eastern India has a potential for growth in several sectors of the economy. This potential lies in a range of endowments, from natural resources to human capital. For a growth strategy it would be optimal to first consider how the resources and endowments that already form a part of the NER resource spectrum can be best leveraged for an engagement that is productive for India, the North Eastern Region and the wider SE Asian Region.)

The North Eastern Region has several inherent strengths, some due to its geographical location and cultural connect with the neighbourhood, others due to its resource potential. A strategy that makes the region a window to the South East Asia and beyond has to develop the local potential build synergies and complementarities with both its immediate Eastern Neighbourhood (Bangladesh, Bhutan, Nepal, Myanmar) as well as with other SE Asian nations. It has to grow the capacity of the NE Region, as a consumption and exporting centre and as an important link in South East Asian trade and exchange with reliable supply chains. At present, NER is known largely for its tea, though it also has oil, natural gas-based and cement industry. The regional economy is largely agricultural with some industrial centres supporting small and medium scale industries. There is also a nascent, but growing, services sector. Diversification of the regional economy is necessary to provide a range of goods and services across borders and enable a wider economic engagement with the regional ASEAN markets.

India has also been engaging with its Immediate Eastern Neighbourhood over the past several decades, first through SAARC, and after differences with Pakistan made SAARC untenable, through its Neighbourhood First Policy, focusing on initiatives such as BBIN, BIMSTEC etc. In the present context, given the Chinese influence and economic and political disruption in Pakistan and Sri Lanka, the Neighbourhood Policy effectively boils down to cover the North Eastern Neighbourhood comprising Bangladesh,

Bhutan, Myanmar and Nepal. Economic links of India's NER with all these countries are critical for any future development scenario in the region. Therefore, India's Act East Policy also needs to be tempered by the imperatives of Eastern Neighbourhood engagement.

For India to engage the Eastern Neighbourhood and SE Asia and beyond through the NER it is also essential that India's Northeast Region itself is able to offer opportunities for international trade and commerce on competitive terms. This would reduce costs of goods and services which could be accessed from the NER itself economically. The momentum so created would open the doors for a wider engagement over time. To that end, it would be well worth considering some obvious strengths of the region and examining some policy imperatives that could pave the way for the future.

The Land Bridge

Trade between India and ASEAN takes place over both sea and land, while that between India and its Eastern Neighbourhood takes place additionally through land and river routes, with Bangladesh seaports providing important potential gateways. Sea routes have taken the bulk of the trade to ASEAN as they can enable movement of large volumes of goods. Such routes, largely flowing through the Bay of Bengal, the Straits of Malacca and for several ASEAN countries, through the South China Sea, have entered into an era of uncertainty with an expansion of Chinese naval might and aggressive posturing over its claims in the South China Sea and the Indian Ocean. There have been attempts by China to militarise and control the South China Sea, in disregard of the established international maritime law that allows the right of peaceful, free passage. At the same time, the Bay of Bengal is increasingly becoming the focus of the Belt and Road Initiative as well as Chinese naval expansion in the Indian Ocean Region. In the uncertain world of today, where established international order and conventions are frequently being challenged and also upended by resort to military might by nation states, it would be prudent to develop alternatives. Land routes to the Eastern Neighbourhood and ASEAN countries, flowing through the NER would complement maritime access for the Region through Bangladesh and build an overland alternative for SE Asia.

Land connectivity is important not only because it is a channel for goods and movement of physical persons but also for transfers of ideas and cultures through social contact. In addition, land connectivity enables electricity transmission corridors and grid interconnections for energy transfer as also for high-speed communications through fibre-optic cables. With adequate and high-quality infrastructure for roads, railways, waterways and related communication networks, land connectivity would also allow several commodities of local economic importance, such as agricultural commodities and food grains, bulk value-added products derived from refineries and Gas Cracking etc. to be directly and economically transported and traded, avoiding costly domestic transhipments at ports. High speed fibre optics communication channels could facilitate services including health and education, trade interactions and financial settlements. Overland connection between production and consumption centres in India, its Eastern Neighbourhood and ASEAN countries would open up the vast markets in India, Bangladesh, Nepal and South East Asia to trade in goods and services, while providing complementarity and balancing out risks and costs arising through sea trade. More than anything, it would leverage local strengths in which the North East has local advantage.

As a result of the local geography, lack of adequate technical knowhow and political turmoil in some countries in immediate neighbourhood, land routes are relatively less developed and have been neglected for long. Though challenges remain, this situation can change with the Act East push, as India gains technological capabilities and financial strength. However, the investments in productive capacity and infrastructure would best thrive if supported by local synergies. The Act East policy offers a great opportunity to address issues relating to NER land potential as well for rationalisation of some major industrial-Infrastructural investments made in the region till date and could well be a key to their survival.

Energy

Oil and Gas: Oil was discovered in Digboi in Upper Assam in 1895 followed by setting up of the Digboi refinery. Later, an oil pipeline was built from Digboi to Guwahati and more refineries set up at Narengi near Guwahati and Bongaigaon. Following the Assam Accord of 1985, a much larger refinery was set up at Numaligarh along with a gas cracking complex near Dibrugarh. Separately gas-based power generation complexes were set up by NEEPCO and ONGC in Assam and Tripura.

While substantial refining and gas cracking capacity has been set up in the Northeast, the existing oil wells in the region, being old ones, are now running out of reserves. There are, however, more oil and gas reserves in the region, but the unsettled law and order situation and territorial disputes between NE States are a constraint to proper exploration, extraction and evacuation. The North Eastern oil based industrial complex, with its substantial refining and gas cracking capacity, now depends on additional oil and gas supplies from outside the region.

Meanwhile, given natural gas discoveries in Bangladesh and Myanmar, it would be logical to establish international gas grids connecting gas supplies from these countries for generation of electricity, providing feedstock for refining and gas cracking capacity already established in the NER. The production from the power plants, refineries and gas cracking units in the North East could then be competitively sold in its neighbourhood. This, however requires extensive agreements with Bangladesh, Myanmar and other adjacent ASEAN countries.

Numaligarh Refinery Limited (NRL)[1] can certainly benefit from such linkages. This refinery, initially set up with a capacity of 3 million metric tonnes per annum (MMTPA), has embarked on a major integrated expansion project to treble its capacity to 9 MMTPA at an estimated investment of more than Rs. 28,000 Crore. However, the crude oil production in the North Eastern Region is now not adequate to sustain even the original capacity. To sustain the augmented capacity following the expansion project, most of its crude oil requirement will need to be imported, for which a crude oil import terminal is being set up at Paradeep Port in Odisha along with a 1640 km long pipeline for transportation of the imported crude oil to Numaligarh.

On the consumption end, production from the initial refining capacity itself was more than what NER could sustain and a sizable quantity had to be taken outside the region, for which a marketing terminal had to be set up at Siliguri in addition to the one at Numaligarh. Once the expansion project is completed, it will be necessary to search for export markets if efficient and viable capacity utilisation is to be achieved. Clearly the cost of production at Numaligarh, loaded with cost of import and transportation of feedstock and re-export of output is likely to become uncompetitive unless the markets in SE Asian Region and Bangladesh are also opened to the Refinery for both supply of feedstock as well as sale of refinery products. In this context, the India-Bangladesh Friendship Pipeline (IBFPL)[2] intended to supply refinery products to Bangladesh through the Siliguri marketing terminal is a worthwhile proposal and needs to be completed expeditiously.

The Brahmaputra Cracker and Polymer Unit, (BCPL)[3], another enterprise set up as a follow through of the Assam Accord was commissioned on

2nd January 2016. It is a huge and widespread petrochemicals complex comprising of several units comprising the railhead at Duliajan, where feed Natural Gas and Naphtha are unloaded, Lakwa where the feed Natural Gas is processed and the main petrochemical complex at Lepetkata, Dibrugarh, where Polymers are produced after processing the feed stocks. The principal end-products of the complex are High Density Polyethylene (HDPE) and Linear Low-Density Polyethylene (LLDPE), totalling 2,20,000 metric tonnes per annum (tpa) and 60,000 tpa of Poly-Propylene (PP). The other products include Hydrogenated Pyrolysis Gasoline and Pyrolysis Fuel Oil.

Again, as in the case of NRL, the production level is way above the absorption capacity of the NER and will require linkages with the rest of India and the proximate and wider markets for the supply of their feedstocks and marketing of their products. With their gas and oil resources, both Myanmar and Bangladesh could be competitive suppliers of feedstock while SE Asia and Bangladesh could provide ready customers, enabling better capacity utilisation and competitive pricing. The petrochemicals complex in Assam could then become a critical value addition node in the overall trade in the ASEAN region. This however, is easier said than done. The investments in Oil and Gas sectors have tended to be developed without taking the possible synergies in the immediate neighbourhood into account. The lack of engagement with Bangladesh and Myanmar has resulted in oil and gas from these countries being exported elsewhere, principally to China who wasted no time in setting up a pipeline connecting Myanmar gas fields to Kunming.

Irrespective of state support, the viability of the investment in oil and gas sector in the North East would become critical for survival of such enterprises. The imperative of planning major investments based on regional, transnational viability is stronger than ever, worth pursuing through the Act East Policy even if it takes major trade and diplomatic effort.

Electricity

Hydro and Thermal Power

In addition to coal and gas based thermal power, North Eastern India has a very large established hydropower potential.[4] While Arunachal Pradesh has the highest hydro-potential, there is considerable potential in Sikkim also along with for small and mini hydro in hill regions in other states which is unexploited. In addition to being renewable, the hydro energy would complement base load generation from thermal energy and provide a balanced power supply addition to the national grid. It would also create local energy surpluses which could be distributed all across the NER and even exported.

While substantial renewable energy capacity is being added in the country, it is likely that oil/gas-based power would be required over the next quarter century or so to supplement hydropower/other renewables and provide a balanced round-the-clock electricity supply profile, optimising mix of base load and peaking power. India has the technical capability of setting up and operating large transmission grids. Energy linkages spanning India, Bangladesh, Bhutan, Nepal and Myanmar have been advocated by experts and planners in various fora. There is, therefore, a good case for investment in generation of electricity and its distribution through a regional, transnational grid, which would include hydro and other renewable energy, to Bangladesh Bhutan, Myanmar and eastwards as complementary to the gas pipeline grid. Such linkages would leverage the natural potential of the North East in terms of resources, geography and know-how.

Apart from linkages with the national grid, a strategy that enables a regional and international electricity grid, along with modern grid management, setting up of electricity exchanges and financial settlement arrangements with neighbouring countries, would not only improve capacity utilisation, provide cheaper electricity for local development but also build up trade in financial terms through energy exchanges. While energy trade is already taking place bilaterally between India and Bhutan and separately with Nepal, regional electricity exchanges would form an important component of wider regional economic development and cooperation. Facilitating such regional, transnational gas and energy grids is clearly another worthy strategic goal for the Act East Policy.

The Land Potential

NER covers an area 2,62,179 sq. kms of land spanning plains areas as well as hills and valleys. This land area is underutilised in terms of its agricultural and horticultural potential. North East is home to a very large number of rice varieties grown in different conditions. Such rain fed, flood resistant and pest resistant varieties have evolved over the ages. In fact, the gene pool available in the region has been used over the last half-century to develop many modern varieties. Geographical diversity enables the proliferation of varieties that are valued for different types of nutritional values and are also attractive in export market. Research and documentation of the genetic makeup and nutritional values of the rice varieties grown in the NER would go a long way towards recognition of NE rice varieties in the international market. ASEAN and Pacific region being essentially rice-eating, the potential of value-added exports covering a range of rice varieties is obvious.

During recent years, the cultivated areas of the North East, largely in Assam, have shown an impressive increase in production of rice. Plains areas of the NE are producers of cereals, legumes and oilseeds and provide the opportunity for value addition through food processing industry by extraction of rice-based products, bran and bran oil, maise derivatives, mustard and other edible oils etc. In fact, such industry exists, but is largely confined to Assam. There is a requirement is of larger capacities with more efficient and modern plant and machinery able to produce diversified products. Given such food processing capacities, NER could well import cereals and oilseeds from Bangladesh and Myanmar for processing and re-export.

With a diversified agricultural strategy linked with post-harvest support and marketing linkages, production levels can increase considerably across the range of agricultural/horticultural crops., which provides the rational for value addition through food processing. This would, however, require considerable scientific and research input to increase yields, improve and certify different varieties combined with specialised supply infrastructure, connectivity and market access in NERs immediate neighbourhood to quickly absorb increased production.

Plantation Crops: North East grows 60% of India's Tea[5]. In addition to meeting the domestic demand, Assam and Darjeeling Teas are Geographically Indicated and are identified as such all over the world. In addition to [6,7] speciality teas are also being grown in some hill states. Production of tea is interlinked with its quality testing and certification, grading auction and movement. In this respect, despite the impressive growth of the Tea Auction Centre in Guwahati, due to legacy issues harking back to the time when Indian tea production and marketing globally was determined by UK based companies, the grading, blending, marketing and export of Tea is closely linked with the tea trade through Kolkata, which provides a window to both domestic and export markets. There is little logic in disrupting this linkage which provides value in terms of matching market preferences to production unless the Guwahati Tea Auction Centre provides value addition through direct exports.

Realising the potential for production of tea in the NER, an Inland Container Depot was set up near Guwahati in 1986. This was a very forward-looking step as it encouraged growth of warehousing, packaging, containerisation and freight forwarding of teas ex-Guwahati. The loaded containers were initially transported by rail. With opening up of water routes via Brahmaputra, these could be transported more economically via river barges. However, the Inland Container Depot is facing a challenge to its financial viability as outward cargo comprising largely of tea is not complemented by enough inward cargo, resulting in empty haulages one way and rising costs. In addition, diversification of out bound cargo beyond tea is also yet to take place. As a result, the Amingaon (Guwahati) inland container depot is by and large a seasonal ICD that mainly handles tea containers for export during the tea[8].

Again, while both Darjeeling and Assam[9] continue as major tea producers, all is not well with the tea plantations with many of them are facing financial difficulties[10]. A part of the problem is due to labour issues and unsettled conditions due to sporadic ethnic unrest. State support in the form of a stable law and order environment and credible framework to resolve labour issues is a must. This would require a very detailed negotiation with both Tea Plantation owners, both corporate and individual, as well as the tea garden labour. The other aspect is the inability to safeguard the tea brand names against inferior teas being pushed in the name of Darjeeling or Assam as the production system of tea is also undergoing a change with small growers contributing an increasing percentage of the production. Therefore, an international scheme of branding and certification to guard against fake branding is necessary. Climate change is also likely to pose a major challenge to the tea industry as the quantity of tea produce, its quality and flavour are strongly environment determined. The Tea Research Institute at Tocklai near Jorhat needs to be developed as a cutting-edge institution for research and development of new, climate resilient varieties of tea.

While efficient supply chains linking Assam to export outlets through Kolkata and various consumption centres across India are no doubt necessary, there is no reason why tea should not form an important component of border trade with Bangladesh and Myanmar. This would require re-orientation of the market structure as well as the processes and technology inputs for production, gradation, pricing, packaging and supply in smaller lots through local trade. Co-opting the Tea Board of India and the state governments would be necessary for safeguarding NE India's tea industry and should be an essential ingredient of the Act East Policy. In addition to Tea, Coconut, Rubber, Betel Nut, Cashew, and Spices are being grown in the region with good results and hold considerable promise and need to be given institutional support as in the case of tea.

While India would itself provide a major market for the consumption of output of such plantation crops, The Act East Policy would be suitable instrument to support value addition and look at consumption centres beyond the traditional ones in UK, Europe, Central Asia and Russia etc. In this respect SE Asia and Western Pacific provide a challenging market place, well worth tapping. A lot would, of course depend upon efficient transportation of bulk goods, primarily through Bangladesh and Myanmar.

Bamboo: NE is home to nearly 45 varieties of bamboo. The agro-climatic conditions of the NE also result in prolific growth. However, while traditionally bamboo has been used widely in the North East for housing construction and various farming and household goods, industrial use of bamboo in the NER has been quite limited.

The global bamboo market was valued at USD 53.28 billion in 2020 and is expected to grow at a CAGR of 5.7 percent between 2021 and 2028. Increasing infrastructure development investments, raised use of sustainable building/construction materials, and rising consumer awareness of the uses and benefits of bamboo are expected to drive the market during the forecast period. Using bamboo and rattan has numerous environmental, economic, and social advantages. Bamboo is a renewable resource that absorbs 40 percent more CO_2 and produces 35 percent more oxygen than trees. Bamboo cultivation also helps in control of soil erosion and is environmentally sustainable in many ways[11].

India is the second largest bamboo-producing country in the world after China in terms of bamboo species and bamboo area, with 136 species in 19 genera covering an area of four million ha. (As against 500 bamboo species in 39 genera, 6.7274 million ha China). Despite being the second largest cultivator of bamboo in the world, India's share in the global bamboo trade and commerce is low at 4 percent. In financial terms, China has bamboo-based industry worth US$ 48 Billion whereas the size of the market for bamboo products in India is barely $4 Bn[12].

Realising the potential of bamboo, the National Bamboo Mission (NBM) was launched as a Centrally Sponsored Scheme in 2006-07. It was subsumed under Mission for Integrated Development of Horticulture (MIDH) during 2014-15 and continued as such till 2015-16. Thereafter its activities were curtailed and funds were released only for maintenance of bamboo plantations raised earlier under NBM. In 2018, the Restructured National Bamboo Mission was approved again as a centrally sponsored scheme. The new Mission envisaged promoting growth of bamboo by adopting "area-based, regionally differentiated strategy: The Mission intends to strengthen marketing of bamboo products, especially those of handicraft items.[13]

A diversified development of a market for bamboo-based products is necessary to create a bamboo-based economy which could be yet another potential source for growth for the NER. While paper making is one potential use of bamboo, large scale use of bamboo for paper making is an inefficient and destructive in the digital age. Besides Bamboo is crushed and treated with large amounts of chemicals to make pulp, releasing various contaminants in the process. India currently produces the most bamboo paper in Asia, with the proportion of bamboo in raw paper making materials as high as 45 to 60 per cent. The Hindustan Paper Corporation, a Central Government public sector enterprise which had set up a large paper production unit in Assam has gone into liquidation. The revival of the paper mill at Jogighopa, (to be revived under the Assam Accord) also made no progress. Unless it is used for manufacture of high-quality value-added paper products, bulk use of bamboo as feedstock for paper production is a poor use of this versatile material which can be used for wide range of products. Another use of bamboo, incineration for electricity generation has proved to be neither environment friendly nor commercially viable.

Primary amongst other options for bamboo use is housing construction for which it is locally available sustainable material. In fact, it has long been used as such for house construction in rural areas in the NER. Its use is well known for pillars and beams and walls. Modern structural innovation has enabled multiple storied houses made of bamboo with innovative development of flooring, panels reinforced bamboo beams etc. Bamboo is increasingly being used for construction of tourist lodges and resorts in the region. This has to be mainstreamed further through design and aesthetic application to floors, roofs and furniture derived from bamboo. In addition, a range of bamboo products can be developed to replace plastics in agriculture while engineered bamboo is used for industrial pallets and lifestyle products such as furniture and many more items of daily use. Bamboo can be a major source of cellulose and other by products that are extensively used in a large number of industries. Rural communities in the NER are well accustomed to use of bamboo in handicrafts, textiles and artifacts and have a fine tradition of craftsmanship in such items. Food products such as bamboo shoots, vinegar, wine represent another growth area based on bamboo.

Research and innovation in use of bamboo for housing is already available in the country but needs to be oriented towards the requirement of a competitive market for bamboo-based goods. Use of bamboo in place of brick and cement-based housing construction needs to be encouraged. Preparation of building codes for sustainable housing incorporating use of bamboo by institutions such as the ISCE (Indian Society of Civil Engineers) or the CSIR Central Buildings Research Institute would go a long way in enabling its acceptability. On the one hand there is a need for bamboo research stations in different parts of the NER to identify, document and propagate local bamboo species, on the other it would be well worth encouraging design and innovation in use of this versatile material for housing. A regional institution for architecture could be a useful vehicle for this effort.

The value of bamboo as a resource can be realised better if its use in a range of sectors is developed in a manner that encourages large scale cultivation, sustainable harvesting and processing. Though NER has a large growing stock of bamboo, much of it is in forest areas. As a result, the yield of Bamboo is quite low since it has not till recently been 'cultivated' as any other agri crop. (In contrast to China's average yield of 50 MT/Ha, the maximal yield range in India lies in the range of 10-15 MT/ha)[14]. Bamboo cultivation, if done as an organised plantation, can yield large quantities of uniform raw material for many bamboo-based industries which consume large quantities of bamboo. While all bamboo species are not suitable for organised cultivation, nine out of the ten bamboo species prioritised by the restructured Bamboo Mission are found naturally in the north-eastern region of the country and it is, therefore, the logical place suitable for propagation of these species.

India's National Bamboo Mission notes that, "the industry in China utilises every single part of the bamboo, with minimal waste. It has transformed the supply chain in bamboo where farmers undertake pre-processing near the source of bamboo. They split the bamboo culms into parts and feed the different parts into separate product chains. The industry in China is also at the fore-front of introducing new technologies in production and development of new products." INBAR notes the employment generating potential of bamboo observing that 7.75 million farmers in China are directly engaged in the bamboo production. In bamboo processing regions, 30 per cent of farmers income comes from the bamboo going up to 50%

in some regions. Further over 8.0 million people are employed in bamboo-based industries.

Clearly focus on developing a bamboo economy would make a major contribution to the economy of the North East.

Scientific Horticulture

The NE Region, due to its diverse geography, is amazingly rich in horticultural crops. Large, sparsely populated land resources particularly in the hill areas, a wide range of soil and other agro-climatic conditions hold out much promise for horticulture which can support food processing industry and horticultural exports into the both the Indian and the SE Asian markets. However, the horticultural potential is hardly tapped.

Horticultural crops available in this region range from tropical and sub-tropical to temperate fruits, vegetables and flowers. Many plant species are indigenous to the region and grow abundantly with a large number of cultivars and land races. It is also little known that the NER is the citrus depository of India.

The diversity of fruits and vegetables in the Northeast is not yet fully documented despite enormous efforts put in by the National Bureau of Plant Genetic Resources (NBPGR) some decades ago. About 16,000 germplasm accessions of different vegetables, tubers, spices and condiments crops were collected through several crop specific and multi-crop expeditions conducted by NBPGR alone or in collaboration with other institutes during the period 1986 to 1994-95. This work faced funds crunch and seems to have lost its momentum[15].

An example of the under-utilised fruit crops of the Northeast is the (Elaeagnus latifolia), local name Soh-Shang. This shrub is mostly grown in semi-wild conditions and sometimes at the household level. The fruit is considered to be a very rich source of vitamins and minerals and other bioactive compounds. It is also a good source of essential fatty acids. It is being investigated for halting or reversing the growth of cancers. Similarly, the region is also home to passion fruit, kiwi fruit, and chow-chow, which are also rich in bioactive compounds and fairly rich in essential fatty acids.[16]

Pineapple cultivation in the North East is a success story that reveals the region's potential as well as pitfalls of not adopting a comprehensive approach. Though not indigenous to the region, pineapple found a very welcome environment in the Northeast. Earlier grown in some selected areas, the support given under the National Horticulture Technology Mission 2001 resulted in a huge increase in area under pineapple so that now NER produces more than 40% of the total pineapple output of India, almost all of it organically. Pineapples produced from this region are said to be compared with the best in the world. Yet inadequate post-harvest, processing and marketing support leads to a substantial part of the crop getting destroyed.

Northeast is known for its rich diversity of Orchids. Of 17,000 species of orchids in the world, about 1,250 occur in India and about 700 occur in the northeastern region, of which around 324 occur in Meghalaya alone. The region with its geographical diversity is also favourable for floriculture in general.

The productivity of horticultural crops can be raised manifold through watershed-based land development and application of practices based on modern science and technology to local conditions. This requires major change of focus in the scientific establishment from cereal crops to horticulture, certification of planting material and a massive extension effort supported by horticulture nurseries selling certified planting material. Unlike cereal crops, however, horticultural produce has shorter shelf life and requires better supply lines with well organised cold chains and quick access to the ultimate consumer. Increased production would need to reach markets and consumption centres quickly, which brings the focus on search for markets and efficient transport and storage infrastructure.

Horticultural potential, however, needs to be viewed not only in terms of fruits and vegetables that can be consumed as such, but also in terms of valuable extracts that form vital ingredients of a large number of nutritional, pharma and wellness products. There is a need for continuous surveys and cataloguing of the local horticultural gene pool available investment in research and development in applications of fruit and plant-based extracts.

Access to markets for horticultural produce comprising of fresh fruits and flowers requires efficient and fast connectivity in addition to post-harvest support such as grading and ambience-controlled storage as well as marketing strategies linking the region's production to markets in South and SE Asia, China and The Pacific Rim. The region is eminently suited to organic cultivation, for which there is wide and growing demand. However, this will require credible certification arrangements close to the production centres which provide access to buyer certification and testing agencies. Tapping the amazing genetic diversity of the North East backed by scientific and technological support structure and marketing input on a sustainable basis would provide considerable comparative advantage to the region and enable value-added trade exchanges with the neighbourhood.

There are, of course, many more areas and sectors where NER can develop competitive advantage, considering the amazing diversity of talent of its people. A full enumeration of all such possibilities would be beyond the scope of this work. The foregoing narrative highlights some of the obvious local advantages that the NER offers. A perspective that extends the region's potential eastwards would build a trade engagement east, regionally and internationally. It would integrate Indian products in the daily consumption pattern of SE Asian countries intimately and provide a major impetus to enduring economic and trade links with the wider SE Asian Region.

Notes to Chapter 6

1. Numaligarh Refinery Expansion Project: https://bcplonline.co.in/

2. The 130 Km India-Bangladesh Friendship Pipeline (IBFPL) project will enable fuel oil products to be exported from India's Siliguri Marketing Terminal in West Bengal State to Bangladesh. The capacity of the 130km oil pipeline will be one million metric tonnes per annum. The project, initiated after the Delhi Dhaka Agreement 2018, is expected to be commissioned by 2023.

3. The Brahmaputra Gas Cracker and Polymers (BCPL) is a Government of India undertaking set up consequent to the Assam Accord 1985; https://bcplonline.co.in/

4. The NE Region has hydropower potential of about 58,356 MW (>25 MW), out of which 2027 MW (about 3.47%) has been harnessed as on 30th November 2021. An additional 2120 MW of hydropower is under construction. The balance of about 92.9 % is yet to be exploited. (NEEPCO report)

5. India produced 945.97 million kgs of tea in 2005 contributing 27.36 percent of world production share in that year and was leading tea producing country in the World. In 2006, China overtook India as world's largest Tea producer. India's total tea production for the 2019-20 was 1367 million kg but dipped to 1283 million kg for the financial year 2020-21 due to the pandemic. However, India remains the second Largest Tea producer in the world. (Tea Board of India)

6. As of a 2018 survey, a total of 6.37 lakh hectares of area was cultivated in India for tea production. India is also among the world's top tea consuming countries, with 80% of the tea produced in the country consumed by the domestic population: Tea Industry and Exports in India; IBEF Report Nov. 2022

7. Assam alone produces more than 52 percent of the India's national production,

8. Report No.16 of 2018 - Performance Audit of Working of Inland Container Depots (ICDs) and Container Freight Stations (CFSs) Department of Revenue Indirect taxes, Customs

9. About tea industries; Govt of Assam, Industries and Commerce

10. Status of Tea Plantation in North-East India: A Review; November 2015 Reter Potom, Gibji Nimasow Rajiv Gandhi University

11. International Bamboo and Rattan Organization (INBAR); "How can bamboo contribute to the circular economy?": INBAR report on the potential for bamboo to contribute to a zero-waste, low-carbon future".

12. 2020 Annual Highlights; INBAR (The International Bamboo and Rattan Organization (INBAR) is an intergovernmental development organisation that promotes environmentally sustainable development using bamboo and rattan. Founded in 1997, with the mission "to improve the well-being of producers and users of bamboo and rattan within the context of a sustainable bamboo and rattan resource base, by consolidating, coordinating and supporting strategic and adaptive research and development." 50 Member States are a part of INBAR. In addition to its Secretariat Headquarters in China, INBAR has Regional Offices in Cameroon, Ecuador, Ethiopia, Ghana and India.)

13. Restructured National Bamboo Mission was approved by the Central Government on 25-04-2018. The Mission envisages promoting holistic growth of bamboo sector by adopting area-based, regionally differentiated strategy and to increase the area under bamboo cultivation and marketing. (National Bamboo Mission; Ministry of Agriculture and Farmers welfare, Govt. of India https://nbm.nic.in/

14 Bamboo: A Potential Resource for Enhancing Rural Economy– A Case Study: Dev I, Ram A, Ahlawat S P, Dhyani S K , Tewari R K, Singh R, Sridhar K B, Kumar N, Dwivedi P; World Agroforestry (ICRAF)

15. Horticultural diversity in North-East India and its improvement for value addition: May 2012Indian Journal of Genetics and Plant Breeding 72(2):157-167: Bidyut Deka Assam Agricultural University Bidyut C. Thirugnanavel Anbazhagan Indian Council of Agricultural Research Ramkishor Patel National Research Centre for Litchi

16. Horticulture in north-east India: Strengths and prospects: Dinesh Sarmah and Parag Kr Deka1 THE ASIAN JOURNAL OF HORTICULTURE Volume 7 | Issue 1 | June, 2012 | 221-228. 13. Horticultural Scenario in North East India; L.C. Dey International Journal of Agricultural Science and Research (IJASR) ISSN(P): 2250-0057; ISSN(E): 2321-0087 Vol. 7, Issue 2, Apr 2017; 243-254

Chapter 7

Organising NER Economy for the Future

(While leveraging the natural potential of the NE Region is bound to yield dividends in the short and the medium term, it is also necessary to look ahead and beyond the traditional sectors to position the region as an economic powerhouse for the future. While all kinds of economic activity is possible in the Northeast, some sectors that can provide a major contribution to the economic growth of the Northeast in the future also need to specifically highlighted. Investment in boosting investment in some critical areas with an eye on the future has to be an integral feature of the Act East Policy. Such investment has to integrate external outreach imperatives with domestic initiatives aimed at human development and boosting employment.)

As services acquire a larger proportion of the Indian economy, the NE Region has to also position itself as an efficient provider of services. Growth contributing value would be created if the local entrepreneurs can customise a range of services to the requirements of end users irrespective of the country, they are located in. This requires a major boost to the nascent services industry in the region along with better connectivity, ease of travel and a communications network of a much higher bandwidth than is available now.

Digitalisation, Internet and Telecommunications

Internet and Telecommunications, being core requirements for service industry, are now central to any strategy for economic growth as well as human development. Digitalisation and reliable telecom services provide a boost to business and trade, education, health and other related spin-off services. Such services, which are of value not only to the region but also to neighbouring countries, depend heavily on digital and communications infrastructure for their growth and sustenance.

Currently, the international digital band-width to India is provided through 15 sub-sea cables1 {17 if Seacom and Middle East North Africa (MENA) are considered separate cable systems}, with 15 cable landing stations in 5 cities across India, namely Mumbai, Chennai, Cochin, Tuticorin and Trivandrum.[1] The nearest landing station to the NE Region is The Cox's Bazar Cable Landing Station located in Bangladesh, owned and operated by Bangladesh Submarine Cable Company (BSCCL). New cable landing stations are planned at Digha (WB), Cochin, the Andaman & Nicobar Islands and Puducherry, all quite remote from the NE Region. As such NER has only secondary or tertiary access to the available bandwidth. These cable systems cater to India's international internet connectivity requirements. However, the market structure is determined by large international tele-communication consortia who have developed these internet cable links and landing stations. The participating telcos have exclusive rights in their home countries and activate the links depending on viability based on available bandwidth, demand and costs involved. Over the years there has been much technological development but the market structure has remained the same.

According to experts, at present (2021), the total installed or operational submarine capacity for India is estimated to be of the order of 20 Terabytes per second (Tbps) and is expected to grow at 25 percent CAGR, thus adding 5 Tbps year-on-year. However, as services based on 5G spectrum and fractional/virtual fibre pairs gain traction in the coming years, it is unlikely that the available cable systems would be ready to meet the emerging hyperscale requirements. On top of that Indian Telcos are facing financial stress due to unpredictable revenue sharing and tax burdens and a competition regulation regime that is still developing. Therefore, mobilising resources needed even to sustain the quality of existing Telecom services efficiently is a challenge. As for the connection through Bangladesh, it is uncertain as to what capacity would be available after meeting local requirements in that country, as the economy of Bangladesh is also growing. The NER, where Internet has covered just 35 percent of the population, is therefore, a part of a comparative digital hinterland which is likely to face increasing capacity constraints[2].

Mobile telephone connectivity is yet another constraint. In 2018, the Central Government had taken up the Comprehensive Telecom Development Plan for North East Region to be funded through the Universal Service Obligation Fund (USOF) which was supposed to facilitate the project of covering the uncovered villages by setting up enough towers. However, the financial and technical roll out of the project has been slow. The intended coverage has not reached the hill areas of the North East which are considerable, covering Arunachal Pradesh, Nagaland, Manipur, Mizoram, Meghalaya (other than Shillong), Sikkim (other than Gangtok) and the hills districts of Assam and Tripura. Border areas, in particular remain uncovered and in border areas, depend on telecom services provided by Bangladesh and Bhutan.

Due to lack of digital access, the IT revolution in India has so far passed the NER by. With the onslaught of the Covid pandemic having resulted in disruption of classroom education in schools and colleges, digital, off-physical classroom education was widely resorted to in many parts of India. Even with the pandemic having waned of late, digital education and remote working has come to stay. However, lack and in many cases absence, of stable and adequate bandwidth has placed NER students and professionals at a great disadvantage[3].

A possible solution is being seen in the development of high-speed, low-latency satellite broadband services to serve rural and remote regions globally, including in India. Experts see India as a top emerging market for satellite internet services as around 75 percent of rural India does not have access to broadband. In many locations in India which are still without cellular or fibre connectivity, satellite-based systems, can be rolled out a lot faster than terrestrial telecom networks. These would ideally fill the gap in rural and remote regions. However, the roll out and impact of such services faces several technological issues and is yet to be seen on the ground.

Enabling digital access would link local human potential with growth and transform the entrepreneurial, business and employment landscape. This would, of course, require simultaneous development of technical and institutional structure, massive investment in providing digital skills along with an MSME policy and financing arrangements suited to local entrepreneurship and start-ups. In the meantime, if the glaring disability caused by lack of digital access is to be addressed, telecom and internet services must improve substantially in the North East. Diplomatic initiatives aimed at securing dedicated access to undersea cable through Bangladesh with land based "landing stations" at different nodes in the NER would have to be pursued. Ministry of Electronics and Information Technology, Government of India; The 'Digital North East Vision 2022' holds considerable promise[4]. However, ensuring quality digital connectivity for the North eastern Region, which will pay a large dividend in the future, is an emerging priority that needs strong support from the Act East Policy.

Diversifying and Modernising Tourism, Travel and Hospitality

The geographical diversity of the region provides a range of tourist options including wildlife and adventure, mountaineering in the eastern high Himalayas, river-based tourism including cruises along the Brahmaputra with rafting and camping experience etc. There is also a growing volume of people visiting the religious destinations such as the Kamakhya Temple in Guwahati, Buddhist shrines in Assam and Arunachal. Another concept as yet largely untapped is History as tourist attraction. There are several archaeological sites of kingdoms and temples of the past. Since the North East was the scene of some of the fiercest battles of the Second World War, the locations of these epic battles, the cemeteries where the fallen soldiers lie buried and the locations from where the war effort was coordinated is of interest to many war historians. Religious, cultural and historical destinations are a resource not only for tourist interest but also for preservation and showcasing of heritage, wildlife and cultures. Cultural exposure to the amazing anthropological diversity across myriad tribes and population groups, cool hills summer destinations, nature, wellness and herbal treatment resorts add to the amazing range of experiences that the modern tourist values. Participative tourism for rural areas, plantations and community immersion is as yet an unexplored area for the NER.

It is well recognised that tourism creates employment, both directly and indirectly, in a cost-effective manner and encourages entrepreneurship and skills development. It stimulates investment, including FDI, across a range of economic options including infrastructure. Eventually good tourist destinations become choices for international events and conferences, enabling their show-casing further. Overall, it has a great multiplier effect by stimulating activity and growth in a number of related services at a miniscule fraction of the cost of, say, a petroleum refinery. The challenge is to leverage tourism as an important plank of the regional development policy.

ASEAN- Tourism as a strategy for economic development.

It is noteworthy that ASEAN has consistently placed considerable premium on the tourism sector as a key component of the strategy for the economic development of the SE Asian region. In fact, tourism has been one of the most important areas of ASEAN's cooperation since the early establishment of the Association[5]. A Committee on Trade and Tourism, as one of the five permanent Committees under the purview of the ASEAN Economic Ministers was established in 1977 itself, followed by the ASEAN Tourism Forum (ATF) in 1981. The ATF was designed as an avenue for the ASEAN governments to engage with private sector and relevant civil society organisations to promote the entire ASEAN region as a single tourism destination. Since then, a large number of agreements have been entered to encourage intra-ASEAN travel and for development and promotion of ASEAN as a single tourism destination with world-class standards, facilities and attractions. These agreements also include measures to ensure the safety and security of travellers, develop human resources in the tourism and travel industry and actively conduct joint marketing and promotion.

As a result, tourism has been one of the key growth sectors in ASEAN. The wide array of tourist attractions across the region has drawn 143 million tourists to ASEAN in 2019, contributing US$394 Bn to ASEAN economies. Till the pandemic hit the world, badly disrupting tourist flows, ASEAN was the fastest growing destination-region in the world. According to the World Travel and Tourism Council, tourism directly contributed to ASEAN's GDP (4.4%) and employment (3.2%) in 2011. In addition, the sector accounted for an estimated 8% of total capital investment in the region. The sector has seen increased interest not only from usual markets in Europe and the Americas but also from Asia's economic giants and emerging markets. ASEAN as a region itself emerged as a top source of tourists with ASEAN countries accounting for about one-third (38%) of the tourist arrivals. The tourism industry was badly hit during the Covid Pandemic but is recovering. While it has still not reached pre-covid levels, the post Covid bounce back is encouraging[6].

ASEAN countries are visited by an increasing number of Indian tourists also every year (Covid disruptions excepted). The reverse, however, is not true. While India has been engaging with ASEAN on tourism (with 2022 designated as the "ASEAN-India Friendship Year" to commemorate the 30th anniversary of ASEAN-India relations) the Indo-ASEAN cooperation on tourism, insofar it is expected to tap into tourists from ASEAN, is yet to move beyond declarations of intent.

Leveraging Tourism Potential through NER

While the North Eastern Region, with its tourism potential, can well integrate into the ASEAN Tourism market, for this role to be realised, it is important for tourism to be recognised as a strategic choice for regional economic development under the Act East Policy, with a coordination across a wide range of activities. Both the Central as well as the State governments have to work in coordinated fashion to meaningfully remove barriers to growth of tourism.

To begin with, access and movement within the North East have to improve, not only to the capital cities but beyond so that tourists can visit destinations of their interest. This is easier said than done. There are a number of restrictions in several NE states such as special or inner line permits. Visitors to the North East are often intimidated by apprehensions regarding their personal safety. There have also been cases of attacks on outsiders by local people in some areas on suspicion of witchcraft or rumours of child lifting or mistaken identity. In some cases, innocent tourists have come to grievous harm due to rumours. Besides access infrastructure, including roads and telecommunications, to the interior areas where most of the wildlife, adventure, community-based tourist attractions are located, is quite limited. All these aspects create negative publicity for the region resulting in potential tourists scratching out most NE destinations.

There is a need to expand and improve the infrastructure at entry as this is critical in forming first impressions. This requires significant expansion and improvement of airports and railway stations. While a number of airports have been established, their capacity is unable to cope with the increasing numbers of flights and passengers. Extreme weather conditions in the NE sometimes lead to disruption of flights increasing the requirement of quality hotels in close proximity to airports to take on stranded passengers. Standards also need to be set for budget, mid and premium range hotels with internationally comparable hygiene standards. Their classification and grading would enable predictable, standardised tariffs and better choices for the tourist. Outreach, by the NE state governments, to domestic and international hotel chains to establish hotels in the region needs to be encouraged.

Tourism involves a very large range of service providers including currency exchangers, tourist operators, hotels, guides, taxi and car hire, equipment and assistance for adventure tourism etc. It is important that these services are provided in a reasonable, safe and credible manner. It would be well worth the effort to establish rule based and accessible registration requirements, competency standards and certification procedures for all types of service providers. A single instance of a travel/ taxi operator, or service provider cheating a tourist creates enough bad publicity to scare off a thousand others. Therefore, it is essential to provide for registration of professional service providers along with a customer rating/grading mechanism.

Concerted efforts need to be taken to map tourist sites for heritage, wild life, religious and cultural tourism with development of facilities specific to the travellers visiting those sites. For example, religious sites may attract large crowds during certain festivals. There should be adequate crowd and facilities management infrastructure for such occasions. Similarly wild life tourism requires peace and quiet, both for animals and humans. Clustering of human habitation and industrial activity in the vicinity of such sites needs to be avoided through regulation. Immersive tourism with food, handloom and handicraft speciality centres.

Northeastern India has to offer tourist facilities and experience comparable to the rest of South East Asia, for which tourism is already an important economic contributor. The task is not an easy one but given the tourist resources of the NE, it is, however doable. North East could be promoted as a brand in the international market with thematic tour packages and attractions. For this, in addition to encouraging visitors from the rest of India, North East should also be plugged into the SE Asian tourist map. Air connectivity between NER and ASEAN, through direct flights to ASEAN capitals from the NE would go a long way in this regard. This has to be combined with efficient immigration and border management services, at all international airports in the region.

Tourism is human interaction intensive and depends on trained human resources for its sustenance. For the tourism and travel industry to grow, significant investment is required in tourism education and training. Tourism education and skills should be recognised as curricula for vocational education along with improvement of language skills in various Indian and foreign languages. Human resource development for tourism in the NER needs to be undertaken with the object of mutual recognition of skills and qualifications in the ASEAN region. The services of professional tourism experts and skilled workers available within the ASEAN region could be secured for the purpose on the basis of bilateral arrangements.

ASEAN-wide promotional events may be supplemented with sports events such as for golf and trans- SE Asian and sub-Himalayan car/ motorcycle rallies, music festivals and films. This has to be complemented with extensive tourist help, information and emergency services. There is also a need to expand digitalisation and communications network so that the visiting tourist can access all kinds of services and stay in touch with friends and family at all times. Apart from formal cooperation with ASEAN, Act East

Policy has to include outreach to the tourism industry, particularly airlines, hotels and resorts, travel agencies and tour operators, in marketing and promoting transnational tour packages including the NER.

Health and Education

With the establishment of Central universities, private universities, IIT Guwahati, NIT Medical colleges and hospitals both in public and private sector as also many other training institutions, the North East is positioned to provide reasonably priced, good quality higher education and capacity building services to students from the SE Asian Region, who would be able to access them easily while studying in a familiar cultural milieu. In fact, Myanmar, Laos, Cambodia, Vietnam and Thailand have, from time to time, expressed interest in availing such services.

Medical Tourism, Services and Education: During the last two decades, the North East has seen a considerable expansion of health facilities with setting up of medical colleges and hospitals, both in the public and private sectors. The NE Region is well placed to provide quality medical treatment, education and services not only to local patients but also from the countries neighbouring it. In fact, many people from these countries actually avail these services. Apart from medical education, reasonably priced specialty medical services would find many takers in SE Asia. Expansion of this activity often has a wide spin-off effect in a number of other sectors as well. Overall, backed by the government's Heal in India7 initiative, Medical Tourism in India currently generates $6 billion which is expected to reach $13 billion by 2026[8]. For the South East Asia, India's North East, with its growing medical and health infrastructure, is well placed to share in this activity.

Medical education and medical treatment represent a growth area for the NER that would help in building enduring relations across borders. Good medical education that may attract foreign students, however, depends a lot on the specialised educational standards, equipment and facilities available and quality of faculty. This requires considerable investment beyond buildings and construction. Further, to establish credibility across borders there is a need to match international standards along with outside evaluation by impartial observers and peer review by other institutions of eminence from both inside and outside the region along with some international participation. In medical science, reputation depends on excellence, which, in turn depends on merit. In this respect, it would be well worth the effort to set up institutions of excellence in medicine with admission based on merit rather than regional residency. Such institutions will also attract students from neighbourhood countries and ASEAN.

Medical treatment services will eventually comprise general and specialised hospitals, centres for basic and advanced diagnostics, nursing and convalescent homes with post treatment facilities, paramedic staff and medical equipment operation along with technical support system to maintain medical equipment. In fact, medical treatment services are as good or as bad as the technical support system available. Nursing care is a critical component of medical treatment. NER offers considerable talent in this regard but is hamstrung by restrictive regulations guiding nursing education, enforced through the Nursing Council of India. There is a good case for liberalisation allowing rapid increase in nursing education without compromising on technical standards and quality. This would improve the quality of medical treatment services considerably.

Digital revolution and telecommunications have changed medical treatment, diagnosis and education by enabling remote participation. This, however, would require internet and digital bandwidth which is not yet available in the North East. Given that many areas of the NER are still remote, digital connectivity can provide major health benefits to the local population. At the same time, it can enable local institutions to access technical expertise and guidance from institutions of excellence abroad.

Generally, institutions set up in the public sector need to meet local, regional, social and economic criteria. While public investment in such institutions should continue to upgrade the services offered by them, it would be appropriate to encourage private institutions also provided they meet national and international standards. There is a need to streamline the present complex system of Accreditation and Continuing Medical Education (CME), prescribe uniform merit and principles-based guidelines and enforce them across the region through a common body of experts.

Engineering and Technical Education: As per the All-India Survey of Higher Education (AISHE).[9] The number of foreign students opting for courses in India continues to rise. In the year 2000, India welcomed only 6,988 foreign students, in 2019-20, the number rose to 49,348. These foreign students come from 168 different countries across the globe. The highest number, however, came from the neighbouring countries — Nepal (28.1 per cent), followed by Afghanistan (9.1 per cent), Bangladesh (4.6 per cent), Bhutan (3.8 per cent). Other students were from the African Continent. While the Indian Institutes of Technology maintained their international reputation, these institutions remained out of reach for foreign students due to their rigorous selection criteria. Therefore, most of the increase has been due to various other engineering colleges in public and private sectors.

Just like medical education, Engineering and Technical education represents another area that is relevant for the future economy of the NER. Companies throughout the world are in search of talented and driven engineers that will help them adapt to the future as new technology advances at an alarming rate. Some disciplines have a great application in the NER where its peculiar conditions can enable development of technologies relevant to the local resources/ productive activity and geo-climatic conditions. These conditions apply across the SE Asian region as well. The technological talent so developed would be a valuable resource for the ASEAN region as a whole.

NER has a sizable range of engineering and technical institutions. These need to be re-oriented from traditional pure engineering disciplines to hybrid ones that will cater to the demand not only in India but also in the ASEAN region. Computer engineering and software development is one such discipline. In the current scenario there is big push in India to manufacture computer and mobile communications hardware in India. NER should be considered a viable site for servicing ASEAN for a range of computers and devices. Software engineers are the backbone of service industry which is likely to be a major growth area for the NE.

Hybridisation of the traditional engineering disciplines would offer greater value to the NER. Given the productive potential of the NER for oil and gas, its refining and cracking and manufacture of downstream chemicals and products and the need for continuous research and development, Chemical engineering has tremendous potential not only for the Oil and Gas sector but also for various environmental sciences; Similarly, given the potential of the region for energy, electrical engineering is relevant for energy management, including grid operation incorporating green/ renewable energy etc. Practical Civil Engineering to meet the challenge of meeting regions infrastructural needs given its complex geography and environmental conditions. Re-imagined Mechanical Engineering, combined with many emerging disciplines with emergence of new composite streams such as robotics (Computers; Artificial Intelligence/ software); Industrial engineering (management), Biomechanical Engineering (medicine) etc. provide avenues of knowledge that would have great applications not only in the North East but also in its neighbourhood.

Engineering education has to be combined with quality Technical and Vocational Education and Training (TVET) to develop involvement of skilled manpower in science and technology as a broad occupational area. There is need to develop the knowledge and skills that will help the workforce become more flexible and responsive to the needs of labour markets in a technological environment. TVET systems must also be open and all-inclusive to give even the most underprivileged access to learning and training.

In a time of continuous economic, social and technological change, skills and knowledge become quickly out-of-date. People who are unable to obtain formal education and training must be given opportunities to acquire new skills and knowledge. An all- inclusive lifelong learning system calls for the mobilisation of increased public and private resources for education and training and for providing individuals and enterprises with the incentives to investing for meeting their learning and skills development needs.

Wellness and Self Care

For the North East Wellness industry has a strong potential. This industry captured global attention during the last decade and according to a study conducted by McKinsey & Company, is currently valued at $1.5 trillion globally[10]. Wellness industry now combines many elements such as personal health, fitness, nutrition, self-care through various products derived from ayurveda, naturopathy, yoga, sleep management etc.

According to the Federation of Indian Chambers of Commerce & Industry (FICCI)[11], India's wellness industry is valued at INR 490 billion. Growing consumer awareness and an increased inclination amongst citizens to adopt a healthier lifestyle have paved the way for the health and wellness industry to evolve rapidly. According to APEDA, India has become one of the largest producers of organic food, apparel and beauty care products in the world. Indian wellness industry has seen a shift in paradigm, where an increasing number of consumers opt for Alternatives to allopathy such as Siddha or Ayurveda substitutes instead of conventional medicine. The global pandemic is also giving rise to a new consumer behaviour called "wellness rebound," where people are becoming more health-conscious and striving to boost their immunity, managing co-morbidities or recovering from an illness. India is expected to become a wellness hub in the global community following a 12 percent growth per annum. This has sparked an increase in start-ups and businesses focusing on the wellness sector[12].

On the one hand this has led to a growing demand for remote medical devices that can constantly monitor their state of well-being, such as digital wearables, telemedicine, and remote patient monitoring services, sleep duration and quality tracking products etc. On the other it has raised a huge demand for organic products for nutrition and immunity building, special dietary supplements for healthcare, beauty, skincare and aromatic products etc.

Genetic Resources of the NE are a vast untapped, unmapped treasure trove whose value is immeasurable. Genetic research and development of new plant varieties offers a huge potential not in terms of production but also in terms of intellectual property. The amazing bio diversity of the NE Region, scarcely mapped as yet has also encouraged plant based ayurvedic and pharmaceutical ingredients and personal care products. While Hindustan Lever was an early mover, of late there has been investment by ayurvedic enterprises such as Dabur and Patanjali in Assam present another opportunity.

With the increase in popularity of telemedicine and remote-patient monitoring, healthcare and the wellness industry are gaining an aggressive online presence. Considering the aftermath of the pandemic, the aggressive implementation of technology, and the constant consumer market in India, the wellness industry will evolve and expand further.

Entertainment: Music and films

A unique feature of the North East is that most local festivals, in addition to traditional dance and music are open to a wide range of musical performances. The Rongali Bihu festival of Assam goes on for several weeks with musical and dance performances in practically every village and town. Similarly, the Hornbill festival of Nagaland provides a musical experience for nearly ten days. Shillong, in Meghalaya is home to singers of international renown. A large number of artistes from the North east participate in the Mumbai film industry and in Delhi. Given the fondness and natural talent of the people of the North east for music, the availability of a wide range of settings for films the entertainments sector is a potential sector for growth.

During the Covid pandemic, as many restrictions were placed on cinema halls and multiplexes, the OTT streaming systems made tremendous progress. It has opened the cinematography and films sector to a very large pool of talent of actors, story and script writers, music directors, special effects developers in all languages and regions. NER with its scenic landscapes and an astonishing range of cultures and customs provides ideal locales and settings for films as well as OTT content across various genres.

While the multiplier effect of the films industry in terms of participating arts, skills and professions is well known, music business is equally a vital part of a complex, growing tourism and entertainment industry and has its own framework of finance, law, publishing, concert promotion, music production, and management and music industry practices. In fact, this is one area of activity which is continuously looking for new business models for talent spotting and artist management, music publishing and marketing, concert promotion, digital streaming and royalty management. It creates a whole new profession of music professionals who produce music for various requirements including films, produce live events, contract talent and manage the business of integrating music into daily life. Eventually music business generates demand for sophisticated audio equipment along with people trained in managing them, production and recording studios, centres for performing arts, concert halls and event management.

Performing arts, films and music represent a great opportunity for the NER. There is a good potential for setting up institutions for education and training in various aspects of films and music in the region. on the lines of Films and Television Institute Pune, or an institute for music management, in the north east.

Integrating the Domestic and Act East Imperatives: Mass Employment first

While digitalisation, telecommunications, tourism, education, music and entertainment would create huge add-on growth benefits, their full potential would take some time to mature as the region gets ready to leverage these sectors for higher incomes. In the meantime, for about a decade or so, there is a need for strategy that would provide mass employment and put purchasing power in the hands of the people. In context of the North East, this would have to be based on agriculture and allied areas of dairy, horticulture, floriculture etc. on the one hand and handloom textiles on the other. In this context North eastern handlooms deserve a special mention.

Handlooms

As in many other parts of India, handloom is one of the oldest and largest cottage industries in the North East with a very long tradition. This industry is essentially household-based and is one of the largest employment sectors both directly and indirectly, providing jobs to lakhs of weavers, mostly female, in the region. The handloom industry is essentially rural, requires very little capital, uses very little electricity and produces environment-friendly products.

The sector is faced with challenges due to lack of effective policy support. Incomes of handloom weavers have been declining across India. According to the Handloom Census, approximately 67 per cent of the weavers still earn less than ₹5,000 a month, which is less than the amount that an unskilled worker earns as minimum wage. There is low penetration of banking facilities for the weavers resulting in poor credit availability. There are also several problems affecting the supply chain, such as in procurement of raw material. Most of the yarn purchased by weavers (approximately 76 per cent) is from the open market and the remaining is from government and co-operative societies. On the marketing side, adequate sales support and proper branding are almost non-existent for the finished goods, due to which most of the sales happen in the local markets. Furthermore, there is no simple way for a consumer to purchase an authentic, certified handloom product via an e-commerce channel.

The handloom cottage industry has however survived because of originality and workmanship of the women weavers of the Northeast.[13] As of now, even with all the difficulties, there are 12.8 Lakh weavers in Assam alone. The North Eastern Region taken together accounts for 61 percent of the total handloom workforce in India. NE has the highest concentration of handloom units in India, with women dominating 88 percent of the adult workforce. Weaving is also culturally significant to NE women, with weaving skills and knowledge passed from mother to daughter (Devi, 2013)[14].

A prudent strategy for employment and augmenting household incomes in the NER should concentrate on handlooms. This would require a major effort to provide design inputs, provide credit and raw material and extend marketing support for sales in the national and international market. Yet the investment required would be but a fraction of a capital-intensive extraction and refining project which could run into thousands of crores. By bringing a balanced compromise between retaining the cultural heritage of the region and the introduction of modern technology, the spin-off in terms of employment and would be huge. The export potential of handlooms that are produced in environmentally ways and reflect the traditional colours and motifs of the wider South and SE region would also be huge. Act East Policy, therefore has to considered in not only in combination with the Eastern Neighbourhood and domestic regional development as well.

Notes to Chapter 7

1. Cable Landing Stations in India; https://www.submarinenetworks.com/stations/asia/india

2. "Northeast states lag behind in internet connectivity": *Times of India* Dec 19, 2018

3. "In the time of online classes, Northeast waits for a faint signal from a distant tower" Rahul Karmarkar, *The Hindu*, June 13, 2020 (Updated December 04, 2021)

4. Ministry of Electronics and Information Technology, Government of India; The 'Digital North East Vision 2022'

5. The ASEAN Secretariat: ASEAN Tourism Sector; https://asean.org/

6. Tourist arrivals in ASEAN countries rose from 89.23 million in 2012 to 143.61 million in 2019. They fell to 26.1 million in 2020 and to 2.91 million in 2021 due to the Sars Covid-19 pandemic. However, the Tourism sector is showing signs of recovery, though reaching pre-pandemic levels will take time; https://www.statista.com; /ASEAN Stats Data portal.

7. https://www.india.gov.in/website-heal-india

8. Medical Tourism in India, in mid-2020, was estimated to be worth around USD 9 billion which makes India stand at Number 10 in the Global Medical Tourism Index. Approximately 2 million patients visit India each year from 78 countries for medical, wellness and IVF treatments, generating $6 billion for the industry which is expected to reach $13 billion by 2026 backed by the government's Heal in India initiative.: Medical Tourism in India; Hindustan Times 03.12.22

9. All India Survey on Higher Education 2019-20, Ministry of Education, Government of India

10. https://www.mckinsey.com/industries/consumer-packaged-goods/our-insights/feelinggood,the future of the 1.5-trillion wellness market

11. FICCI -EY Report on "Wellness and beauty: an ecosystem in the making," This Report focuses on future trends and opportunities this segment holds and outlines the market size and opportunities, including the sub-segments such as alternate therapies;https// www.scribd.com/document/449067981/Wellness-and-Beauty-An-ecosystem-in-the-making

12. https://globalwellnessinstitute.org/

13. Weaves of North Eastern India; Textiles Value Chain; Aug 25, 2021

14. Handlooms for Livelihood in North-Eastern Region: Problems and Prospects; Devi, 2013, Ch. V, pages 427-438; Journal of Rural Development, volume 32.}

Chapter 8

Getting Infrastructure Right-I

(Only 15.51 percent of the total population of North East India live in towns, while the remaining 84.49 percent people live in about 45000 rural settlements. About 90 percent of the rural settlements are small, having less than 1000 population in each. The challenge is to raise the productivity of this pre-dominant segment of the population. At the same time NER is also urbanising. A policy framework that enables cities to act as engines of future growth is equally essential for the region. While assessing infrastructure requirements of the region both rural and urban requirements are relevant and should be addressed along with the critical aspect of annually recurring floods and erosion in the region).

Tackling Floods

The NER is a very high rainfall area with huge volumes of surface water evacuating through a system of rivers and tributaries, largely falling into the Brahmaputra and some into the Barak River systems. Some of the northern tributaries of Brahmaputra, flowing in from Arunachal Pradesh, bring down enormous discharges of water and soil during the monsoon months. As a result, Brahmaputra, Barak and their numerous tributaries are highly flood-prone. Several million hectares of land in the plains areas of the NER including cropland, transportation infrastructure, villages and even urban settlements, are inundated every year by floodwaters, causing loss of life and serious economic damage. According to an estimate made by the Rashtriya Barh Ayog (National Flood Commission)[1], the flood-prone area in Assam is c. 3.15 million ha, which is 40.16 % of the total geographical area of the state. (However, in 1998, when floods were particularly severe, as much as 3.83 million ha area i.e., 48.85 percent of the total area was affected.) High flood waters also cause severe bank erosion in certain stretches of these rivers sweeping away agricultural land, roads and village settlements, breaching protective embankments and causing extensive water logging over large areas, seriously disrupting life and the economy of the state. The hill areas of the North East are, on the other hand, affected by heavy rainfall and surface run-off degrading the land, causing mud-slides, road subsidence and damage to various infrastructure and residential structures.

The strategy of flood control in Assam over the past several decades has mainly comprised construction of embankments to constrain the rivers and protecting the adjoining land, including floodplains from inundation. About 5000 and 600 km of embankments have been built on the Brahmaputra and Barak River systems, respectively[2]. While these structures have indeed offered some protection from floods, RBA[3] noted several shortcomings of this strategy. According to them, the silt load carried by the rivers, which was earlier deposited in the floodplain, now gets deposited inside the river channel, resulting in elevation of the riverbed. This in turn necessitates frequent raising of the height of the embankments. Embankments also have an adverse impact on the biodiversity as they act as barriers to the lateral migration of river flora and fauna. Several fish species traditionally found in Assam are facing a rapid decline. The embankments have also prevented the deposition of nutrient-rich alluvial sediments in the floodplains, thereby decreasing their natural fertility. The existing embankment infrastructure in the region is also prone to high maintenance costs as, being earthen, it suffers frequent breaches[4].

Deforestation and shifting cultivation in the hill areas of the Northeast in Arunachal Pradesh, Nagaland, North Cachar Hills and Karbi Anglong Mizoram and Manipur are also partly responsible for increasing the surface run-off with a heavy silt load. The increase in population and paucity of flood free agricultural land has resulted in encroachment of flood plains and riverine areas resulting in demands for embankments even where they are unsustainable. Encroachment and reclamation of wetlands, which could otherwise serve as storage areas for the surplus floodwater have greatly impaired their drainage ability, resulting in aggravated flooding.

The problem of annual flooding in the north East would require a blend of several approaches comprising a wholistic approach. A major component has to focus on afforestation and soil conservation in both the hill and plains areas of the region. This has to be done through micro watershed planning and management of catchment area of each tributary/ stream/ river system in the region. Floodplains also play a very important role in the ecology and economy of this region, as they serve as storage areas for excess floodwater, as fishing grounds, as groundwater recharge areas, and when the floodwater recedes after monsoon, as fertile agricultural land for the production of winter rice and other crops. It would be necessary to identify and protect flood plains from settlement and encroachment, combined with wetland restoration and management. The siltation choke points and obstructions to the river valley drainage have to identified and removed annually. Overall, an ecologically compatible solution may need to be devised by combining several approaches rather than depending upon structural approach alone.

Construction of dams is also suggested as a solution to the problem of flooding. Several dams on the tributaries of the Brahmaputra and one on the Barak (at Tipaimukh) are either commissioned or under consideration. While dams, along with their reservoirs provide a damping system to control water flow fluctuation, it would be necessary to design the reservoirs to absorb sudden extreme rainfall/cloudburst events that are frequent in the North East. In the past suddenly rising water levels have caused dangers to the dam structures resulting sudden opening of sluice gates. This has caused serious flooding downstream. Large dams result in several issues like loss of biodiversity, displacement of people, and also face high seismicity that may result in dam failure. A combination of small check dams with soil conservation work upstream would need to be incorporated in dam project design to ensure safe operation of the system.

While developing a comprehensive plan for flood management in the North East it would be necessary to manage the existing embankment system more scientifically and efficiently. For this remote sensing technology offers many solutions for identifying vulnerable spots and taking preventive action. Where the embankment system is found to be ineffective or detrimental, it may have to be modified to allow for flood plains and wetlands to provide natural absorption of flood waters.

Some experts have suggested that the solution lies in channelising the discharge of the Brahmaputra through canals, aqueducts, tunnels, and linking it to other rivers. A proposal to link the Brahmaputra and the Ganga through a feeder channel is also under consideration by the Government of India. These are very long term and expensive options. Modification of natural drainage systems can have unintended, and sometimes disastrous consequences. More important would be to develop "river training" infrastructure that guides the river waters and silt formation in a manner that restrains the river between reasonable boundaries.

The annual scourge of floods in the region has to be dealt with, not only to save the local economy but also the considerable investment being made in infrastructure in the region. This is a major planning and governance issue that has to be addressed if the credibility of the NE Region as a potential economic bridge is to be established[5]. In addition to tackling annual floods comprehensively and effectively, there is also to build disaster management and resilience including improved flood forecasting and warning systems, creation of flood shelters on high ground where available, speedy evacuation of flood affected population and livestock, flood proofing of homesteads through innovative building technologies, building raised flood shelters for clusters of villages in flood prone areas and effective drainage for the cities. Road, rail and bridge design and technology has to take into account high flood incidence in the region. Another important component of this strategy would be to make agriculture flood resilient by introducing deep water paddy varieties having higher yields during flood period, rapid growing and high yielding pre-flood and post-flood varieties, cultivation of pulses, vegetables and winter rice in the flood-free period.

Rural Infrastructure

Rural infrastructure has the potential of unlocking the local economy by improved mobility and access to various services and amenities, enabling rural producers to get access to market centres, better skills, inputs and raw materials at competitive prices. The resulting human development unlocks entrepreneurship essential for powering growth and development.[6]

The rural subsystem of the NER economy consists of some 35 thousand villages inhabited by over 32 million people who constitute about 85 percent of the total population in the region. Of approximately 10.6 million main workers in the NER economy, about eight million workers are directly engaged as cultivators or agricultural labourers.[7]

There is huge requirement of Rural infrastructure in the North Eastern region encompassing rural roads, soil conservation, irrigation and drainage, rural housing, water supply, health, electrification and telecommunication connectivity all over the region. The infrastructural interventions required therefore, need to focus on human development as well as physical infrastructure. This requirement has to be met to enable the region to reach its productive potential.

Thinking Rural

Roads and bridges

For agriculture and related activities to open up in the region and to grow further, rural roads infrastructure becomes a critical requirement. There is a need to overcome the disruptions and discontinuities caused by myriad river systems and hill ranges, criss-crossing the region. Physical mobility and connectivity are also critical in breaking the isolationist mindset and the feeling of deprivation amongst people. In addition to providing a boost to rural production systems they equally open up employment in non–agricultural sectors and ensure better public services including health and education. Rural areas and cities also need to be interconnected for growth. NE's rapidly-growing urban areas cannot succeed without reliable and economic links to sources of food raw materials and markets. To maximise the potential of urban economic growth, investment in rural-urban supply chain routes, including transport links, is vital.

Rural electrification

Most of the Northeast, villages and dwellings are dispersed over large areas, particularly in Hill areas8. Essentially all human capital and lifestyle enhancing inputs and productive efforts depend upon use of electricity. Apart from agriculture, it is vital for other activities including small and medium industries, khadi and village industries, cold storage chains etc. While the rural electrification program has extended electricity lines to villages, household access, particularly where there is an absence of cluster dwellings as in the Northeast is an issue. In addition, there are issues of quality of supply, maintenance, metering, billing and collection in many rural areas. As a result, utilities see rural electrification as a loss-making business and try to subsidise it from extra high tariffs for urban and industrial consumers.

While access to the grid is critical, decentralised energy generation and distribution systems need to be encouraged to supplement the grid energy, with skill development at the local level for its operational and financial management. Advances in renewable energy enables a combination of solar, small hydro and biomass-based energy generation. For this, government and utility-based planning and investment that favours big projects and big contracts, needs to be re-oriented towards investment in decentralised energy generation and access. The electricity regulatory system would equally need to develop the regulatory regime required for such electrification and its interface with the grid system.

Rural water supply systems

Clean drinking water is critical for public health and rural water supply systems need to be developed keeping an eye on sustainability of such systems and sources and to tackle the problem of water quality and sanitation arrangements.[9] North East has abundant water resources. But the seasonal and geographical dispersion is uneven. There is huge surplus over the extra-long rainy season, followed by an equally long dry season. In hill areas, the surface run-off results in loss of water at a very rapid rate. Water quality is also a major issue as deforestation and unscientific mining in several areas has resulted in leaching of chemicals into the soil.

Management of water in the Northeast will require a major scientific, technical and planning effort. An intensive grid of water testing facilities will have to be established, mining and deforestation controlled, water recharging strategies through check dams and small reservoirs implemented up, small sized water treatment plants, capable of being operated in remote locations for populations of 500-1000 developed along with piped water supply is possible. This needs to be complemented by easy availability of household water treatment and purification systems.

Rural Health Systems

With introduction of new technologies, increasing specialisation and clustering of health services into urban based systems and networks, rural health systems remain relatively weak and insufficient. The market and governmental schemes policies have attempted to address some of these disparities but major constraints remain. Policy has to address the key dimensions of access to health care in rural areas and constantly evaluate and improve potential ease with which consumers can obtain health care at times of need. Access needs to be seen in all its dimensions i.e., availability, geography, affordability, accommodation, timeliness, acceptability and awareness.

The national and state policies in India support universal health coverage with implementation of the primary healthcare approach.[10] In the rural areas of the Northeast, however, these are not adequately supported by the availability of doctors, infrastructure, medical equipment, budgetary resources and skills necessary to sustain an effective and responsive rural health system. As a result, NER rural health systems are generally weak with poor working conditions which impacts negatively on the quality of care as well as staff morale and retention.

Generally, health sciences curricula carry an urban bias.[11] Medical students are mostly taught by specialists who concentrate on specialised advanced individual treatments rather than on wider public health issues. The Central government had set up and promoted special health missions at national level for child immunisation and to eradicate polio, malaria, tuberculosis, leprosy and blindness amongst the Indian population. These special missions, though still in existence have tended to lose the race for funds and attention to facilities for specialised care. The growing urban middle class has pulled health investment towards itself, both in the public and private sectors.

This trend, equally noticeable in the North East, discourages local students from embarking on a career in rural health. Students only spend short periods of their training in rural areas, (if at all) and the rural imperative for clinical leadership training is usually not acknowledged. This is further compounded by the fact that there are much lesser material benefits in rural areas.

For the rural health system to function, training needs to be viewed as a core function of health service delivery. In the NER training is usually not well integrated into service delivery. Besides there is little support for rural trainers, number of training sites limited and, where such sites do exist, services are often underfunded and constrained by poor infrastructure and support services. Therefore, it is imperative that an Institutional framework and cadre of rural health doctors and professionals be built up along with better health awareness in rural areas and training facilities for public health services in the NER.

Urban Infra

"Urbanisation and growth go hand in hand, and no one can deny that urbanisation is essential for socio-economic transformation, wealth generation, prosperity and development." – Joan Clos, Under-secretary General, UN-Habitat.

As countries, and regions, move through the development process, agriculture declines as a share of gross domestic product (GDP), and manufacturing and services begin to dominate the economy. Goods and services are often produced most efficiently in densely populated areas that are organised, in terms of sites, manpower and services for organised production. In addition to access to a pool of managerial talent and skilled labour, a network of complementary firms grows around such areas acting as suppliers of not only outsourced components, but also for a variety of services. In the new age economic activity that is likely to grow through innovation in services and knowledge-based activity, such compact urban industrial clusters also provide a critical mass of customers. Even though digital communications-based technologies are geography neutral in terms of outreach to customers, sustained economic growth is invariably powered by urbanisation. Globalisation and localisation have not diminished the importance—or the pace—of the urbanisation process. As cities grow, they help their citizens hook up with the global economy and eventually become reliable links in the global supply chain, particularly of services and become attractive consumers and destinations themselves. It has been estimated that urban areas generate 55 percent of gross national product (GNP) in low-income countries, 73 percent in middle-income countries, and 85 percent in high income countries. The way cities manage development, including the arrival of industries, goes far in determining the rate of economic growth.

Currently North-East India is the least urbanised state of India with only 18 percent of the region's population living in 414 towns of variable size, many of which are actually classified as semi-urban or rural. Guwahati, the capital of Assam, is the only million-plus city in the region. Besides, there are half a dozen towns with a population of over 100,000. The largest number of towns falls in the group having a population of 5,000–10,000 people.[12] Urbanisation in the NER is a comparatively recent phenomenon, with levels having shot up in second half of the 20th Century. Data from the 2001 Census reveals, medium and small towns (towns of class III, IV and V), which together account for over 80 percent of towns in the region, are quite evenly distributed and display an encouraging potential for growth. The uneven urbanisation suggests a high potential for a more balanced pattern of urbanisation in future.

Like the rest of India, the North Eastern Region is also urbanising. The pace is slower but increasing numbers of people are moving from open rural areas to urban or semi-urban areas. If managed well, this urbanisation, with its concentration of people, talent, innovation and enterprise can create a wide range of new economic activity.

However, urbanisation in the NE also brings with it significant challenges. Most population centres in the North East grew as small towns with low population density and limited infrastructure. Sustained investment in infrastructure is necessary if cities are to provide the basic services necessary for economic growth. Pressure for investment is particularly heavy during the urban transition—the years of rapid urban population growth fuelled by rural-urban migration. As towns in the NE transform into cities, there is a need to invest into and build, maintain, and upgrade extensive transport, power, water supply and sanitation, telecommunication networks, health and education facilities in order to keep up with the demands of economic development and population growth. The challenge is all the more complex as it involves transforming the limited and aging infrastructure to serve much larger populations today while anticipating the needs of the future.

The problems of integrating new improvements or systems with existing urban infrastructure require significant investment in time, planning and funds over a long-time perspective. While public financing will remain central to addressing the infrastructure shortfalls, government will increasingly need to rely more on private sector investment. If approached well, risk and return on infrastructure investment will become better managed and boost economic growth. This in turn should stimulate further investment, creating a virtuous circle of development and improvement.

Managing Urban Growth

Land Use Policies

Freedom of mobility, or the lack of it, profoundly affects urban economic growth. Agglomeration economies, by definition, require proximity—firms to firms, households to places of employment etc. The ability of firms and households to sort themselves into efficient location patterns requires an active real estate market in which land prices reflect the different economic values of various sites. Urban planners need up-to-date information on land use and transactions in order to design and implement effective land use plans.

There is a need for development of an efficiently organised and regulated land market in the NER cities. This would require a considerable planning and capacity building input to educate governments at city and state level. In this regard state governments' role is vital as a repository of claims to land ownership, clear and easily accessible title arrangements and a well-kept land registry where ownership rights are clearly established and all transactions are recorded. This would also demarcate the public portion of urban land which would be critical in determining the spatial configuration of a city. The land use pattern, on the other hand, would relevant for assessing its transport and logistic requirements and for zoning for regulating and guiding economic activity in the city. The city governments control over public land and transportation systems would enable critical planning to build up city development and its economic activity.

This would require significant support to NE states in terms of capacity building and training in urban planning, development of necessary legal framework, modern systems and procedures that enable measurement and digitalisation. While institutions that can provide such capacity building to successive batches of urban administrators can be accessed in other parts of the country, they may also be set up in the NER itself on twinned with institutions of excellence elsewhere. Since most NE states would not be able to finance such wide-ranging effort on a sustainable basis, funds for the purpose may be accessed through the central government, either through budgetary support or through intermediated multilateral funding. Making such support available to NER states would be a very useful aspect of the Act East Policy.

Urban Financing Needs

Cities have to provide institutional and administrative infrastructure, centres of commercial activity such as markets and business centres, institutions for human development and education from primary school to university, health, diagnostic and life support facilities, housing for different income levels, transport linkages and infrastructure, utilities i.e power, water, and telecommunications. The financial investments required on the journey for urban transition are considerable. Obviously, this is going to require financing at a large scale which would be far beyond the capacity of the NE States. This will, therefore, require not only a judicious mix of public and private financing but also innovation.[13]

Local governments can finance their new responsibilities in several ways. Development fees, connection charges, and local tax revenue can all generate funds that can be used for investment. This is an avenue that is hardly used in the NER. The statutory financial and operational environment that allows for levy of user fees or viable tariffs is inadequate. In this case debt financing may be required, though accessing it is likely to be a challenge in the North East.

While municipal bond markets are emerging in some developing countries, in the North East, this would not be a viable option at this stage as few of the conditions necessary for functioning of such instruments, such as capital markets geared to handle municipal debt, well-established financial track record of the borrower, exist. More suitable would be financing through Municipal Development Funds (MDF). Central/State governments can set up these funds through a mix of contributions from the public exchequer and market borrowings and lend to municipalities for specific well-defined projects, subject to the state governments contributing a certain percentage of the funds and enacting a suitable legal framework for financial and operational sustainability of projects so financed. Since the central/state governments would bear the ultimate risk of municipal default, they would be well within their rights to impose risk mitigating conditionalities.

Co-opting Local Governments

Centrally determined spending, even at the state level, can produce arbitrary, lop-sided or inefficient allocations across cities and tends to sever the links among investment, operation, and maintenance. In contrast, local governments, including municipalities that participate in investment decisions can respond better to local needs. While inputs most relevant to urban economic development are often beyond the control of local governments—through managing labour costs and skills, natural resources, climate, and energy prices, local governments can facilitate urban economic growth in their areas. For this they will need to invest in trunk infrastructure for transportation and energy, create a well-functioning and open land market and provide capacity building for maintaining infrastructure and public services needed to create an attractive, and responsive, environment for both businesses and households.

An effort also needs to be made particularly by the state governments to establish an environment that gives local governments the opportunity, incentive and ability to become worthy borrowers. This would require a revamping of the legal and regulatory system that enables institution of accounting, auditing, and disclosure practices that are compatible with national and even international standards.

Notes to Chapter 8

1. The Rashtriya Barh Aayog (RBA), or the National Flood Commission (NFC) was set up by the Ministry of Agriculture and Irrigation of India in 1976 to study India's flood-control measures. This was done after the projects launched under the National Flood Control Program of 1954 failed to achieve much success. RBA (or NFC) is responsible for flood control problems in the country and draws out a national plan fixing priorities for implementation in the future.

2. Irrigation, Flood Control and Water Shed Management; North Eastern Council

3. RBA questioned the effectiveness of the methods adopted to control floods, such as embankments and reservoirs, and suggested that the construction of these structures be halted till their efficacy was assessed. RBA recommended a dynamic strategy to cope with the changing nature of floods. RBA recommended consolidated efforts among the states and the Centre to take up research and policy initiatives to control floods.

4. River flooding and erosion in Northeast India; Background Paper No. 4 October 2006; Northwest Hydraulics Consultants, Edmonton, Alberta, Canada; Input to the World bank study "Development and Growth in Northeast India: The Natural Resources, Water, and Environment Nexus".

5. Flooding in India's Northeast Reveals Weakness of the Act East Policy; Angshuman Choudhury, The Diplomat: July 20, 2022

6. Infrastructure and Development in Rural India, Madhusudan Ghosh; Journal of Applied Economic Research 11: 3 (2017): 256–289; Sage Publications

7. Rural development in the North-Eastern Region of India: Constraints and prospects Mishra, SK (1999): Rural development in the North-Eastern Region of India: Constraints and prospects.

8. Energy and Energy Access in NORTHEAST INDIA-A Factsheet; Centre for Science and Environment; 2016

9. Drinking Water in Rural India: A Perennial Crisis; Shamsher Singh 2019; Foundation for Agrarian Studies.

10. Healthcare Access in Rural Communities; Rural health Information Hub; https:// www. ruralhealthinfo.org /

11. Rural Health Care System in India; National Health Mission.

12. Urbanisation and Urban Landscape in North-East India. In: North-East India: Land, People and Economy. Advances in Asian Human-Environmental Research. Dikshit, K.R., Dikshit, J.K. (2014). Springer, Dordrecht; Financing

Strategies for Urban Infrastructure: Trends & Challenges, Harun R Khan; Reserve Bank of India, Mumbai, July 18, 2013; Conference on Financing Strategies for Urban infrastructure

13. Financing Urban Infrastructure for Implementing Urban Resilience; Alok Shiromany; www.teriin.org/projects/apn/pdf/day2 /Financing of Infrastructure Development TERI Goa.pdf

Chapter 9

Getting Infrastructure Right-II: Connectivity Within

The considerable land mass comprising the NE region and its geographical complexity makes for a transportation and logistics challenge. Landlocked between Bangladesh, Bhutan, China and Myanmar, the NE Region also has to find a way of ensuring that it enables efficient and cost-effective interchanges with and between neighbouring countries and contributes constructively to a sustainable and positive dialogue with all of them conducive to friendly relations and economic growth. Critical infrastructure will have to be designed and implemented that overcomes the disadvantage of geographic isolation and meets not only domestic requirements but also that of international regional trade and international regional connectivity. In addition, infrastructure has to meet the operational requirements of the security forces not only for internal but also for external security by maintaining lines of supply for reaching geographically remote areas and defending land borders stretching over thousands of kilometres of difficult terrain.

Railways

The earliest railway tracks in the Northeast (then largely Assam province) were laid in the Dibrugarh area in 1882, initially for the transportation of tea and coal. However, most of the subsequent track connecting destinations outside Assam was routed through the then undivided Bengal province of colonial India.

With the Partition in 1947, railways in Assam got delinked from those in the rest of India as the connections to Assam, running through the then East Pakistan and later Bangladesh, were lost. North Eastern region was connected to the rest of the country through the narrow Siliguri corridor. Indian Railway took up the Assam Link project as early as in 1948 to re-build rail connection to Assam through this corridor. Meanwhile, construction of the Saraighat Road and Rail Bridge over the Brahmaputra started in

1958-59 and was completed in 1962. This was followed by a road bridge at Bhomoraguri at near Tezpur. Another road- cum- rail bridge came up at Jogighopa after the Assam Accord. Recently the Dhola Sadia and the Bogibeel rail-cum -road bridge have also been completed, supplementing the ones at Guwahati and Jogighopa.

Continued investment in railway infrastructure in the NER, has resulted in the region, particularly Assam, now being well connected by railways with the larger Indian railway network through a number of long-distance railway routes. Meanwhile, the broad-gauge conversion program in the North East, which was a part of the national gauge conversion programme started in 1992, picked up pace over the last decade. Assam now has broad gauge railway lines running in a loop along both the northern and southern banks of the Brahmaputra. Broad gauge links have also been extended from the Brahmaputra valley to Silchar in the Barak valley and southwards to Agartala in Tripura. Railways services have also started within Tripura, linking Dharmanagar, Agartala and Sabroom. The broad-gauge railway network presently connects the state capitals of Assam, Tripura and Arunachal Pradesh. The next stage, connecting the state capitals of Manipur, Mizoram and Meghalaya is expected to be completed by 2025.

Meanwhile, Indian Railways in the North East (through its NE Frontier Railway Division) faces the challenge of project delays and burgeoning costs and financial sustainability of its infrastructure. There is also a lack of interfaces with road and river transportation systems for handling both passenger and goods traffic. Extending railway lines through difficult hilly terrain poses unique engineering challenges which require detailed and comprehensive knowledge and study of the terrain, its geology and local climatic conditions. This may require specially engineered tracks and trains and needs to be done by analysing engineering requirements specific to the geography of the region.

Waterways

The North East is dominated by the Brahmaputra and Barak River systems. Both the rivers have their navigable portions falling entirely in Assam and are fed by a system of tributaries, some of which are also perennial. Both Brahmaputra and Barak are major international rivers that flow through India and Bangladesh. Eventually, Barak joins up with Brahmaputra (Jamuna in Bangladesh) as it flows into the sea.

The river Brahmaputra runs along the entire 640 Km length of the Assam valley, practically bisecting it into two. On the stretches of the river in between bridges, connectivity between the North and South Bank depends largely on river transportation. A large number of ferries move across and up and down the entire length of the river on, transporting a very large number of passengers and a considerable tonnage of agricultural produce. In addition, a large number of fishing boats move up and down the river, providing livelihood to several communities of fishermen. In the lean season, Brahmaputra throws up several large sand banks and islands known as chars, which are inhabited by shifting population and are cultivated. For people living in the char areas of the river, river transportation provides outlet to the agricultural produce of the area as well as physical connectivity to the outside world.

All along the Brahmaputra River there are several routes that are commercially important, some for carriage of goods, others for passengers. The river also provides a good route for transportation of heavy machinery and equipment from Kolkata and Haldia Port in West Bengal to Assam and for export of commodities from Assam such as tea. Of late the river has also become popular for tourist river cruises through large sized boats. In other words, vessel traffic on the river Brahmaputra is growing and is likely to increase in future with large vessels, carrying heavy cargo and large number of passengers plying up and down and across the river. There is a strong case for modernising the river transport sector in the North East which has been suffering from neglect in terms of institutions, enforcement, infrastructure and capacity.

Keeping Rivers Fit for Navigation

In India, the navigable part of river Brahmaputra after traversing the length of Assam east to west, enters Bangladesh, where it joins with Padma and then River Meghna further downstream forming a single massive outlet to the Bay of Bengal. The average annual discharge of the Brahmaputra is about 19,200 m3/sec. However, the discharge shows tremendous seasonal fluctuations, from a lean season flow of c. 4000-6000 m3 /sec to 48,160 m3 /sec during monsoon. In some extreme years, the fluctuation can be even higher. China, through its 14th five-year plan has included building dam on the lower reaches of the Brahmaputra River over which India and Bangladesh, the riparian states, have raised concerns. As a lower riparian state with considerable established user rights to the waters of the trans-border rivers, the Indian government has consistently conveyed its views and concerns to the Chinese authorities and has urged them to ensure that the interests of downstream states are not harmed by any activities in upstream areas. This aspect needs careful monitoring and sustained diplomatic efforts in international fora as construction of dams by China over the portion of Brahmaputra flowing through Tibet, if used for diversion of water, could affect the lean season flow.

The Brahmaputra River and its tributaries produce enormous sediment loads, as they flow through geologically young and unstable terrain. The Brahmaputra, however, has a gentle gradient which results in a highly braided channel with huge sand bars and riverine islands, which change their shape and location during floods. The banks of the Brahmaputra and its tributaries are also extremely unstable and subject to widespread erosion and subsidence. The river also forms several riverine islands, of which the largest and the most important is the Majuli island in Sibsagar district. The other major river of the state, the Barak, flows for a distance of 192 km through the flat valley areas of Cachar and Karimganj districts. This river also has a low gradient and a meandering channel.

In the circumstances, the unstable nature of these rivers provides a huge challenge in maintaining a predictable, safely navigable channel. This will require a huge engineering effort for extensive and continuous river mapping and dredging to maintain the requisite depth through the length of the river. At the same time, river bank stabilisation would be necessary along commercially important stretches.

The River Transportation Chain

The transportation chain across the river includes not only the river vessels but also interconnection between other forms of transport; e.g. road, rail etc. and the junction points such as the ghats and ferries where the passengers and goods traffic are managed. The true economic potential of river transportation requires multi-modal interfaces with the road and railway networks, systems for passenger ticketing and movement; goods storage infrastructure; efficient cargo handling; provision of supporting freight forwarding, customs and financial services, enforcement of safety regulations; provision of river navigation along with movement, communications and pilotage services to be fully unlocked.

River Port Management

The management of River Ports and Ghats (which are mini-river ports serving a large volume of passengers on a daily basis) requires urgent modernisation. While any transportation system would require these ports to be properly constructed (compare with bus terminuses, railway stations, airports etc.) There is absence of infrastructure such as jetties, fixed or floating, that would facilitate the docking of vessels and allow movement of passengers and goods to take place in a safe and orderly manner.

In the NER, river ports (including Ghats) are the take-off points for passenger and goods traffic and are managed by various agencies. The principal agency for regulation of inland waterways for shipping and navigation and development of terminal infrastructure along National Waterways such as the Brahmaputra (NW2) is the Inland Waterways Authority of India (IWAI), about 87 by the Assam Department of inland Water Transport (ADIWT) and the rest numbering several hundred by local Panchayat bodies.

IWAI has fixed terminals only at one location, Pandu. The remaining nine principal ports along the Brahmaputra are served by floating terminals. There is an absence of adequate multi modal connectivity to road and rail infrastructure, cargo handling and indeed practically all the requirements for a modern port. ADIWT on its part has limited resources and has not been able to channelise much investment in river ports under its charge, build adequate related infrastructure or to manage them properly. The Panchayats, who are supposed to manage minor river ports under the Assam Panchayats Act and Assam Panchayat (Financial Rules) 2002 have, of course, not seriously recognised the need as they tend to see this as a resource that should be exploited for revenue only. In any case, the Panchayats are hardly the appropriate institutions for enabling modern river port development and management. This river port infrastructure therefore suffers from neglect, absence of modern and properly designed infrastructure and facilities.

Modernise the Statutory Framework

The river transportation sector is regulated by The Indian Vessels Act,1917, The Northern India Ferries Act, 1878, Control and Management of Ferries Rules 1968. These enactments are quite old- largely British period. When these statutes were enacted, the river transportation was important but the pressure on this sector in terms of goods and passengers was lower as the economy was oriented more towards colonial needs. Yet these enactments did provide a broad framework that could be effectively implemented during the colonial times. The interactions required by a rapidly changing and growing economy are far more. The requirement now is to respond to provide a much more extensive, efficient and safe service to the rapidly increasing goods and passenger traffic.

The regulatory framework based on these enactments does not provide for a modern institutional framework for regulation and development of the sector and is inadequate in addressing its safety concerns, encouraging investment in development of safe and efficient infrastructure in the waterways transportation chain. The inspection-based regime of enforcement through the local state ADIWT which is overburdened by a complex mix of enforcement, regulatory, developmental and commercial functions is proving to be unsustainable while dealing with the large volumes and growing complexities of the river transportation sector.

The entire river transport sector needs to be re-organised substantially. There should be separation of regulatory, developmental, enforcement and operational functions in the sector to enable greater focus in each.

Fresh legislation should be enacted to provide for development and management of river ports through a State River Ports Authority. All locations that function as river ports, handling passengers and goods through mechanised vessels, or vessels above a particular size, should be identified and notified as river ports and should be managed by the Authority to be set up under such legislation. The Authority should be charged with providing necessary infrastructure and services for passenger and cargo handling, charging fees and levies etc. for services provided. It should be enabled to raise financial resources and invest them in development of river port infrastructure, enable private investment in such services as may be appropriate.

River transport regulation needs to improve drastically, covering all aspects including licensing, vessel fitness, operating and safety regulations. Such a regulator should have statutory powers to regulate, enforce as licensing conditions and impose penalties. Therefore, the proposed legislation, in addition to establishing a River Ports Authority, may also establish a River Ports Regulator as a statutory regulator.

The enforcement of statutory river transportation framework should be entrusted to a state agency, such as the AIWTD. This body should carry out route management, including mapping and registering existing river routes, registration of vessels, enforce standards that result in vessel fitness and safety, provide essential services and facilities in particular, facilities for vessel testing, safety instructions & requirements, pilot and crew training, establish control rooms, provide River traffic monitoring and pilotage facilities, Infrastructure for navigation safety etc.

Modernizing River Navigation

River Route management on the Brahmaputra River needs to be urgently modernised in order to ensure safety of the vessels and their passengers. River routes need to be carefully charted and the course to be followed by a craft/vessel using that route demarcated. Basic Navigation data, suitably priced, should be available to licensed river route operators. The movement of various vessels and crafts should be monitored through GPS/Satellite and should be available through communications on monitors of all vessels plying in the river. Pilotage services should be provided for safe day and night operation. A system of buoys and markers- including those emitting light and radio signal should be maintained across length and breadth of the river to assist in navigation. A River Communications system needs to be established to provide pilotage services, route management and traffic monitoring, safety information, weather data, storm warnings etc. In the absence of proper communication service, the chances of accidents, collisions and disasters caused by freak weather events or otherwise may increase.

Disaster Management

The responsibility of developing and implementing the disaster management plan for the river transport sector, establishing quick response procedures and enabling the same if the situation demands, maintenance and operation of vessels for rescue and recovery should also be entrusted to ADIWT. It should have close communication links with the Indian Meteorology Department (IMD) for providing weather related data to the river ports as well as various ferries, passenger and cargo boats and other river craft plying on the river on real time basis is important for safety. Such information needs to include information relating to other disturbances including cyclonic storms over the Bay of Bengal. IMD should immediately set up a system for broadcasting of weather bulletins over radio frequencies that would provide ongoing weather information not only to Deputy Commissioners'/ police, ADIWT control rooms, the River Port/Ghat managements but also to all radio affected or interested persons over radio receivers, which may also be fitted on board all kinds of river vessels. Storm warnings should also be made available through mobile phone.

ADIWT should also enable quick response to river craft disasters through coordination with various agencies The river port infrastructure is critical to safety of river vessels as they ply over the river and they must be so organised, to provide safe havens to vessels braving inclement weather or other distress situations. launching rescue and recovery efforts and extending medical aid to the wounded, providing boat mounted machinery for rescue of vessels etc.

Capacity Building

Worth emphasising that the establishment and operation of a modern river transportation system would require capacity building at all levels – regulation, enforcement, technical testing and evaluation, disaster management etc.

Roads and Highways

Road connectivity and transport infrastructure in general is at the heart of the supply chains necessary to develop the economy. This applies to urban, semi urban and rural areas equally. In fact, many semi- urban and rural areas are intimately connected to the cities and depend upon them for economic welfare. A good rural roads system unlocks the productive potential of rural areas and provides access to the population living in such areas to healthcare facilities, education, and many other facilities The pattern of development in the NE has been such that educational and health facilities have grown largely in the cities and urban centres. Hill areas, which dominate most of the North Eastern land area, contain far flung villages with very low level of services and facilities for human development. They could also be production centres provided they find outlets and markets for their produce.

The infrastructure plan for the North East has to cater to multi-modal mobility on account of its geography and interplay of various means of transport operating in different areas. Along with greater integration of the North Eastern states with each other and with the rest of the country, it has to provide greater access to rural, hill and border areas within the North East to enable realisation of the region's agricultural and horticultural potential. The perspective for infrastructure should not be limited to roads and bridges but should be diversified to meet the changing economic and demographic profile of the region.

The Domestic Roads Network

District and Rural roads: While National Highways tend to corner most of the attention, investment and effort, it is critical that secondary and tertiary road systems comprising of district, rural and village roads also be developed as these roads serve as feeder roads to the main roads network and link rural production and market centres. The same applies to roads along borders with Bangladesh, Bhutan, Myanmar, China, as also interstate borders. These are critical in improving accessibility, enabling border management, regulating trade and immigration and in maintaining internal and external security in the difficult terrain in the North-eastern border areas.

For such roads there is a need for technology that requires low maintenance along with skill development in road repair and maintenance amongst local population. Prioritisation of repair and directing local effort is best done through local government involvement and funding support.

State Highways are arterial routes of a State linking district headquarters and important cities within the State and connecting them with National Highways or highways of the neighbouring States. State Highways serve district headquarters, sub-divisional headquarters, major industrial centres, places of commercial interest, places of tourist attraction, major agricultural market centres and ports. As such they deserve the same investment as National Highways. The State highways network came up in the North East long ago with colonial expansion and in some cases, such as Assam, even prior to that but is in a sorry state for the most part. It requires investment for upgradation and maintenance to provide seamless and smooth transition from National highways to the interior. There is also a huge requirement of all-weather bridges over myriad rivers and streams criss-crossing the region, if the accessibility beyond the trunk routes is to be opened up. However, the smaller NE states do not have the necessary financial resources for the purpose. Therefore, it may be better to subsume at least the important state highways in the NH network and have them maintained through central funds.

National Highways

There has been considerable investment in national highways stretching over the NER and linking the region to the rest of India. North East has 8480 (2842) km of national highways with an intensity of .032 km/ sq. km against the All-India average of .046 km/sq. km. However further

134

extension of 2637 km to the National Highway network are planned. While the network is progressing and the quality in some stretches is quite good, the issue is that of quality in hill areas which dominate most states of the region. The highways in the hilly regions have been cut through and built over newly uncovered, unstable soil in places which is prone to shifting and sliding. The region is subject to heavy rainfall over a long monsoon season which causes floods and landslides, leading to disruptions. Road design, engineering and technology need to be ramped up to address these challenges.

One set of highways that are critical for connectivity to Arunachal Pradesh lie on the North Bank of the Brahmaputra River. These highways are frequently disrupted by flash floods in the rivers flowing down from Arunachal to Assam. In fact, the North Bank highway system comprises a major transverse road (NH 15) from which several highways take off towards the north into Arunachal Pradesh, right up to the Line of Actual Control with China. This highway, is particularly vulnerable to flash floods in the rivers flowing down from Arunachal into Assam and needs to be redesigned and strengthened. More East - West highways are planned north of and running parallel to NH15. These highways are likely to pose greater engineering challenges due to the local geography, climatic conditions and their alignment. Successful construction of these roads would require considerable research in terms of design and construction technology employed.

Another strategic node for internal North East connectivity is Silchar in Assam. This town lies at the end point of the East West Highway (NH27) and at the confluence of National highways connecting it Guwahati via Shillong (NH6), to Agartala in Tripura (NH8), to Aizawl and then to Tuipang in Mizoram (NH306), and to Imphal in Manipur (NH37 which also extends westwards to Sylhet in Bangladesh and north west via Imphal, to Kohima in Nagaland as NH137). All these highways are of vital importance as they connect to state capitals. However, most of these highways lie in hill areas and are frequently subjected to landslides and subsidence during the long rainy season.

A Technology Mission under the Act East Policy could look specifically into the engineering challenges involved and come up with solutions that would allow for stable construction and efficient maintenance. Meanwhile a considerable investment has been made in the past to construct bridges over the Brahmaputra in the Assam Valley and Barak in the Barak Valley. These bridges have come up at Saraighat/ Jogighopa/ Dhola Sadia/

Bhomoraguri/ Bogibeel / Dhubri-Phulbari/Silchar. Now the challenge is to provide seamless multi-modal connectivity linking various modes of transport, e.g. waterways, airports, railways etc, within the NE as well as for improving international connectivity. The transport infrastructure has to be complemented by efficiently managed logistics parks all along the major trading points to facilitate goods traffic.

Domestic Air Connectivity

Over past few decades, air connectivity of the NER with other parts of the country has improved considerably. Today airlines connect various NE State Capitals like Guwahati, Shillong Dimapur, Itanagar, Aizawl, Imphal and Agartala to a large number of cities in the rest of India. Air traffic to these destinations has also been increasing. More airports are being added, such as Pakyong airport in Sikkim and Tezu airport in Arunachal Pradesh. Both are yet to be fully utilised due to technical constraints, but when they finally do, will give impetus to air travel all over the North East.

However, domestic airlines do not find their North East operations profitable and require Government mandates backed by subsidies to make them possible and affordable. Many reasons are cited for lack of viability for NE routes including periodical demand, high operational costs and low passenger volumes. In the 1990s, Route Dispersal Guidelines (RDGs) were issued by the Central Government under which airlines compulsorily had to fly routes to destinations in the erstwhile state of Jammu and Kashmir and/or the North East (including Sikkim). Most airlines included such mandated destinations to their other profitable routes and brought air connectivity to some major NER destinations like Guwahati. Later, in 2016 Government launched the regional connectivity scheme (the UDAN scheme) to encourage airlines to fly un-served and underserved routes in the country via economic incentives. The regional air connectivity scheme, which is quite complex, is applicable on route length between 200 to 800 km with no lower limit set for hilly, remote, island and security sensitive regions. The incentives offered include a reduction of certain taxes and charges, Viability Gap Funding (VGF) and cash subsidies for a portion of seats on the aircraft. A Regional Connectivity Fund (RCF) is set up to fund the scheme via a levy on certain flights. States are expected to contribute 20 per cent to the fund. Market-based reverse bidding mechanism is proposed to determine least VGF requirement to select the appropriate airline operator. The VGF is intended to be reduced if passenger load factor remains high and will be discontinued after 3 years when route becomes self-sustainable.

Airline industry being quite competitive as it is and with the losses incurred during the pandemic, Indian domestic airlines have generally continued to face financial problems, with several airline failures. As a result, dependence on subsidies, particularly for non-profitable routes such as those for most destinations in the North East, is likely to continue for a long time to come.

Connecting the North East also requires aircraft that are fit for purpose, smaller in size, capable of operation in the hill areas and able to take off and land from small runways. The airports, whether large or small, need better technology for flight operations management and improved passenger handling facilities. The other aspect needing to be addressed relates to air connectivity planning. Regional and consumer trends in the NER are not quite similar to patterns seen in routes connecting other more densely populated parts of India and metro-cities. Here in addition to the principal cities or state capitals, the need is also to connect far flung, remote and sparsely populated areas through cheap flights which can be vital in providing emergency health care or disaster relief when other means of transport are suspended due to natural calamities. Air connectivity plans, therefore, have to be geared to specifically address the requirements of the region. In absence of a carefully devised regional plan, the UDAN scheme, though well meaning, may also not be able to keep on supporting such connectivity on a sustainable basis. As a result, even with the progress made, the region continues to have many unserved and underserved destinations, without the ability to make day trips.

Challenges to Infrastructure Development

While the cost of initial construction is being borne by the Central Government, the expanding network will require continuous annual outlays for maintenance. The existing traffic and commerce over national highways, barring one or two, is inadequate to sustain tolling arrangements. Therefore, there will have to be adequate budgetary outlays for the purpose, unless a more financially sustainable solution is found.

Construction costs for infrastructure are very high in the North East compared to other parts of the country. In addition, infrastructure is subject to high cost and time over-runs. The geography and soil structure of the region, periodic disruption of work due to law-and-order situations and lack of skills required for modern construction locally combined with antipathy to personnel from outside the region complicates matters further.

Some other factors resulting in slow implementation of the projects are inadequate technical data and project evaluation at the DPR stage leading to faulty design. The geological, climate and soil conditions in North East are quite different from the rest of the country and are given to extreme events. There is a need to adapt road construction technology and techniques to local conditions. Difficulties in contracting also contribute to poor quality of road infrastructure is due to the. Most contractors in the NER do not have the financial strength or the technical ability to take on large, complex infra projects. Getting large contractors from outside the region creates local political problems. Often, the unevenness of repairing the same highway is said to be the result of multiple contractors working on the same project.;

There are wide disparities in the availability and quality of infrastructure between hills and plains areas. Most of the NER has hilly terrain where the problems involved in construction and maintenance of infrastructure are aggravated even further.

To yield full potential in form of efficiency in logistics, national highways need to be supported by logistics parks and service centres. There are plans to set up such facilities but project formulation is slow, with land availability issues acting as delaying factors. A problem is also of ribbon and cluster development along national highways leading to congestion and reducing efficiency of movement. There is a lack of properly planned supporting roads.

Safety and security continue to be a major issue in various parts of the NER. Goods carriers get intercepted and looted, with operating staff/drivers etc. being killed or injured. With police and other security forces having been engaged countering extremism and terrorism, there is a lack of adequate police follow up and investigation in such occurrences. This creates various problems for transporters who are not able to claim insurance in absence of such follow up.

Roads projects also suffer from land acquisition delays. In many cases, these are caused by lack of communication with the local people leading to obstructions and protests. North East also faces lack of local expertise and skilled labour and difficulties in securing skilled personnel from outside. Law and order and public safety issues compound the problem further. Project delays lead to recurring inadequacies and disruptions in funding;

Competitive Infrastructure

There are several Central Government infrastructure development schemes in addition to UDAN-RCS such as *Bharatmala*, a road development scheme which includes development of tunnels, bridges, elevated corridors, flyovers, interchanges, bypasses etc. to provide optimised connectivity, *Sagarmala* for unlocking the potential of waterways and the coastline, Dedicated Freight Corridors, a network of broad gauge freight railway lines intended to solely serve freight trains, to make the freight services faster and more efficient, Industrial corridor, *BharatNet,* for the establishment, management, and operation of the National Optical Fibre Network to provide broadband connectivity to all 250,000-gram panchayats in the country (covering nearly 625,000 villages), *Digital India,* aimed to ensure that Government's services are made available to citizens electronically through improved online infrastructure and Internet connectivity to make the country digitally empowered. Taken together, these schemes provide a comprehensive infrastructure platform, provided they include some of the infrastructural weaknesses and choke-points in the North East in their ambit. While the scope of these schemes is nationwide, the Act East Policy can provide the necessary policy impetus for identification of NE regional needs and providing necessary resources to address them through concerted action under various initiatives.

The diverse infrastructure requirements of the North Eastern region have to be met in a financially and operationally sustainable manner. Therefore, all aspects relating to governance, technology and financial sustainability issues will need to be addressed together. While there is enough technical manpower available in the North East, capacity building for modern infrastructure planning and implementation is required along with skills for operation of the relevant mechanised equipment.

While big ticket infra projects will need to be handled by the Central Government, there is no alternative to making State Governments accountable as they have to ensure availability of land (land acquisition can drag on for years); ensure safety and security of project staff, enable logistics and supply lines to the project to function without disruption.

Notes to Chapter 9

1. From New Bongaigaon, the old metre gauge ran to Guwahati, over the Saraighat Bridge. This was eventually converted to broad gauge in 1984.

2. Assam now has six large bridges over Brahmaputra River connecting its North and South Banks, constructed post-independence: Saraighat is the oldest bridge over Brahmaputra River. This bridge is located in Pandu area of Guwahati city and connects it to Amingaon in the North Bank of the Brahmaputra. It is 1.492 km long and was opened to the public in 1963; the Kolia Bhomora Setu, 3km long road bridge that links Kaliabor with Tezpur was inaugurated in 1987; The Naranarayan Setu which links Jogighopa (Bongaigaon district) and Pancharatna (Goalpara district) was opened in 1997. It was the third bridge built over the Brahmaputra and is about 2.284 km long; Bhupen Hazarika Setu (Dhola Sadiya Road Bridge) opened in 2017; New Saraighat Road Bridge, opened 2017, a 1.49km beam bridge that exists parallel to the old one, was built to augment the road traffic handling capacity between Pandu and Amingaon, which had grown considerably over the years opened 2017 The Bogibeel bridge, a 4.94 km long road and rail bridge that links Dhemaji and Dibrugarh district opened to traffic in 2018.

    For instance, to provide a rail link to Chittagong port, the then Assam Bengal Railway constructed a track between Chittagong and Comilla (Bangladesh) which was opened to traffic in 1895. This was followed by the Comilla–Akhaura–Kulaura to Badarpur section 1898 which was then extended to Lumding (Assam) in 1903. A branch line was constructed to Guwahati, connecting the city to the eastern line in 1900. By 1910, the Eastern Bengal Railway had built the Parbatipur (now in Bangladesh)- Golakganj–Amingaon (on the North bank near Guwahati) line connecting the north bank of the Brahmaputra to the rest of India. This was later extended to Tezpur

    This was in the form of broad-gauge railway line running through north Bihar and northern West Bengal via Katihar, Kishanganj, New Jalpaiguri and thence to New Bongaigaon in Assam, partly through new construction and partly gauge conversion.

    The challenge of engagement East would be extending the railway network through Bangladesh and Myanmar. While Myanmar poses obvious challenges due to the unsettled conditions, progress has been made in extending rail connectivity to some destinations in Bangladesh by restoration of some old rail links that existed before the Partition.

    An East-West Industrial Corridor Highway is proposed from Bhairabkunda in Assam located at the tri-junction of Bhutan, Assam and Arunachal Pradesh, to Ruksin in East Siang district of Arunachal Pradesh, lying at the base of the Eastern Himalayan Mountain ranges. Yet another 2000 Km highway, the Mago-Thingbu to Vijayanagar Border, also known as Arunachal

Frontier Highway, in Arunachal Pradesh India is proposed to be built along the McMahon Line (international border between India and China) by the Government of India. This road is considered important for strategic national defence purposes and is under construction.

UDAN is an acronym for the Ude Desh ka Aam Naagrik Scheme. It is a regional airport development program of the Government of India and part of the Regional Connectivity Scheme (RCS) for upgrading under-serviced air routes. Its goal is to make air travel affordable. The UDAN scheme is intended to expedite the development and operationalisation of India's nearly 425 unserved, under-served, and underdeveloped regional airports with regularly scheduled flights. Launched in 2016, it has undergone five phases.

Chapter 10

Act-East Connectivity

(To realise benefits of such infrastructure, whether for connectivity or otherwise, continued strategic investment would be needed across various sectors. The challenge is to enable a pragmatic and mature coordinated approach among various ministries and technical agencies not only within India but also on a trans-border basis, putting aside national prejudices that have prevailed for decades. Building a common vision on a regional basis is a task made more complex by internal politics of respective countries, not the least due to the upheavals in Myanmar, the land interface with India. The speed of implementation of projects also needs to improve drastically, as the excruciatingly slow pace of implementation not only erodes credibility, making competitive options attractive, but also gets overtaken by events).

The post-pandemic world is marked by nation states withdrawing behind their borders, perceiving their security and wellbeing as being threatened externally. This siege mentality is reflected in many aspects of international relations- such as harking back to a glorified image of the national past, suspicion of global institutions and the rule based global order, growing geo-political rivalries, some seen as harbingers of a New Cold War, seeking national economic self -reliance irrespective of the inefficiencies it breeds and so on. These trends are likely to eventually lead to global economic crises and conflicts, with comprehensive national power soon reducing to raw military power. Opposed to this is the approach of co-operation and interdependence based on comparative strengths and a more diverse and nuanced perspective of national power and the means of projecting it. The latter approach is based on mutually constructive engagement. In this respect, borders can be viewed as opportunities for engagement rather than fortifications against all things external. The trans-national infrastructure projects are a case in point. These projects carry contents of sub-regionalism based on physical contiguity, socio-cultural bonds and exchanges and seek to create a mutually beneficial situation for the parties concerned. They stand as prime examples of how shared economic interests can lead to sustainable cooperation and thereby build a nation's beneficial influence.

International Connectivity

Road connectivity of the NER with ASEAN Countries has been tested several times with Trans-ASEAN Road rallies. In all such events, road connectivity has proved to be easy and welcome. There are, however, issues of varying road quality with some sections of the proposed links being in very poor condition. The Trans-National Highway is one project that seeks to connect ASEAN countries with India via NER through a modern highway system. This highway would also connect with other highway systems across SE Asia.

There are proposals for other international projects as well, intended to improve international connectivity. These, however, face a number of difficulties arising out of a lack of shared common vision amongst the proposed participating countries, difficulties in ensuring smooth entry and exit across national borders, financing issues, technical issues including maintenance and road traffic management etc. In addition to financial and operational sustainability, political turbulence in participating countries and its overhang over international relations imposes considerable disruptive risks on these projects. In this context the proposed India-Myanmar-Thailand Trilateral Highway and the Kaladan Project demonstrate the constraints and challenges and are worth looking at in some detail.

IMT Trilateral Highway

The India-Myanmar-Thailand (IMT) transnational highway was envisaged in 2002 under the Look East Policy to enable additional trade routes from India to Myanmar and through Myanmar, to other ASEAN nations. The total length of the highway, intended to link Imphal in India to Bangkok in Thailand was estimated as 1813 km. The construction/upgradation work required was on the 1408 Km stretch from Moreh (India)-Mandalay (Myanmar)-Mae Sot (Thailand). The planned connectivity was expected to generate an estimated US$70 billion in incremental GDP and incremental aggregate employment for 20 million persons by 2025 across the three participating countries.

While some sections of the proposed highway were in good condition, the proposal required significant upgrade of several sections that were in very poor shape with scores of dilapidated bridges. A start was made with the 160 km long Moreh-Tamu-Kalemyo-Kalewa section which was built by Border Roads Organisation and maintained by it till 2009 when it was handed over to Myanmar. The Government of Myanmar, however failed to continue the upgradation work and, following the 2015 Myanmar elections, withdrew the country's commitments. Thereafter, India took upon itself the task of upgradation of the stretches from Moreh to Monywa as well as from Kalewa to Yagyi.

The highway evoked considerable interest and enthusiasm in all quarters. It was still a work in process when in 2015, India proposed a trilateral Motor Vehicle Agreement to facilitate seamless movement of passenger and cargo vehicles among the three countries. In early 2018, with work still going on, a visa agreement was signed for the citizens of two nations to travel by road for education, medical assistance, tourism and other purposes. An Imphal-Mandalay bus service was also envisaged. Meanwhile, India and ASEAN drew up plans to extend this route to Laos, Cambodia and Vietnam. In December 2020, Bangladesh expressed official interest to join the highway project. Subsidiary network comprising Imphal-Moreh-Mandalay national highway upgrade was also planned to provide Imphal with direct access to the trilateral highway. Strengthening of Zokhawthar-Mandalay Road and Mizoram-Kalemyo Highway was planned to provide multiple access to Mizoram to the IMT Highway.

However, the Army takeover in Myanmar threw the country into turmoil and all these initiatives, along with construction work on the main highway remained suspended pending return of peace to that country. Therefore, the IMT Highway remains a work in process even 20 years after being envisaged. While India views this highway as important to achieve seamless connectivity to ASEAN and is still committed to the project, getting it through will require renewed commitment from Myanmar, and much better and faster project implementation. Chances are that even if Myanmar re-commits itself to the highway, it will not be able to fund its portion, requiring new financing mechanisms. Besides the engineering, it requires signing of and operationalisation of the Motor Vehicle Agreement (MVA) and the Cross-Border Transport Agreement (CBTA) to fully yield its benefits. Despite all that, it is worth persisting with the project as the benefits will eventually compensate for the long wait.

Kaladan Multi Modal Project

The Kaladan project was jointly initiated by India and Myanmar to create a multi-modal platform for cargo shipments from India's eastern ports to Myanmar and from there to Mizoram. This project connects Sittwe port in

Myanmar, located on the mouth of the Kaladan river where it debouches into Bay of Bengal, and then through the Kaladan River to Paletwa, also located in Myanmar. After Paletwa the route continues overland to Zorinpui on Mizoram-Myanmar border. Finally, the plan is to connect Zorinpui to Aizawl and thence to India's National Highway-27 (part of the larger East–West Corridor connecting North East India with the rest of India) at Dabaka in Assam.

Prior to the Project, talks between India and Bangladesh had long taken place for transport and transit rights through Bangladesh to the North-Eastern states including access to its Chittagong port, which is less than 200 km (120 mi) away from Agartala. However, as these efforts did not make any headway, the Kaladan project was developed to provide an alternative to the narrow Siliguri corridor for transportation of goods to the NER. The Project includes port upgradation, river dredging, jetty construction, inland water terminal, power stations and eventually Industrial parks. The Kaladan project opened the possibility of several other associated projects with integrated linkages such as the Sittwe Special Economic Zone, Thathay Chaung Hydropower Project, Sitwe–Gaya gas pipeline etc.

The project is being piloted and funded by the Ministry of External Affairs (India). The agreement for the Kaladan project was signed between the governments of India and Myanmar in 2008. Originally, the project was scheduled to be completed by 2014, later extended to March 2023. However, the project could not be completed by the extended date and may take additional 3-5 years to be commissioned. The cost of the project, initially estimated at 536 Cr is now likely to be upwards of 3200 Cr.

The Project initially faced problems such as underestimation of the road length in Myanmar. A bigger delaying factor was the plan by India's Power Ministry to construct hydro-electric projects — Chhimtuipui and Lungleng — on two tributaries of the Kaladan river followed by another project downstream- Kolodyne II. These proposals also involved some submergence within Myanmar territory which required further negotiations with Myanmar. Another impact of these projects is dam management to ensure sufficient water is released by the HE projects to enable navigation in the Kaladan River, failing which, a barrage may be required to regulate sufficient discharge for navigation as well as to ensure peaking operation of these HE projects.

As a result of the lack of coordination in project design and changing technical requirements, there were several upward budget revisions and delays in finalising contracts for various elements of the project. The contract for the road connecting the Paletwa river terminal to Zorinpui in Mizoram border could be awarded only by 2017. There were also coordination issues as different components were being handled by different contractors.

While India is pressing ahead with the project, delays in project implementation have resulted in altered political and economic environment of the project. The political situation changed in Myanmar post-military coup and imposition of international economic sanctions on that country. The route of the project around Paletwa and along the Kaladan river was in any case troubled with Chin insurgency. Following the Rohingya crisis, the Myanmar region where the project is proposed has also become prone to insurgency with the formation of the Arakan Rohingya Salvation Army (ARSA) and the Arakan Army. ARSA/Arakan Army cadres have clashed with Myanmarese troops on many occasions with majority of the skirmishes occurring in close proximity to the Kaladan project. There have also been instances of Arakan Army cadres targeting the shipment of materials for the infrastructure project or attacking Myanmar troops providing security to the project. The Thai military has also reported seizure of consignments of Chinese-made weapons, including AK-47 assault rifles, machine guns, anti-tank mines, grenades and ammunition, in Mae Sot district bordering Myanmar's Karen state. The weapons, were meant to be supplied to the Arakan Army and Arakan Rohingya Salvation Army (ARSA).

The growing insurgency in the region surrounding Kaladan project and illicit flow of weaponry into Myanmar poses a security threat to regional stability and has implications for the Kaladan project.

Meanwhile India and Bangladesh have been working to enable access to India's North-Eastern states through the Chittagong (Chattogram) port in Bangladesh. India and Bangladesh had signed a Memorandum of Understanding (MoU) as far back as 2010, to allow for using Chittagong and Mongla Ports in Bangladesh to transport goods to and from India. However, Bangladesh approved the agreement for the purpose only in 2018. With resumption of trade after waning of the Covid Pandemic, both the countries re-affirmed the agreement in 2022. Access through Chittagong port would definitely be more cost effective for India and may have an impact on the viability of the Kaladan project.

While the IMT Trilateral Highway and the Kaladan project continue to face a challenging environment, India has been pressing ahead with various arrangements that would eventually facilitate movement to

ASEAN countries. An Integrated Customs & Immigration Check post at Zorinpui in Lawngtlai district was made operational in 2017. In early 2018, visa agreement was signed for the citizens of two nations (India and Myanmar) to travel by road for education, medical assistance, tourism and other purposes. Indians and Myanmar citizens with valid passport and visa can also pass through two official Land Border Crossings at Moreh in Manipur (Tamu in Sagaing Region of Myanmar) and Zokhawthar in Mizoram (Rikhawdar in Chin State of Myanmar).

In 2015, India proposed a trilateral Motor Vehicle Agreement to facilitate seamless movement of passenger and cargo vehicles among the three countries. The draft of the trilateral agreement has already been prepared. The signing of Motor vehicle agreement is still pending.

However, there are many challenges such as land acquisition and security issues resulting from unlawful activities of armed insurgent groups. It would however be appropriate to develop the infrastructure on the Indian side, right up to Myanmar border to be linked to these transnational projects once the environment becomes conducive to their implementation.

International Waterways

Nort East rivers provide an outlet to the North Eastern land mass which is otherwise land locked, to the sea and provide low-cost alternative for evacuation of bulk goods to sea ports. Vibrant waterway connectivity would provide a big boost to regional trade, commerce, and tourism. Realising their importance, the Central Government has declared as many as 19 new waterways in NE as National Waterways. Of these, 11 are in Assam, 5 in Meghalaya, and 1 each in Arunachal Pradesh, Mizoram and Nagaland. In line with the "Act East" policy, India has also taken up several infrastructure projects on National Waterways-1, Indo-Bangladesh Protocol route, and NW2, to improve the waterway connectivity with North Eastern Region (NER).

Bangladesh features the world's largest river delta, formed by the junction of three great rivers – the Ganges, the Brahmaputra, and the Meghna. The Government of Bangladesh has formulated the Delta Plan to eliminate extreme poverty, create more jobs and sustain gross domestic product (GDP) growth until 2041. The Plan envisages increased trade and navigational opportunities. The target is to develop 10,000 km inland waterways navigable for all seasons by 2030. This will lead to better integration and connection between India and Bangladesh. In addition to economic growth, the Plan includes elements of environmental conservation, enhanced climate resilience and disaster risk mitigation. Meanwhile cargo transportation through National Waterway 2 has been rising with exports to Bangladesh using IWT having gone up in recent years.

The Eastern Neighbourhood: Indo Bangla Protocols

The Protocol on Inland Water Trade & Transit (PIWTT) between India & Bangladesh is a unique example of bilateral cooperation between India and Bangladesh. The Protocol also includes additional ports of call and specifically grants India access to Chittagong and Mongla ports for shipping goods to NER. (Bangladesh has already allowed the use of Chittagong port for the NER) Meanwhile the Coastal Shipping Agreement between the two countries provides for direct connectivity between seaports of eastern India and Bangladesh. Further, two stretches of IBP routes are being developed to provide seamless navigation to NER via the IBP route. Meanwhile Patna to Pandu River route via Bangladesh is already operational. However, to unlock the value from the cargo trade on a sustainable basis in the region, there is a need for diversifying the trade basket.

River Ports

Dhubri, Assam, India's fastest growing terminal, is now well connected with Narayanganj (in Bangladesh) through this inland water route and there has been regular sailing of cargo vessels. Neighbouring Bhutan has also been using this route for trade with Bangladesh. The development of Dhubri port has led to cross-border and transit trade of stone chips, boulders and coal between India, Bangladesh and Bhutan. The local traders are now focusing on agricultural products like ginger, oranges and other products such as waste cotton. Fresh investments are however needed to convert river terminals along the river Brahmaputra into full-fledged river ports.

With the development of the Karimganj river port and the revival of the Mahishasan railway transit point and the Integrated Check Post at Sutarkandi, Karimganj, Bangladesh can connect with other north-eastern states. Improvements are underway in both Bangladesh and India to improve several IWT terminals, including Ashuganj river terminal, which has road links and custom facilities for transit cargo to NER via Akhaura-Agartala land border and also links to Chittagong port terminal. While there are possibilities of developing more protocol routes, these can be well supplemented by several small-haul trade routes, opening up employment opportunities in inland water navigation, trade, and tourism that would be more inclusive for the informal economies in trans-boundary river basins.

Making International Waterways viable and sustainable.

Dredging is also one of the important aspects that need to be taken into consideration. Also, there should be synergy and sequencing in route maintenance from both sides. Measures need also be taken to remove low-height bridges that pose a significant challenge in the movement of vessels and to design flat bottom or low superstructure base ships. Measures need to be taken to up-scale the tonnage of the vessels and stretch the waterways further to service production centres.

There are hard and soft challenges relating to navigation and pilotage that need to be addressed, such as navigation quality along the protocol routes, loading-unloading facilities at ports, pilotage and night navigation facilities and others that need to be developed. To promote safe navigation, electronic charts, night navigation aids and Differential Global Positioning Systems (DGPS) stations along the rivers are also needed

Cargo diversification Vessels carrying steel and ODC (Over Dimensional Cargo) for enterprises such as Numaligarh Bio-refinery are already using Inland Waterways via IBP route. A major task is to develop IWT terminals with appropriate cargo handling equipment and to establish Road-Rail link including a roll-on roll-off facility. Multi-modal ports need to be developed to provide connectivity to people and to traders that connect productive centres along the rivers.

Trans-boundary river basins are also sensitive to climate change, such as floods, river erosions, and others. Intergovernmental Panel on Climate Change (IPCC) has released its sixth assessment report titled 'Climate Change 2021: The Physical Science Basis' that states the impact of climate change at a regional scale. Hence, it is important to consider and develop climate-resilient trade and tourism infrastructure on the river basins. Various minor rivers and tributaries may also require investments for flood control and river training along with periodic dredging.

River basin systems are complex mechanisms that need scientific water governance. Importance has to be given to enhancement of livelihood opportunities and participation of local people with attention to ground-level issues faced by water dependent activities such as agriculture, fisheries, transportation etc. The agenda on water governance must also align with the one on climate change adaptation and mitigation through sustainable basin-wide management.

Trans National Railways

Reviving railway links with and through Bangladesh: Pre-Partition, an elaborate railway network operated seamlessly over territories now comprising India and Bangladesh. As described earlier, these rail links spanned both the territories falling within present-day India and Bangladesh. A major effort is now underway in both India and Bangladesh to undo the disruption of the Partition and the 1965 war with Pakistan. This requires reopening pre-partition railway links with Bangladesh, such as the old Kolkata and Agartala rail link through Bangladesh.

As a result of special initiative taken over the last two decades, India and Bangladesh currently have re-started five operational rail interchange points and started new train services between West Bengal and western Bangladesh. Linking Chittagong and Cox Bazar to destinations in Assam via Tripura and completion of the rail link between Agartala and Akhaura will improve rail connectivity further and also enable NER to start using Chittagong as the region's main port, which was indeed the situation before 1947. India is also developing railway route from Cox's Bazar deep water port to South Tripura district by rehabilitating the railway link from Santirbazar in India to Feni in Bangladesh, where a road and rail bridge is being built to connect the Belonia (India)–Parshuram (Bangladesh). This will reduce traffic through Sittwe, but will provide strategic redundancy if there is a war or internal disturbance. There are many more proposals on the cards linking railway networks in Bangladesh and India, which if carried to fruition would create a large interconnected rail grid in the Eastern part of the Indian Subcontinent and provide immensely better access to the North East and beyond.

Rail Links - Myanmar and beyond

With the construction of a 51.38 km long stretch of broad-gauge railway line between Bhairabi on Assam-Mizoram border and Sairang near Aizawl expected to be completed by end of 2023, Aizawl is due to come on to the Indian railway map. Encouraged by the engagement with Myanmar prior to the military takeover, Aizawl was being considered as the new railway hub for rail connectivity to Myanmar. With this in view, several new connections were planned from Aizawl to destinations in Myanmar such as Wuntho, Kalaymyo, Kyauktaw-Sittwe. While these projects are now delayed and would require a major re-engagement with Myanmar, NEF Railway plans to revive an earlier proposal to construct a broad-gauge line from Sairang to Hmawngbuchhuah in Mizoram's Lawngtlai district, near the Myanmar border.

There are several other proposals for linking Indian railway network to Myanmar. Tinsukia-Myitkyina railway is a proposed new railway link between the existing rail stations at Tinsukia-Doom Dooma in Assam, India and Myitkyina in Kachin State of Myanmar, via Shin Bway Yang and Sumprabum. Imphal-Kalemo railway is yet another proposed new railway link between the existing rail stations at Imphal in Manipur of India and Kalay in Myanmar. These proposals remained at the planning stage with Myanmar withdrawing from such engagements post military coup. Reviving them would be an uphill task and musts await a more outward looking regime in Myanmar.

Proposed Rail Links - ASEAN

The land connectivity through Myanmar is critical for building rail links to other destinations in ASEAN. Several such proposals have been envisaged in the past and represent potential links. There is a proposal for an India-Myanmar-Thailand railway link that envisages connecting Aizawl to existing railway lines in southern Myanmar and thence to the Thailand rail network. This link, if and when completed, could be extended to Laos as well through a rail network reaching just 20 km east of Vientiane and built by State Railway of Thailand during 2007-09.

India-Myanmar-Thailand-Malaysia-Singapore railway is yet another proposed railway link as part of the Trans-Asian Railway, parts of which already exist. While India Myanmar section is proposed but has run into difficulties as noted above, the connection beyond Myanmar envisages using existing metre-gauge connections of Thai railway network to railway network in Malaysia and eventually to the Kuala Lumpur–Singapore high-speed rail (under construction).

The Track Ahead

Building up transnational railway connectivity, however, is going to be a gargantuan task. To begin with, there are several missing links in India itself, particularly between the Railway network in the Assam Valley and the Myanmar border through Manipur, Mizoram and Nagaland. With the disturbed law and order situation following ethnic strife in Manipur and a restive Mizoram, this itself is going to be a long-drawn affair. Once normalcy is restored this part of the Region, rail connections to Aizawl which are under implementation would need to be completed. This will need to be followed up by electrification of railway tracks in the NER along with introduction of more intercity trains connecting all the NER capital cities and more long-distance trains originating therefrom. As Aizawl is being positioned as a hub for further connectivity with Myanmar it is critical to complete this section first.

The most challenging cross border rail connectivity issues are with Myanmar, which has a rail network that runs north-south but is not connected to the Indo-Myanmar border. There are also many missing/ damaged links. It is however the key to connectivity with the rest of ASEAN. Still considerable progress had been made in discussions with Govt. of Myanmar prior to the military coup, which may have to be taken up once again. With the disruption in Myanmar following the takeover by the military junta and the threat of economic sanctions hanging over Myanmar it is not clear, at least in the short/ medium term how the railway connectivity is going to be set on track. Apart from the hilly terrain, the law-and-order situation in Myanmar does not lend itself to easy project implementation.

Another issue in cross border rail connectivity is gauge uniformity, or lack thereof. Indian Railways uses broad gauge (1,676 mm or 5 ft 6 in), while Myanmar, Thailand, Vietnam and Malaysia mostly use narrow gauge (1 meter). However, Indian railways have considerable experience in gauge conversion and may well offer that to neighbouring countries.

Rail links with Bangladesh are, however progressing, albeit at a slow pace. Activation of colonial period railway lines through Bangladesh with trade and transit agreements would give regional rail networks a big boost. Needless to say, as rail connectivity actually takes shape there will be need for dry ports, Inland Container Depots, Customs and immigration,

In December 2017, India offered a US$1 billion line of credit to build connections to ASEAN nations. Events in Myanmar and the Covid Pandemic has put most rail connectivity initiatives on the back burner. While revival of the India Myanmar rail link is awaited, it would be strategically beneficial for India to be invested and engaged in the growing South East Asian rail connectivity plans. It would be a considerably complex and difficult exercise to revive them again but it will be something that is worth undertaking. Given adequate policy, diplomatic, financial and operational support, are possible.

International Energy Corridors and Exchanges

Energy is a sector with great potential for mutually beneficial international cooperation in India's Eastern Neighbourhood and with ASEAN. In the NER, energy can be sourced from hydropower, coal, oil or gas. While Bhutan and the states of NER have large hydro energy potential, neighbouring Bangladesh and Myanmar have considerable natural gas resources. India's NER shares common borders with all its Eastern neighbouring countries and is well placed to be a transit corridor for power exchanges with them. Power exchanges between India and countries neighbouring NER can help in achieving competitive tariffs and efficient load management by power consuming systems, better use of the existing power transmission and load dispatch infrastructure and market diversification by the power producers. With diverse sources of energy, there is potential of building energy trade between India, Bhutan, Bangladesh and Myanmar and even beyond. The recently released Hydro Carbon Vision 2030 for North East India makes a comprehensive attempt in relocating the NER in the energy map of India, recognising cross-border exchanges as a core strategy.

In fact, SAARC realised the potential of energy exchanges in South Asia as far back as 2004 at the Islamabad summit, repeated in declarations made in several following summits till 2014. A SAARC Energy Centre was also set up at Islamabad and a South Asia Energy Dialogue was started. There was talk of regional hydro potential, grid connectivity and gas pipelines and also evolving an appropriate regional inter-governmental framework. In 2014, Nepal and India signed an Agreement on Electric Power Trade, Cross-border Transmission Interconnection and Grid Connectivity and also set up a Joint Working Group for the purpose. Meanwhile a number of technical entities engaged in power generation and transmission in several SAARC countries started working to foster cooperation in energy sector, an initiative that was well supported by international organisations such as World Bank and the ADB.

The Bangladesh-Bhutan-India-Nepal (BBIN) sub-region faces persistent power shortage and has historically had relatively low per capita electricity consumption. These countries have been importing a significant portion of their commercial energy requirement, mainly hydrocarbon. With prices of fuel rising across the world cooperation with immediate neighbouring countries makes economic sense. emerged as a key instrument. At the same time the energy market structure is also changing with power sector reforms that include a role for the power sector as a whole, development of power exchanges and cross border power purchases. Electricity generation is also attracting cross border private investment.

Transnational Generation Projects

India and Bangladesh have entered into extensive bi-lateral energy related cooperation that could well be a model for the larger Indo-ASEAN region. These initiatives include energy exports from India that starting in 2013; Construction of a grid inter-connection between Bheramara (Bangladesh) and Behrampur (West Bengal): Construction of a 1,320-MW coal-based unit at Rampal in Bangladesh by National Thermal Power corporation (NTPC, India); export of earmarked share of electricity (100 MW) to Bangladesh from Palatana Project in Tripura. The power exchange between Tripura and Bangladesh from the 726 MW Combined Cycle Gas Turbine (CCGT) at Palatana (Tripura) is an excellent example of bilateral cooperation. The project included a 47-km-long, 400-KV double circuit transmission lines from Suryamani Nagar Power Grid, in Tripura to Comilla in Bangladesh, constructed by PGCIL. This project was facilitated by Bangladesh through transportation of related equipment and goods and service through its waterways and roads to the project site. The level of confidence this project has generated is demonstrated by the fact that simultaneously a 10 gigabit per second (GBPS) bandwidth gateway of internet connectivity for the entire North Eastern states has been secured via Bangladesh. For the first time, India's Northeast region gets bandwidth through the Bay of Bengal base far away from the traditional sources of southern and western India.

Most of the HE projects in Bhutan (Chukha, Kuricchu, Dagachu, Basochhu, Tala) have been built with Indian financial and technical support. Bhutan today has the highest per capita consumption of 2,400 kWh in South Asia but still has huge amount of surplus power which it exports to India, with very welcome export earnings for that country. The challenge now is to extend the scope of such initiative multilaterally.

Energy trade linkages with Myanmar are also emerging such as the buy-back arrangement of 80 percent of India's 1,200- MW Tamnthi Dam (Chindwin river in western Sagaing region) in Myanmar initiated with NHPC of India in 2007.

Broadly five models of power exchanges are now emerging internationally. These include: i) exclusive bilateral exchanges such as those between India and Bhutan, and Bangladesh and Nepal respectively; ii) subregional initiatives like among the countries in Greater Mekong Sub-region (GMS); iii) regional power pool proposals like that in Southern African Power Pool

(SAPP); iv) integrative exchanges like generation-load centre location based model between Palatana (Tripura) and Bangladesh; and v) wheeling facilitation like that done by India between the Eastern and Western Bhutan through the adjoining territories of Darjeeling and Jalpaiguri Districts in West Bengal and Assam.

Overall, generation of energy through various sources would need to be accompanied by evacuation arrangements as well as regional transmission and grid management arrangements along with energy trade agreements and mechanisms for international metering, billing and settlements. This would require integration of a diverse mix of hydro, thermal, renewable generation along with a mutually agreed coordination for monitoring operations, collecting data, planning and disseminating technical and financial information to members etc.

Interconnection of power systems of contiguously located countries and their coordinated operation would provide immense technical and economic benefits. The Pool-based approach similar to one adopted by South Africa and its neighbouring countries and regional power pools successfully operating in several parts of the world could be another major forward-looking venture for the BBIN sub-region. In fact, India's Power Grid Corporation has worked out the interconnections required, their feasibility and the cost and benefits to the participating countries in the BBIN sub-region. Therefore, establishing a trans-BBIN Subregional power trading entity could launch a market mechanism that pools surplus power generated by individual plants in the participating countries and transports it to deficit ones by a coordinated exchange mechanism. It would be well to study the possibility of applying some or all the above models to build up power exchanges covering India-BBIN- ASEAN.

Air Connectivity

International Air connectivity

While land connectivity opens up many avenues for movement of goods and persons, in today's world air connectivity is critical for quick and convenient movement of people and high value cargo. For the NER to open up to SE Asia it is necessary that both business and leisure travellers have option for easy air travel access to North eastern destinations.

While several efforts have been made to improve domestic air connectivity to the NER, the greater challenge, however, is to build international connectivity between NE Region and the neighbouring countries and

ASEAN which would contribute greatly to various kinds of tourism including health and wellness. NER's airports are mostly yet to be connected internationally. So far there are only two airports in the North East with limited international connectivity- Guwahati and Imphal. Earlier, in 2019, six international destinations were approved ex-Guwahati to Singapore, Kuala Lumpur, Bangkok, Dhaka, Yangon and Kathmandu to be supported under the UDAN scheme. These were suspended in early 2020 due to the Covid pandemic. While Bhutan's Druk Air has resumed flights from Paro to Bangkok via Guwahati, efforts are also being made to resume other flights on these routes. More services, such as the Imphal-Kalay-Mandalay flight are proposed but are yet to take-off.

Obviously, international air connectivity to other SE Asian destinations will depend on demand rising in the NE Region, which is possible as economic links of India's NER deepen with SE Asia. In the meantime, it would be well worth the effort to develop Northeast specific plans for regional air connectivity such that they do not depend upon subsidies indefinitely.

Economic Development, Sustainability and Disaster Resilience

NER must develop modern, cross-border, integrated supply chains to unlock value and create business opportunities. The expansion of physical infrastructure needs to be complemented with e-commerce supply chains and start-ups to pave the way for further visibility globally. To achieve this the design and vision of future infrastructure development has to be commercially and financially viable, incorporate latest system management, materials handling digital and communications technology, and go beyond national borders. Given the ecologically sensitive geography of the region, high rainfall, interspersed with massive rivers prone to annual flooding and a general propensity for extreme weather events, infrastructure development also has to address environmental concerns and be disaster resilient. India has the technical ability and the financial strength to facilitate such development, with the Act East Policy providing a suitable platform for the purpose.

Notes to Chapter 10

1. The India–Myanmar–Thailand Trilateral Highway (IMT Highway) is a highway under construction under India's Act East policy that will connect Moreh, India with Mae Sot, Thailand via Myanmar. Imphal-Mandalay-Bangkok 1981 km route consists of Imphal-Mandalay (584 km) and Mandalay-Bangkok (1,397) km segments.

2. India has also proposed extending IMT highway to Cambodia, Laos and Vietnam. The proposed approx. 3,200 km long route from India to Vietnam is known as the East-West Economic Corridor (segments linking Thailand to Cambodia and Vietnam are already operational.) This highway will also connect to the river ports being developed along the way at Kalay (also called Kalaymyo) and Monywa on Chindwin River.

3. The Kaladan Multi-Modal Transit Transport Project was the result of a Framework agreement entered into by the Ministry of External Affairs (MEA), Govt. of India with the Govt. of Myanmar in April 2008. The Detailed Project Report (DPR) for development of the Project was prepared by M/s RITES during 2003. The transit route envisaged between Kolkata (nearest Indian port / commercial hub) and Mizoram as per the current implementation programme (after revision of the DPR for Port & Inland Water Transport components by Inland Waterways Authority of India in 2009) comprises of following segments.

i) Kolkata to Sittwe port in Myanmar (Shipping)539 km; ii) Sittwe to Paletwa (River Kaladan) Inland Water Transport (IWT) 158 km; iii) Paletwa to Indo-Myanmar Border (in Myanmar) Road 110 km; iv) Border to NH.54 (Lawngtlai) (in India) Road 100 km.

M/DONER   https://mdoner.gov.in/kaladan-multi-modal-transit-transport-project-inland

4. The sustained effort to rejuvenate the historical trade routes via Bangladesh got a fillip under PM Gati Shakti Scheme. On the Indian side the Eastern Waterways Connectivity Transport Grid project is being implemented with the support of the World Bank to provide seamless connectivity between National Waterway-1 (NW-1) and NW-2 through the Indo-Bangladesh Protocol routes. This concept is adopted to leverage and connect waterways in a logistic grid and transportation network, linking the Yamuna Economic Corridor with the Eastern Waterways Connectivity Transport Grid project.

5. Sirajganj-Daikhowa and Ashuganj-Zakiganj are also being developed at a cost of Rs. 305.84 crore on an 80:20 share basis (80% being borne by India and 20% by Bangladesh)

6. This involves rivercraft sailing from Patna on NW-1 (Ganga) via Kolkata, Haldia, Hemnagar, through Indo Bangladesh Protocol (IBP) route through Khulna, Narayanganj, Sirajganj, Chilmari, and joining up with National Waterway-2 (Brahmaputra) in India through Dhubri, and Jogighopa covering 2,350 km. Once the IBP Route no. 5 & 6 from Maia near Farakka in India to Aricha in Bangladesh open up, the IWT distance connecting NW1 to NW2 (North Eastern Region) will further be reduced by nearly 1000 km, which will reduce time and cost to a great extent.

7. These are Petrapole- Benapole; Gede -Darshana; Singhabad-Rohanpur; Radhikapur-Birol; Haldipur -Chilahati. Of these, two, namely Radhikapur-Birol and Singhabad-Rohanpur are also notified for use of Nepalese transit traffic. Three new train services: Jalpaiguri-Haldibari-Dhaka (Mitali Express); Kolkata-Khulna (Bandhan Express) Kolkata-Dhaka (Maitree Express) have also been operationalised.

8. In addition, there are many more proposals on the cards linking railway networks in Bangladesh, India. Some of these are the Sabroom-Cox Bazar railway, connecting Sabroom on the Tripura- Bangladesh border to Khagrachari-Rangamati-Bandarban district headquarters in the tribal areas of Chittagong Hill Tracts, then to Cox's Bazaar via Satkania. (Cox's Bazar is now one of the official ports for transit to India); The Shillong-Sylhet railway via Shillong and Dawki in India to Sylhet in Bangladesh; Dhubri-Jaria railway via Dhubri, Tura, Barengapara and Durgapur in India to Jaria in Bangladesh. These proposals

9. India-Bangladesh-Myanmar railway from Sabroom in South Tripura via Chaggalnaiya (Bangladesh) to Lunglei, Aizawl, Zokhawtar to Kalemo (Myanmar); Bandarban-Tuiping-Gangaw railway Route for this will be Bandarban (Bangladesh)-Tuiping (Mizoram), Niawhtlang (Mizoram-Burma border)-Gangaw (Myanmar);

10. 75 percent of total generation in Bhutan is surplus and is exported to India. (5,179.26 million GWh in 2014) earning over Nu 10690 million (1 Nu= 1Indian Rupee) in 2014 and thereby contributing over one-third of government revenues and over nine percent of the country's GDP. has a target of generating 10,000 MW 17 by 2020 at a total cost of

Chapter 11

Financing Development in the NER- Past and Future

(Economic development has been an element of the strategy adopted by the Indian state to address separatism and insurgency along with military action and political accommodation in the NER. While several arrangements were made over the last half-century, investment in the region picked up pace at the turn of the century. An elaborate financial architecture was devised to channel resources for the economic development of the North East. A survey of these arrangements reveals the recognition of the needs of the region. However, going forward more innovative financing options, combining both public and private sources, would have to be looked at to enable the development of a modern economy in the NER.)

The Evolution of Financing Arrangements

Soon after independence, the nation was confronted with an enormous requirement of resources for economic development. Post WW II, economies were shattered across the globe and the new international institutions-the World Bank and IMF were engaged in reconstruction of the economies of Europe and the Pacific Rim. India, having emerged from colonial rule as a part of which it incurred the cost of war in terms of men, materials and money, the trauma and disruption of the Partition, the devastating famines of the 1940s, was steeped in poverty, with hardly any investible resources. New institutions of a modern state were being set up and reorganisation of the states, (which was finally done in 1956) was on the anvil. Even after re-organisation, the states had hardly any capacity to raise resources to meet their revenue expenditure, leave alone raise funds for development. The private sector in India was also in a fledgeling state, short of capital and finding its way around the sterling companies left behind by the departing colonial rulers. In the circumstances, the task of mobilising resources fell largely to the Central Government.

With the coming into force of the Constitution, constitutional arrangements for sharing the resources between the Centre and the States came into play. The Finance Commission was constituted in 1951 and charged with the allocation of resources raised through taxation and other measures, between the central and the state governments. It was also given the responsibilities of examining the liabilities and resources of the states, their budgetary commitments and the effort undertaken to fulfil their commitments. The first Finance Commission was followed by others, constituted regularly every five years, to carry out their constitutional duties.

The National Planning Commission was also established in 1950 to look into the problems of financing national development. In course of time, the Commission was enabled to provide assistance to states to implement specific development priorities identified under the Five-year Plans. The first five-year plan was launched in 1951. In the decade that followed the newly independent nation sought to mobilise its resources through constitutional arrangements and chose the path of planned economic development and growth. In the initial decades, the new states forming the Union of India, all faced revenue and capital scarcity and depended, to varying degrees, upon resources mobilised by the Central Government and provided to them through the Finance Commission awards and Plan assistance through the Planning Commission.

As for the North East Region, then comprising of the composite Assam and the former princely states of Manipur and Tripura, the task was all the more difficult due to its geographical isolation post-Partition, abysmal lack of infrastructure of all kinds, the challenging task of nation building in the backdrop of strong local identities with early insurgency breaking out in the Naga Hills. Over the two decades following India's independence, as insurgency and militancy spread all over the region, it was realised that there was a need to go beyond military action and political accommodation and address the poverty and economic deprivation of the region.

The Gadgil Formula and the Special Category States

The first Five-year Plan was followed by two more Five-Year Plans till 1966. However, the period 1966-68 saw the country face an acute agricultural and food crisis resulting in the five-year Plans being suspended. When the Fourth Five-year Plan was being formulated, it was felt that the central assistance provided for in the first three plans and annual plans of 1966–1969 was not able to address the developmental issues facing the respective states and particularly the NER.

In 1969, the Fifth Finance Commission, recognising that certain states, such as those located in the NER, had a low resource base and could not mobilise resources required for development at the same pace as the rest of the country, sought to provide such states with preferential treatment in the form of special central assistance and tax breaks. Taking into account the recommendations of the Fifth Finance Commission, a new formula, named after R.C. Gadgil, then Dy Chairman of the Planning Commission, was arrived at for plan transfers to the states which recognised the special problems of the North East and Jammu & Kashmir. As per this formulation the special problems facing the states of Assam, Jammu and Kashmir and Nagaland were recognised. These were classified as Special Category States. It was decided that their needs be given preference and should first be met out of the total pool of Central assistance.

For the Special Category states, the Central government bore 90 percent of the state expenditure on all centrally-sponsored schemes and external aid while rest 10 percent was given as loan to state at zero percent rate of interest. Further, the Special Category States were allowed to use up to 20 percent of the Central Assistance for Non-Plan expenditure.

Initially, three states; Assam, Nagaland and Jammu & Kashmir were granted Special Category status but from 1974 onwards, as the state of Assam was reorganised and new states came into being, more states were added under the Special Category. These included Himachal Pradesh, Manipur, Meghalaya, Mizoram, Sikkim, Tripura and Arunachal Pradesh, in addition to Assam and J&K. This formula was tweaked from time to time but continued in its basic form till 2014 when with the setting up of the NITI Aayog in 2015, the Planning Commission was dismantled and the Gadgil formula-based grants discontinued. In its place, the allocation to all states, including NER, was made from the national Divisible Pool of Resources.

NEC, the Special Regional Planning Body for the North East.

While the recognition of the political aspirations of the peoples of the NER led to the region being politically re-organised, it was recognised that some of the new states would be quite small in terms of population and resource base and would not be able to adequate mobilise resources on their own. It was felt that these states would also benefit from regional development given their interconnected nature due to the geography of the region. This led to a regional development strategy for the North East whereby additional allocations of Central assistance would be made to benefit the North eastern region as a whole.

The North Eastern Council (NEC) was constituted in 1971 by an Act of Parliament as the nodal agency for the economic and social development of the North Eastern Region which eventually included Sikkim as well as the States of Arunachal Pradesh, Assam, Manipur, Meghalaya, Mizoram, Nagaland, and Tripura. The intention was concerted and planned effort to remove the handicaps and bottlenecks that stood in the way of rapid development of the NE Region. This body was headquartered at Shillong and was placed under the Union Home Ministry, with membership comprising of Governors and Chief Ministers of the constituent states. The funding of the Council is historically 56 percent contributed by the state governments and the rest by the Central govt departments. The central assistance provided to the NEC is over and above that provided to the individual state governments.

Thus, post reorganisation in 1972, the development requirements of NE States, as Special Category states, were pursued through a variety of means such as the Finance Commission awards, by the respective Five Year and Annual Plans of the states supported by central transfers recommended by the Planning Commission, as well as through Centrally Sponsored Schemes of the Union Ministries and Central Agencies and through projects of inter-State nature in the region funded by the North-Eastern Council (NEC), which had a separate additional budget for the purpose. In addition, the states could resort to market borrowings, in a carefully structured manner commensurate with their ability to service the same, within limits and as supervised by the Reserve Bank of India.

Non-Lapsable Central Pool of Resources(NLCPR)

In the 1990s, with the emergence of the Look East Policy, it was felt that the NER required major investments in both physical and social infrastructure sectors such as Irrigation and Flood Control, Power, Roads and Bridges, Education, Health, Water Supply and Sanitation etc. The states of the NER could not meet the financing needs of such investments. It was also difficult for the NEC to identify, prepare, finance and implement infrastructure projects at this scale. It was decided that large infra projects of critical importance would be implemented through central ministries through large central public sector organisations that had the necessary expertise.

Scaling up of Infra projects in the NER faced another problem. These projects also took a long time to implement in the NER whereas the normal budgetary resources provide by the Central Government were on annual basis. Reallocation and re-release under the budgetary process tended to disrupt funds flow and caused further delays. To obviate this difficulty, in 1997, the Central Government created the Non-Lapsable Central Pool of Resources (NLCPR), a pool of non-lapsable funds for the North-Eastern States. In addition to increasing the flow of budgetary financing for new infrastructure projects/schemes in the region, which received priority, this arrangement also provided continuity, as unspent money under Central schemes for NER did not lapse. In 2001, the Ministry of Development of North Eastern Region (DoNER) was established by the Government of India ministry to function as the nodal Central Government Department to administer the Non-Lapsable Central Pool of Resources (NLCPR) and coordinate with the Central Ministries and the State Governments of the NE states on developmental matters. DoNER was also declared the administrative ministry for the NEC.

The accruals in NLCPR were utilised by Ministry of DoNER under the two Schemes of NLCPR (State) and NLCPR-Central for which annual budgetary allocations were provided in the normal budgetary process. Utilisation of funds under the two schemes was debited annually to the resource pool. Under the NLCPR (State) Scheme, priority projects of North Eastern States were funded and under NLCPR-Central Scheme, funds were provided to Central Ministries for implementing projects of national and regional importance.

A National Committee headed by Secretary, Ministry of Development of North Eastern Region was set up to oversee NLCPR with representation from Ministries of Finance, Home Affairs and Planning Commission. Representatives of Union Ministry/Departments, whose proposals were to be considered in a particular sitting for funding under NLCPR, were also invited. The Planning and Development Department of the state concerned was refashioned as the nodal department for NLCPR and DoNER's interface with all other departments of the state.

North East Special Infrastructure Development Scheme (NESIDS)

In December, 2017 a new Central Scheme namely, "North East Special Infrastructure Development Scheme" (NESIDS) was launched to replace the NLCPR Scheme. With adoption of NESIDS, no new project was to be taken up for funding under the NLCPR Scheme. However, funding for ongoing projects under the Scheme was to be continued till March,

2020 for their completion. Under the Scheme guidelines of NESIDS, 100 percent centrally funding is provided to the State Governments of North Eastern Region for identified projects of physical infrastructure relating to water supply, electricity and connectivity enhancement, tourism and social infrastructure relating to education and health.

The Fifteenth Finance Commission

The 15th Finance Commission has recommended devolution of 41 percent from the divisible pool to states. The transfer of funds to states takes place as per established procedure. The Central Government makes provisions in the budget for the amount to be transferred to the states as part of devolution. Based on Finance Commission recommendations, the Centre also transfers to the States various grants such as the Revenue deficit Grants, Sectoral grants, incentives, etc. These grants form part of the Union Budget. However, the actual transfer is based on the extent of tax collected. (A shortfall in the tax collection could result in a fall in the actual amount received by the states through devolution as witnessed in 2020-21.) Apart from these, Centre's transfer to States may take place through Centrally Sponsored Schemes, funded by the Central Government but implemented at the state level. As per 2021-22 budget estimates, the expenditure on Central Sponsored Schemes was around 9 percent of the total central expenditure.

Other Central assistance -Beneficiary Oriented Schemes

The assistance extended by the Centre is also in the form of direct benefits to beneficiaries under various centrally sponsored and central schemes. The transfer to the beneficiaries can be through (i) direct transfer by the Central Government or agency to the beneficiary (ii) transfer of funds to the states who implement the scheme and spend the funds on the same. In a few other cases, the states add their share to the central transfer before spending.

The Regional Development Initiative

The North Eastern Council was created to complement and supplement the developmental efforts of the NER States. Through its Regional Plan, NEC has attempted to identify thrust areas as well as critical gaps for taking up as many development initiatives in different kinds of infrastructural facilities including highway and bridge building projects, transport and communication, power generation and transmission etc. Apart from infrastructure, the Council has demonstrated considerable achievements, mostly in health and education, by establishing several institutions of excellence and funding several engineering and medical colleges. NEC's 3-year plan issued in 2017, envisaged an annual budget of INR 2500 crore, 40 percent from the government and the rest 60 percent from the Non-Lapsable Central Pool of Resources (NLCPR)

NEC Institutions

Ever since it was set up, NEC has been instrumental in setting up organisations and institutions critically required for the development of the North Eastern Region. These include the North Eastern Electric Power Corporation (NEEPCO) set up in 1976 as a power generation company in the region for tapping its enormous power potential. It has developed and set up Hydro/Thermal/Renewable Energy Projects with adoption of new technologies for generation of electricity and schemes for efficient utilisation of installed energy capacities etc. NEEPCO operates 6 hydro, 3 thermal and 1 solar power stations with a combined installed capacity of 2057 MW.

Other NE Regional institutions include the North Eastern Development Finance Corporation (NEDFi) - a Public Financial Institution and a registered as NBFC with the RBI- provides financial assistance to micro, small, medium and large enterprises for setting up industrial, infrastructure and agri-allied projects in the NER as also Microfinance through MFI/NGOs. Besides financing, the Corporation conducts sector or state specific studies and offers Consultancy & Advisory services to the state Governments, private sector and other agencies. Similarly, the North eastern Regional Agricultural Marketing Corporation (NERAMAC) was set up to maximise the potential of the North East for Agro Food Processing, Horticulture, Floriculture, Farming, livestock etc. In addition, NEC has been instrumental in establishing several institutions of excellence in the North East such as the North Eastern Hills University, (NEHU), North Eastern Indira Gandhi Regional Institute of Health and Medical Sciences; (NEIGRIHMS); North Easter Regional Institute of Science and Technology, (NERIST);

Meeting Future Funding Requirements

Central Government Transfers: As the foregoing narrative shows, the Indian Central Government has devised various modalities to fund development in the North East from time to time. This was in recognition of the disturbed conditions in the North East, lack of growth and employment generating economic activity in the region. Most NE States, with the possible exception of Assam, are revenue deficit and are unlikely to be able to spare any funds for capital expenditure, nor do they have any significant independent borrowing power. Therefore, investment requirements to boost their economies to a level where they can meaningfully participate in the SE Asian regional value and supply chains would require continued support by the Central Government. Currently this support is flowing through a mix of enhanced Finance Commission allocations, direct funding of large infrastructural projects, food subsidies, employment support and direct transfers through beneficiary-oriented schemes

However, this dependency would not be sustainable in the long term. As a strategy it would be important to focus on the fiscal sustainability of the NE States. Insofar as large infrastructural projects, vital for the economy or the security of the region are concerned, it would be difficult for NER states to fund such projects on their own and Central Government support would be critical.

However, large projects, with their time and cost over-runs tend to hog the attention and resources disproportionately while there are infrastructural requirements at small and medium levels, both in urban and rural areas that can be efficiency enhancing. Besides large projects have operational and maintenance costs to be met on recurrent basis. Therefore, a strategy has to be devised to secure funds for various small and medium infra projects based on local needs on the basis of efficiency and income and employment generation criteria while ensuring their financial viability and sustainability. Financial instruments and modalities, systems and institutions that make such infra projects sustainable would have to be devised. These may include a combination of benefits in terms of lower cost of funds, taxation relief and user charges. Capacity building amongst the local population to execute such projects would go a long way in securing local support and timely completion.

While Finance Commission allocations would be made available to states, they may not necessarily ensure desirable level of growth. The tendency amongst the NER states (as in many other parts of the country as well) is to create Government and public sector employment as a means of distribution of incomes. This may create limited employment and encourage consumption but is not outcome oriented or economically efficient. In addition to placing a huge revenue burden on the state through salaries, wages and cost of administration, it also tends to discourage individual capacity enhancement, entrepreneurship and innovation, eventually securing less growth for the investment done. An option could be to make a part of the central transfers targeted and contingent upon outcomes, particularly for public health, child nutrition and school education including primary education. Eventually employment, income generation and thereby access to food and services would depend on human development and use of local talent and capacities.

Regional Development

Institutions such as DoNER and the NEC have been successful in bringing about a regional focus to NER as a geography that is divided into several state jurisdictions and in that sense has opened up the combined potential of the region for the future. NEC is a useful forum for bringing together, political leaderships of constituent states on a common platform. It has also set up excellent institutions with a long-term value for the region. These regional institutions are of great benefit for the smaller states where institutions of such size and stature would not otherwise be feasible. Its success in forging a common development agenda however, remains a work in progress, as individual state priories invariably take centre stage in respective states.

Foreign Multilateral and Bilateral Funding

In addition to Central budgetary resources or transfers through Finance Commission awards, the Central Government can also facilitate funds through borrowings from multilateral development institutions such as the World Bank and ADB. Indeed, the Central and state Govts. have been availing such funding in the past, though the quantum would have to be raised considerably to meet the future financing requirements for rapid growth to enable NER to engage with the SE Region. Multilateral funding requires detailed project planning and comes packaged with policy recommendations to be implemented together with the project. The need therefore for the Centre and the State governments to work together to tap this resource. This would be a valuable addition that would help the NER to build a vibrant market economy that can participate on competitive terms in the ASEAN markets.

There are also opportunities for bilateral funding from countries such as Japan and South Korea for specific infrastructure projects in transportation, energy etc. These projects carry a certain amount of currency risk and are most cost effective if implemented quickly, and are intended for purposes where the donor technology or project implementation is much superior to any other available. It is however possible to minimise risks in such cases with careful project selection, detailed project planning and commitments at the state level with regard to land acquisition, utilities planning including shifting where necessary, un-interrupted logistics and security at project sites.

Leveraging Government support for Investment in infrastructure

Budgetary support is not the only option for the Government nor is it necessary that all such projects be implemented directly by public sector agencies. However, to overcome the delay and cost escalation cycle of projects in the NE, Central Government agencies need to make a beginning with proper turn key execution with financial and administrative accountability for poor performance. Government can also involve private sector in such projects through the Public-Private Partnership (PPP) mode with better designed Build Own Operate (BOT)/Build Own Operate Transfer (BOOT) modalities. However, as per the World Bank, few PPP projects are viable without some form of government technical or financial support. Infra projects in the NER, with their long implementation periods and attendant risks, are not likely to be financially viable for private investment, at least in the initial stages. Yet it is important to work towards more efficient and sustainable arrangements for financing and implementing projects.

Efficient financing of PPP projects involves government support in many ways to ensure that the government bears risks which it can manage better than private investors and to supplement projects which are economically desirable but not financially viable. There are many instruments for the Government to extend such support where such projects are envisaged on Public Private Partnership mode. This can be through, through specially tailored subsidies/grants, equity investment and/or debt. Government may also support by waiving for specified periods certain fees, costs and other payments which would otherwise have to be paid by the project company, provide tax holidays, provide financing for the project in the form of loans Debt/equity or viability gap funding, and where user charges are envisaged, subsidise tariffs to be paid by some or all consumers. In some cases, instead of funding, government may take on certain contingent liabilities, for example through guarantees, including guarantees of debt, exchange rates, convertibility of local currency, tariff collection, termination compensation etc.

Where the Government is extending support, it should also manage the provision of such support, insist on performance obligations with penalties and liquidated damages for non -performance. This will require a huge effort for gathering and analysing information, setting government policy and creating and enforcing appropriate incentives for those involved. Given the complexity of these tasks, it would be necessary for the Government, at both Central and State levels to create specialist teams for project management and to manage fiscal risk arising from contingent liabilities, in particular those associated with PPP.

Financial Intermediaries

The government could also consider support to mobilise private financing as such financing will not be available on its own for infrastructure projects. It can consider intermediation of debt from commercial financial markets, creating an intermediary sufficiently skilled and resourced to mitigate the risks that the financial markets associate with lending to infrastructure projects. Such intermediaries could be private financial institutions with commercially oriented private sector governance, having appropriately skilled and experienced staff and a credit position sufficiently strong to mobilise financing from the market.

There are examples of such intermediaries such as the Infrastructure Development Finance Company (IDFC) set up in 1997 by the Government of India to connect projects and financial institutions to financial markets and develop a long-term debt market. It offers loans, equity/quasi equity, advisory, asset management and syndication services and earns fee-based income from advisory services, loan syndication, and asset management. IDFC also develops projects through feasibility studies, financial structuring, managing the bidding process generating success/development fees from the winning bidders, or in some case monetising developed projects by transferring to suitable project implementing entities. India Infrastructure Finance Company Limited (IIFCL), is yet another wholly Government owned Company set up in 2006 for financing and development of infrastructure projects in the country.

Project Development Funds

The government may wish to develop a more or less independent project development fund (PDF), designed to provide funding to grantors for the cost of advisers and other project development requirements documentation, project selection, feasibility studies and design of the financial and commercial structure for the project, through to financial close and possibly thereafter, to ensure a properly implemented project.

The PDF may provide grant funding, require reimbursement and levy some charges and fees to create a revolving fund. Tamil Nadu Urban Development Fund (TNUDF) is an example of a state level financing intermediary is the Tamil Nadu Urban Development Fund (TNUDF), which attracts private finance for on-lending to local governments for infrastructure projects, and encourages private-sector co-financing of such projects.

Private Domestic and Foreign Investment

Both Domestic Private and Foreign Direct Investment (FDI) trigger entrepreneurship, enable induction of new technology, assist human capital formation. By creating a more competitive business environment and enhancing enterprise development, such investment contributes to higher economic growth and international trade integration. It is time avenues for private investment to be looked at seriously in the NER. By and large, such investment has come in trade, real estate, housing and commercial construction. In time it is likely in pharma, wellness, tourism, food processing, higher education and hospitals. Private investment in infrastructure has been negligible as there are several financial, implementational and operational risks involved with an absence of a framework for viable tariffs, tolls and user charges. For private investment to take place, the overall business environment has also to improve through improved connectivity and laws, courts and administration that do not act arbitrarily and protect legitimate business activity and interests. Getting NER ready for private investment would require major efforts in ensuring safety of persons and property and resolving the plethora of local rules and restrictions.

Empowering local bodies

Better accountability and financial discipline at the state and sub-state levels e.g. municipalities. Many cities in developing world are putting into place mechanisms to improve their credibility for securing finance by leveraging the financial strength of their urban bodies through Municipal bonds and Development funds. With a radical restructuring of the fiscal framework for the Urban Local Bodies (ULBs) so could the growing cities in India, including the North East.

The 74th Constitutional Amendment Act (CAA) provided a constitutional framework for decentralised functioning of ULBs. The Act also introduced the Twelfth Schedule in the Constitution, which lists18 subjects or functions which should be falling under the jurisdiction of municipalities, including urban planning. However, the Act has not provided them with any powers directly and has instead left it to the discretion of state governments to bestow ULBs with adequate powers, authority and responsibility to perform the functions entrusted to them by the Act. As in many other parts of the country, democratically elected urban local governments have been introduced in Assam Tripura and Mizoram. In other states such polls have not been held and the ULBs are managed directly by the state governments.

However, on other aspects of the CAA, many state governments have remained reluctant to transfer all the functions listed in the Twelfth Schedule of the 74th CAA to ULBs. Even with regards to the functions that have been transferred, necessary fiscal powers have not been devolved. As per the Act it is for the state legislature to authorise a municipality to levy, collect and appropriate such taxes, duties, tolls and fees etc or if such levies are collected by the state to assign them to respective municipalities through grants-in-aid from the Consolidated Fund of the State. It is also provided that the State Finance Commissions shall review the financial position of the Municipalities and make recommendations to improve their financial position. However, experience in the NER has shown that recommendations for financial devolution to municipalities have largely been ignored at the state level, as states themselves face financial difficulties. Therefore, the framework provided by the Act has not led to any substantive transfer of resources to ULBs to match their responsibilities. Further, the passage of the Goods and Services Tax (GST), effective from 1 July 2017 has generally made the financial position of ULBs even more precarious. While GST is silent on the financial share of ULBs it has subsumed many of the local taxes such as entry taxes, octroi etc. This has left many municipalities financially weaker than before and even more dependent on the states and practically carrying a large unfunded functional mandate. Therefore, the reform intended through the 74 Amendment has to be carried forward through further legislation so that a firm foundation is available for financial sustainability of urban governance.

However, leveraging parastatals like municipalities to raise resources to even complement those received through devolution is a distant but not unachievable goal. In fact, North east with its relatively small urban areas can provide an opportunity for experimentation before devolution is applied to much larger and politically complex civic bodies. Central Government can facilitate responsible and thorough auditing framework with statutory backing through technical assistance to be provided through the state government for specific projects at municipal level. Similar assistance can be provided for urban data management that would be the basis for a host of urban services. States can be incentivised towards greater functional and fiscal devolution by grants tied to progress made in such reform and metrics that measure actual devolution. The Act east Policy can provide a suitable platform for such reform.

Getting the Job Done

One of the factors retarding infrastructure development of the North East is the hesitant appreciation of the needs of the region, slow pace of implementation and cost escalation of all projects, much to the annoyance of the local public and loss of credibility with international donors and financial institutions and where the projects are trans-national, amongst the neighbouring partners. As a result, there is growing popularity of initiatives like the BRI of China (despite its attendant long-term costs). Very often the story of the institutional and infrastructural implementational architecture is that of 'too little, too late'.

While the financial arrangements made to finance development in the NER in the last half century have served the region well, the requirement is likely to be much more if a positive engagement with ASEAN is to be sustained as the levels of infrastructure, public and business facilities and human development in that region is at a much higher level. Given multifarious demands on Central Government resources, continued budgetary support for the NE projects may not be sustainable after some time. Therefore, it would be necessary to prepare and empower the region to mobilise resources, to fully meet its revenue expenditure and infra investment at least partially, on its own steam. This will require a sea change in the governance and indeed in all policies and ways of doing things. The financial and technical capacity of the administration will have to be built up, along with suitable checks and balances and accountability, to carry out a complex process of developing, competitive awarding, financing and monitoring of projects with incentives for good performance and disincentives for delays and poor quality of work. The task is difficult but not impossible as the experience in many developing, and indeed even in ASEAN countries has shown.

Part III

Chapter12

Strategic Interplay- Economic Development, National Security and International Engagement

(For the North Eastern region to play a significant part in India's Act East Policy, to the extent it encompasses engagement with South East Asia, will require a confluence of development initiatives and strategic thinking. The experience gained through past initiatives needs to be sustained and leveraged, taking into account the dynamically evolving situation in South East Asia.)

The cultural connect and geographical proximity of India's NE Region to the SE Asian Region would definitely help build India's comprehensive national power in South East Asia in a manner that is beneficial and acceptable to the countries in the region. However, to engage meaningfully with the South East Asian Region and to overcome challenges of internal security and international engagement in a rapidly changing geo-political environment, it would be necessary to overcome the narratives of the past, which have dwelt largely on tribal and local identities and look towards the possibilities of the future. While building upon local strengths, it must facilitate mutually beneficial economic growth that enables widespread gainful employment, rising incomes and standards of living of the people of the region as a whole.

Ensuring good governance, building up human capital, establishing and operating stable and credible institutions, maintaining a credibly fair and efficient criminal administrative system and responsive machinery for ensuring law and order and public safety within the entire NE Region are critical facilitators for future growth. These would also be the foundations of the strategic aim of national and international economic and trade relations and help India build long-term friendly relationships with the ASEAN region.

To match up to a positive interaction with SE Asia, the strategy for economic development of the North Eastern Region needs to invest heavily in connectivity, encourage innovation and establish technology-based systems for production, trade and commerce. Such development, however, would require many arrangements to meet the complexities of regional trade exchanges. While acting as interface of trade with SE Asian Region, it has to plug into and bring value into supply chains for the ASEAN region as well as its immediate neighbourhood comprising Bangladesh, Nepal and Bhutan. The task is made all the more challenging by the post pandemic situation, the ongoing war in Ukraine and the consequent emergence of the New Cold War.

Building International Interfaces

The entire Eastern Region of the Indian Subcontinent, including the Indian North East, not very long ago, was interconnected and interdependent. It underwent a partition in 1947 creating international boundaries across a region that had been a single entity for millennia. East Pakistan, now Bangladesh, is a new 20th century nation state interposed between the NER and rest of India, but for a narrow land corridor. It shares borders with India, stretching almost 4096 km of which 1,880 kms are with north-eastern states of India, namely Assam, Meghalaya, Tripura, and Mizoram and the rest is with West Bengal. The legacy of the Partition in terms of communal, linguistic and ethnic conflict, subsequent wars and sensitivities over migration have resulted in a new reality, with challenging imperatives for international relations across borders.

Soon after the Partition, it was perceived in some quarters that the fractured nature of Eastern/Northeastern India needed to be overcome by new arrangements. However, bitter memories of the Partition, the sub-continental conflicts which took place post de-colonisation and in the background of the Cold War resulted in these initiatives losing steam. Yet the concept of sub-continental economic engagement remained. The need now is to look forward and find ways to overcoming the obstacles posed by the legacies of the past to build cooperation and shared prosperity beyond the Indian sub-continent over the extended Southeast Asian Region.

SAARC, SAPTA and SAFTA

Effort to promote trade with a view to enable economic growth, social progress and cultural development within the South Asian region had been discussed in several international conferences as early as the 1950s. However formal efforts to establish a grouping of South Asian countries started in 1979 and culminated with the establishment of the South Asian

Association for Regional Cooperation (SAARC) in 1985[1] when the Heads of State of Bangladesh, Bhutan, India, Maldives, Nepal, Pakistan and Sri Lanka formally adopted the charter. Afghanistan joined as the 8th member of SAARC in 2007. The focus of SAARC, however, was on the South Asian Region rather than SE Asia. Still, the agreements reached, to the extent they involved India, Bangladesh and Bhutan, recognised the need for economic cooperation in the immediate vicinity of the NE Region and laid the groundwork for future groupings.

Agreement on SAARC Preferential Trading Arrangement (SAPTA)[2] was signed in Dhaka on 11 April 1993 and provided for the adoption of various instruments of trade liberalisation on a preferential basis amongst the SAARC members. In 2004, SAARC the South Asian Free Trade Area (SAFTA)[3] was established with a view to promoting and enhancing mutual trade and economic cooperation among the contracting States. The SAFTA Agreement was an elaborate one and provided for broad ranging trade facilitation measures such as Trade Liberalisation Programme, mutually accepted Rules of Origin, Institutional Arrangements, Consultations and Dispute Settlement Procedures etc.

SAARC had a promising start and resulted in several institutions and organisations with South Asian Regional reach[4]. However, the Kargil conflict between India and Pakistan in 1998, followed by several attacks by terrorist organisations based in Pakistan in different parts of India, resulted in relations between India and Pakistan deteriorating, bringing diplomatic cooperation and trade between the two largest members of SAARC practically to halt. In any case Pakistan did not extend MFN status to India, leaving SAFTA in doldrums. All these developments stymied attempts to build SAARC as a viable regional grouping. In the second decade of the 21st Century, China launched its China-Pakistan Economic Corridor (CPEC) and the Belt and Road Initiative, leading to Pakistan and some other SAARC member countries turning towards investments through expensive Chinese loans for large infrastructure projects rather than economic development through regional trade. Gradually, economic relations of many SAARC countries with China soon outpaced trade within the SAARC region. Eventually this had its shadow on the SAARC as a grouping of nations with a common vision and economic interest. As SAARC declined, a search was necessitated for other mechanisms to promote trade in the South Asian Region. However, SAARC continues as an important platform for South Asia and is supported by many multilateral institutions. There is a continuing international effort to sustain the SAARC concept in the hope that eventually, the need for regional cooperation would overcome local differences. Meanwhile, many ideas and initiatives launched through SAARC formed the basis of cooperation in new sub-groupings that followed.

BBIN

The Bangladesh, Bhutan, India, Nepal (BBIN) Initiative came up as a sub-regional architecture of countries in Eastern South Asia. It originated in May 1996, when India, Nepal, Bhutan and Bangladesh agreed to set up a sub-regional body (comprising of these four nations) as the South Asian Growth Quadrangle (SAGQ). Later in 1997, in the Malé summit, it was agreed to co-ordinate efforts catered to the special individual needs of three or more Member States, and formalised procedures focused on the subcontinent's north east to develop intra-regional trade and investment, tourism, communication, and energy resources.

BBIN comprises official representation of member states to formulate, implement and review quadrilateral agreements across areas such as water resources management, connectivity of power, transport, and infrastructure. It focused on specific projects especially for road and rail transportation and power (electricity) trading. Over years its objectives expanded to incorporate land and port connectivity. In May 1996 the participating countries approved a sub-regional body of Nepal, Bhutan, north east India and Bangladesh as the South Asian Growth Quadrangle (SAGQ). Later, when Asian Development Bank was approached for funding of BBIN projects, it led to formulation of the ambitious South Asia Sub Regional Economic Cooperation (SASEC) Program. It was envisaged to link West Bengal and North Eastern states through Bangladesh by rail, highway and maritime corridors, alongside north–south transport routes that spanned Nepal, Bhutan and Indian hill states to northern Bay of Bengal ports. These grids were to bridge other regions throughout member states and eastwards beyond BBIN. The ADB involvement expanded the BBIN initiative with accession of Maldives and Sri Lanka to SASEC in March 2014. This made the grouping unwieldy and pushed the originally envisaged quadripartite integration on the back burner. As it was, the SASEC program remained a non-starter.

Eventually, renewed focus by India and several rounds of informal discussions led to renewed consensus on the original BBIN initiative. Initially India had proposed a SAARC Motor Vehicle Agreement during the 18th SAARC summit in Kathmandu in November 2014. Due to objections from Pakistan, an agreement could not be reached. India instead pursued a similar motor vehicle agreement with the BBIN. The BBIN Motor Vehicles Agreement (MVA) was finally signed on 15 June 2015 at the BBIN transport ministers meeting in Thimphu, Bhutan. The MVA once implemented will facilitate seamless cross border movement of trucks with less regulatory and paperwork requirements without the need for trans-shipment of goods at the border. World Bank has observed that these measures could bestow enormous benefits on the countries of the sub-region. As per the World Bank, at present a plethora of documents and approvals are required to trade between India and Bangladesh. Repeated submission of documents to authorities leads to unnecessary and long delays which add to the costs. Under the MVA, however, a truck traveling from Agartala in India's north east to Kolkata port will take 65 percent less time and be 68 percent cheaper. In Bangladesh, for instance, seamless connectivity with India could raise national income by as much as 17 per cent, while India would gain by 8 per cent. All BBIN partners can be expected to see similar results, spurring robust, resilient, and sustainable growth across the region.

The BBIN MVA has been ratified by Bangladesh, India and Nepal. Bhutan did not ratify it but requested other members to proceed with the agreement without Bhutan. Efforts are ongoing to secure full participation of Bhutan. Meanwhile, an existing bilateral agreement between Bhutan and India permits seamless vehicle movement between the two countries.

BBIN has endured a phase of prickly relations between India and Nepal. However, having seen the economic disasters shaping up in Pakistan and Sri Lanka, Nepal is wary of the "costly borrowings" route to development and is more supportive of sub-regional arrangements. While maintaining equidistance from India and China, Nepal, of late has also opened up to financial assistance from the US and India for infrastructural projects. While Bhutan is still hesitant in allowing sub-regional open access, it is not playing the spoiler for the MVA initiative. Cost advantages of trade facilitation would eventually provide a compelling argument for participation while use of technology can ensure adequate supervision regarding movement of goods and persons. Recognising this, a meeting of three countries on the BBIN Motor Vehicles Agreement (MVA) on March 7-8, 2022 in New Delhi, where Bhutan participated as an observer, decided to proceed with the plan to operate the Kakarvitta-Kolkata-Dhaka or Biratnagar-Kolkata or both the routes in the next six months.

Meanwhile several other BBIN initiatives are progressing in parallel. Bangladesh has confirmed Bandwidth to Bhutan for the Third Internet Gateway through Bangladesh territory at a special low tariff. The deal offered by Bangladesh will come into effect once an MoU is signed between competent authorities in Bhutan and Bangladesh Submarine Cable Company Ltd. (BSCCL). This would enable IT industry to develop in Bhutan. This also opens the door to investment opportunity for Indian IT companies in digital infrastructure which would develop platforms for better data infrastructure, leading to a seamless flow of data and information, automated customs processing systems, electronic cargo tracking and risk management systems etc. This digital infrastructure would contribute to trade and multi-modal connectivity in the region as better data infrastructure will provide traceability through improved shipment visibility and enhance the safety and security of the cargo including Single Window systems,

Other BBIN initiatives include rail links with Bangladesh and Nepal, opening of ports of Chattogram and Mangla for the shipment of products to and from India such as organic food, silk, crude oil, fish and food grains etc. India has also been steadily been pushing for enhancing close cooperation in developing Multi-modal transport connectivity within India's neighbourhood.

BBIN has the potential of transforming India's NER from a landlocked to a land-linked region with the Eastern Neighbourhood. Well integrated development of BBIN would provide a strong spring board for trade with ASEAN, who in turn would find economic depth for their trade and investment initiatives. The task ahead would be to transform BBIN physical connectivity into wide ranging economic cooperation through business ventures and exchanges. There is also potential for expanding the cooperation and to more regional joint projects including for addressing climate change and enabling disaster management.

BIMSTEC

The initiative to establish Bangladesh-India-Sri Lanka-Thailand Economic Cooperation (BIST-EC) was initially taken by Thailand in 1994 to explore economic cooperation on a sub-regional basis involving contiguous countries of South East & South Asia grouped around the Bay of Bengal. Myanmar was admitted in December, 1997 and the initiative was renamed as Bay of Bengal Initiative for Multi-Sectoral Technical and Economic Cooperation (BIMSTEC). Later, in 2004, Bhutan and Nepal also joined.

The initiative involves 5 members of SAARC (India, Bangladesh, Bhutan, Nepal & Sri Lanka) and 2 members of ASEAN (Thailand, Myanmar).

BIMSTEC is visualised as a 'bridging link' between two major regional groupings i.e. ASEAN and SAARC. BIMSTEC member countries agreed to establish the BIMSTEC Free Trade Area Framework Agreement in order to stimulate trade and investment in the parties, and attract outsiders to trade with and invest in BIMSTEC. A Trade Negotiating Committee (TNC) was in 2004. TNC's negotiation area covers trade in goods and services, investment, economic cooperation, as well as trade facilitations and also technical assistance for LDCs in BIMSTEC. It was agreed that once negotiation on trade in goods is completed, the TNC would then proceed with negotiation on trade in services and investment. Meanwhile 2 Working Groups were setup to work on technical aspects of Trade in Goods, namely the Working Group on the Rules of Origin (WG-RoO) and the Working Group on the Dispute Settlement Mechanism (WG-DSM).

The BIMSTEC Trade Negotiating Committee (TNC) has held 19 sessions of negotiations. The negotiations are spread over the areas of (i) tariff concessions on trade in goods, (ii) customs cooperation, (iii) services and (iv) investments. However, after twenty-three years of its journey, the Bay of Bengal Initiative for Multi-Sectoral Technical and Economic Cooperation (BIMSTEC) still suffers from a sluggish pace of growth.

BIMSTEC started out as an important element in India's "Act East" strategy and expected to add a new dimension to India's economic cooperation with South East Asian countries. Observers have, however, noted a lack of a common strategic vision among BIMSTEC members. BIMSTEC at present serves more as a forum for the exchange of ideas among the countries which participate in its summits and, from a strategic point of view, engage in limited projects and activities on areas such as disaster management.

Meanwhile China has pushed large, expensive loans for various infrastructure in BIMSTEC countries. Now some BIMSTEC members are facing severe internal economic crises on account of their ability to service such loans. The current economic crisis in Sri Lanka caused by indiscriminate borrowings from China for costly infrastructure projects with doubtful viability has completely crippled its economy and created serious internal disruption. While India is stepping in with essential supplies and financial assistance to enable Sri Lanka to buy and import food and some essential goods there is no further support coming forth from China, the principal lender to Sri Lanka. Sri Lanka has not been able to negotiate moratoriums, waivers, debt restructuring in any form or direct financial aid. The revival of Sri Lankan economy appears to be beyond the scope of any bilateral aid, and will now require major support from various international organisations like WB/ IMF etc. to be saved from imploding.

On the other hand, the military coup in Myanmar has thrown the country into an era of turmoil and instability. Myanmar was also a recipient of Chinese loans but the massive exploitation and expropriation of its natural resources by China led to resistance developing in that country against Chinese financial dominance. Now with the military takeover and application of sanctions following the brutal suppression of the pro-democracy movement, its economy is in shambles and it is very doubtful if the military regime of Myanmar will have enough diplomatic and economic credibility to attract and sustain foreign investment or meaningfully participate in any trade arrangement. While Thailand, the originator of this concept, maintains its interest in expanding its foot print in the Western part of South East Asia, is likely to be wary of the situation in Myanmar. In any case it is unlikely that it will be able to sustain any initiatives beyond ASEAN on its own.

There are other constraints also facing the BIMSTEC strategy. As events have evolved, Thailand and Myanmar continue to be "economically and strategically closer to China". Meanwhile, Nepal, Bhutan, Sri Lanka and Bangladesh also have extensive economic engagement with China and would prefer to balance their engagement with India and China, without offending either.

Despite various constraints it might still be relevant to keep the BIMSTEC concept diplomatically alive. This would depend largely on Indian support. As things stand, it is doubtful if the participating nations can reach and operationalise any major trade or infrastructure initiative. Still, a fresh beginning could be made with small cooperation initiatives. The establishment of international cooperation and trade links around the Bay of Bengal region would complement the initiatives to provide interlinkages and open up access to the sea through BBIN. As all the members of the BIMSTEC group gradually return to a "neighbourhood first" approach, there is hope of future revival and engagement between South and South East Asian regions.

ASEAN

Ever since the enunciation of the Look East Policy in 1991 and its development into Act East Policy in 2015, India's engagement with ASEAN has been going from strength to strength, with India graduating from being ASEAN Sectoral Dialogue Partner in 1992 to a Summit-level Partner in 2002.

Trade relations have continued to expand between India and ASEAN despite the East Asian crisis of 1997-98 and the global financial crisis of 2008-09. In fact, the free trade in goods agreement was signed between India and ASEAN in 2009 when the world was still struggling with sub-prime crisis. The Free Trade in Goods Agreement facilitated the development of supply chains and production networks in many products such as electronics and automobiles, including vehicle and component manufacturing.

Following the Indo-ASEAN Summit in 2012 the India- ASEAN engagement was elevated to one of a strategic partnership and a dialogue was initiated on investment and trade in Services. In 2014, with a view to speeding up the engagement India renamed its Look East Policy as the Act East Policy. The ASEAN India Agreement on Investment and the ASEAN India Agreement on Trade in Services were both finalised and signed in 2015

India has engaged with ASEAN at both regional and sub-regional levels by signing economic cooperation agreements with its different members. Bilateral agreements with various other members such as Thailand, Singapore, and Malaysia have also been signed, all of them aimed at deepening economic integration with the region.

The value of trade between India and the ASEAN region had grown from US $ 64.3 billion in 2016 to US $ 96.8 Bn in 2019. It dipped during the Pandemic to US $ 78.9 billion in fiscal year 2021. Earlier, between 1995 and 2016, trade between India and ASEAN had grown at a compound average growth rate (CAGR) of about 11.9 percent.

The India ASEAN cooperation has also been buttressed by several projects and funds such as the ASEAN-India Cooperation Fund; ASEAN-India S&T Development Fund (AISTDF); ASEAN-India Green Fund: ASEAN-India Projects: India has also been cooperating with ASEAN by way of implementation of various projects in the fields of Agriculture, Science & Technology, Space, Environment & Climate Change, Human Resource Development, Capacity Building, New and Renewable Energy, Tourism, People-to-People contacts and Connectivity etc.

India's engagement with ASEAN has been growing steadily, disruption caused by COVID notwithstanding. For one, as India's vaccination programme reaches practically universal coverage and credibility of

Chinese and Russian vaccines declines, it is possible for India to extend support to ASEAN countries through its vast and state of the art pharma manufacturing capacity. Meanwhile the world is finally emerging from the debilitating effects of the Pandemic. With milder strains of the virus dominating, many countries have abandoned zero-covid and lockdown-oriented approach. Trade and travel having opened up, India is well positioned to provide a wide range of services to the region.

Separately events in other parts of the world are equally casting their shadow over the ASEAN region. The war in Ukraine has given a totally new and dangerous perspective to claims made by China, the local superpower, over territorial disputes with some ASEAN countries. Groupings such as the QUAD have found meaning in context of the threat to security in the Asia-Pacific region. This has led to cooperation in various other spheres as well such as trade, as witnessed by the recent Indo -Australian Trade Pact and growing investment in India by Japan and South Korea. Meanwhile recent financial woes of Pakistan and Sri Lanka have rung warning bells in some ASEAN economies that were in the process of becoming Chinese dependencies, encouraging to diversify their trade and economic engagement. It appears that while ASEAN countries would continue their engagement with China, they would like to counter-balance it and would welcome economic cooperation that is mutually beneficial and non-threatening manner.

Border Trade

Border trade, as it has evolved post redrawing of the national boundaries in the Region, is "over-land trade" by way of "exchange of commodities" from a bilaterally agreed list by people living along both sides of the international border. Trade with Bangladesh and Bhutan takes place under a Free Trade Agreement (SAFTA), through Land Customs Stations (LCSs) situated on the Bangladesh and Bhutan border while separate Border Trade Agreements have been entered into with China and Myanmar.

India's North East region's documented border trade with its neighbouring countries is relatively quite small though there is likelihood of informal trade taking place. However, border trade is beneficial to the wellbeing of people living in the border regions and with some liberalisation and facilitation can grow further. Bangladesh is India's most important border trading partner accounting for 87 per cent of the border trade followed by Bhutan with a share of 11 per cent. The others account for only 1 per cent

Bangladesh

In terms of its economic impact, while the Partition seriously disrupted the formal economic life of India's eastern region, informal links across the new borders continued in the form of informal border trade. This has manifested itself in the form of border bazaars (Haats). Such Haats provide the much-needed forum for exchange of surplus local produce and create many local livelihood opportunities. Local people and state governments have long realised the value oof such trade and have moved repeatedly to allow it greater freedom. As yet only four Border Haats are in operation, two in Tripura and two in Meghalaya. After a long dialogue facilitated by improving relations between India and Bangladesh, the two governments have entered into an MOU to set up such Haats at six additional locations.

Even though a small start, the recognition of the value of border trade is a welcome development. However, there is a need to liberalise this regime further. For instance, upper limits of purchases at such Haats and restrictions on the range and quantities of commodities to be traded need to be relaxed along with the 5 km restriction for participants. There is also no logic for banning sale of local handicraft items.

There is also a need to put into place appropriate infrastructure that provides access from both sides, basic amenities including shelter, gender sensitive toilets and clean drinking water as well as arrangements for shelter and storage of commodities. Both countries need to enter into protocols that enable the Indian Border Security Force and the Bangladesh Border Guards to better monitor safety and security to participants.

India Myanmar

Myanmar would be a key player in any Indian strategy leverage its North Eastern Region to strengthen trade, investment and other forms of economic cooperation with ASEAN. India shares a 1643 km long border in four northeastern states – Arunachal Pradesh, Nagaland, Manipur, and Mizoram - with Sagaing and Rakhine provinces of Myanmar. This geographical proximity provides an opportunity for the north-eastern states of India to build on their strong historical sociocultural and economic linkages with Myanmar and access economic opportunities and markets in the east.

Border trade constitutes an important part of Myanmar's overall trade with its neighbours. In 2017-18, Myanmar's border trade was US$ 8.4 billion, being 46 per cent of its total bilateral trade with its neighbours. China is

Myanmar's most important border trading partner, accounting for 87 per cent of Myanmar's border trade while Thailand accounted for 19 per cent. India accounts for only 1 percent of Myanmar's border trade[11].

For permitting locally produced commodities to be traded as per prevailing customary practices on both sides of the India-Myanmar border, an agreement on border trade between India and Myanmar was signed on 21 January, 1994 and operationalised on 12 April, 1995.

India-Myanmar bilateral trade has grown from US$ 994.45 million in 2007-08 to US$ 1.6 billion in 2017-18, an approximate increase of 61 per cent. However, in 2017-18, there was a significant decline of 26 per cent in India Myanmar trade from the previous year. The key reason for the decline in imports from Myanmar has been the import restrictions on certain agricultural commodities such as peas and lentils levied by India.

Historically India has adopted a very restrictive border-trade policy framework with Myanmar, with trade being permitted only in a limited number (62) of locally produced items through barter. In December 2015, however, there was a shift from "Barter Trade" to "Normal Trade" [12] and along with a greater emphasis on Normal Trade as compared to Border Trade[13].

However, a closer study of the Border trade pattern between India and Myanmar reveals that border trade is not really a subset of bilateral trade between India and Myanmar[14]. While no reliable estimates of border trade are available, according to some sources, border trade including the unofficial trade was actually much more than the overall official bilateral trade between the two countries. The composition of overall bilateral trade between India and Myanmar is different from the composition of border trade, with the latter including a fair amount of third country goods e.g., from China and Thailand. Meanwhile there is also confusion regarding the allowable items of border trade subsequent to switch to normal trade.

Border Trade - the Future

Border trade, though small in financial terms[15], is a very good avenue for establishing cooperation and trust between people on both sides of the border and reviving age-old ties that existed before the South Asian Sub-continent was torn apart. It also tests and points out requirements for further improvement and facilitation in terms of trade, transit of goods and persons, security monitoring, currency exchange, banking, credit and financial settlements etc. As it makes its impact on local employment and trade grows in physical and financial terms, infrastructure and institutions, along with necessary organisation follow, leveraging it further.

Allowed to take its course and facilitated along the way, border trade opens up the gateway for much wider normal trade between the countries and may eventually be subsumed in it. There are a large number of projects planned for interconnection of roads, railways, waterway networks between India and neighbouring countries, particularly Bangladesh and Myanmar. The geographical and economic rationale for these projects could be founded on the requirements of border trade. Incremental approach towards building trade facilitators would build far more enduring links than big-bang large mega projects (witness their failure in Sri Lanka). These would eventually grow, provided they are sustained with continued financial, institutional and technological support as well as diplomatic commitment through the ups and downs of political upheavals in the participating countries.

Global Turbulence and Neighbourhood First

SAARC revisited

The last two decades have seen a markedly low interest in SAARC on the part of South Asian nations. A major cause has been the intense animosity between India and Pakistan which prevented agreement being reached on any subject. India has also been insisting on financial and diplomatic isolation of Pakistan on account of its support to terrorist activities in India and in 2016, in protest, even refused to attend the SAARC summit scheduled in Pakistan. Meanwhile Sri Lanka and Nepal turned towards China for loans to meet their development plans, which China was more than happy to provide to the extent that such borrowings caused a serious debt crisis in both the countries. As a result, South Asia is today one of the least integrated regions in the world with intra-regional trade at barely 5% of total South Asian trade, compared to 25% of intra-regional trade in the ASEAN region. According to a Brookings India study, most South Asian nations are now largely dependent on China for imports despite geographical proximity to India. However, the economic meltdown in Sri Lanka and the growing threat of an economic crisis in Pakistan and Nepal, both in the process of becoming Chinese dependencies, have forced South Asian countries to re-evaluate their options.

Meanwhile India's political interest in SAARC has also dipped significantly. With SAARC receding into the background, India focused on broader security issues through the Indo Pacific security groupings such as QUAD and bilateral trade agreements with Australia and Japan. Meanwhile India has started investing in other sub- regional instruments, such as BBIN/ BIMSTEC. However, a fresh effort was made in March 2022 to get SAARC nations together through a video conference of SAARC leaders, where Pakistan was also represented. The Conference organised by India, welcomed Prime Minister Modi's proposal for an emergency fund with India's contribution of $10 million for dealing with the crisis caused by the Pandemic. The leaders of SAARC also agreed not only to pool their best practices, share their experiences and coordinate their efforts to work together in fighting the virus, but also to mitigate its long-term economic and social consequences. However cross border terrorist incidents continue to bedevil Indo-Pak relations.

Like ASEAN, SAARC region can benefit from higher intra-SAARC investment flows. There's a need to resuscitate the negotiations on a SAARC investment treaty, pending since 2007. However, the road to revival continues to be uncertain and thorny.

COVID -19: The global COVID-19 coronavirus pandemic has already had a severe adverse impact on the global economy. While the pandemic is receding, its impact, it appears, will continue for some more time to come. 2021 estimates pointed to a to a global GDP loss of 3.4 percent, or based on 2020 global GDP of $ 84.54 trillion in 2020 with almost $ 2.87 trillion of lost economic output. Industries such as travel, tourism, airlines, hospitality etc were badly hit as many countries placed restrictions on travel. Lockdowns imposed to slow down the spread of virus disrupted supply chains and industrial production with consequent loss of employment and demand compression. Government resources were diverted to provide food and income support to low-income population groups as well as small and medium businesses. At the same time major investments had to be channelled to launch and sustain research and production of vaccines followed by vaccination campaigns to cover entire national populations. The COVID virus mutated and new variants caused successive waves of infection that carried the mayhem started in early 2020 well into 2022. Even today many countries are reporting fresh infections though the severity of the virus mutants appears to have reduced. Eventually re-opening of industrial activity, travel and movement, e-commerce, food retail, IT, and the healthcare industries have begun the revival of the global economy but the damage to all countries, including India, in terms of lost GDP has been huge.

In general, COVID forced countries to think national to ensure welfare of their respective populations. The Pandemic disrupted the globalised trade and economy to the extent that pre COVID globalised economic and trade engagements, such as through WTO, appear to have virtually dissolved. Many countries, especially with large economies sought to create production and supply arrangements within their borders to reduce dependence on extra- national sources. In India too this trend found expression through the *Atmanirbhar* (Self-sufficient) campaign. Even today serious debates are taking place on the restructuring of WTO to be relevant to post-Covid world. Meanwhile recurring waves of COVID infections in many countries, though milder than before, continue to disrupt supply chains leading to inflationary pressures.

The War in Ukraine: Barely had the global economy started recovering with removal of the pandemic related restrictions and revival of trade when it got a rude shock due to the war in Ukraine which started in Feb 2022. This resulted in economic sanctions being imposed on Russia, causing fresh disruption to global supply of food, fertiliser, metals, oil and gas etc. Economists fear that as war continues and sanctions become more extreme, this could lead to serious inflationary pressures globally with consequent damage to weaker and developing economies.

Noting that the disruption of grain exports from Ukraine could have serious adverse effect on the world's grain supply, World Food Program (WFP) Executive Director David Beasley stated in April 2022 that the shipping challenges following the war in Ukraine have already caused WFP to halve rations for millions around the world. As the war induced crisis persists, more cuts might have to take place.

Recently the World Bank Group president David Malpass, IMF managing director Kristalina Georgieva, WFP executive director David Beasley and WTO director-general Ngozi Okonjo-Iweala issued the following joint statement ahead of the Spring Meetings of the IMF and World Bank Group 2022:

> *"The world is shaken by compounding crises. The fallout of the war in Ukraine is adding to the ongoing COVID-19 pandemic that now enters its third year, while climate change and increased fragility and conflict pose persistent harm to people around the globe. Sharply higher prices for staples and supply shortages are increasing pressure on households worldwide and pushing millions more into poverty. The threat is highest for the poorest countries with a large share of consumption*

from food imports, but vulnerability is increasing rapidly in middle-income countries, which host the majority of the world's poor. World Bank estimates warn that for each one percentage point increase in food prices, 10 million people are thrown into extreme poverty worldwide."

"The rise in food prices is exacerbated by a dramatic increase in the cost of natural gas, a key ingredient of nitrogenous fertiliser. Surging fertiliser prices along with significant cuts in global supplies have important implications for food production in most countries, including major producers and exporters, who rely heavily on fertiliser imports. The increase in food prices and supply shocks can fuel social tensions in many of the affected countries, especially those that are already fragile or affected by conflict."

"We call on the international community to urgently support vulnerable countries through coordinated actions ranging from provision of emergency food supplies, financial support, increased agricultural production, and open trade....."

The turbulence in international relations due to the war in Ukraine and the resetting of the Global order with China and Russia drawing together on the one hand and unprecedented unity amongst NATO members as well as with US and the Western World (U.K., Canada, Australia etc.) on the other is bound to radically reorder the geo-politics and the global economy for a long time to come. The response of the Western World has so far been in terms of military aid to Ukraine and economic sanctions on Russia. These developments have already created conditions of a new cold war and threaten globalisation, world trade and economy, leaving no nation unaffected. As India emerges from the economic slowdown due to the Covid pandemic, the pressures imposed by opposing camps of nations are likely to affect growth negatively. India, due to its relations with both USA and Russia has adopted a neutral stance so far.

Regionalism and Neighbourhood First

In context of the global developments influenced by COVID 19 Pandemic and the Ukraine War, attention in India, as in some other parts of the world, is shifting again towards securing national interests in context of the disrupted global trade arrangements post Covid and now big power rivalry in the era of economic sanctions and the New Cold War. In this scenario, national perspectives and regional groupings have gained importance once again. The "Neighbourhood First" approach is seen as not only bolstering economic zones with short supply lines but also to secure immediate neighbourhoods against unpredictable security threats. As the global trade and exchange institutions continue to be disrupted, there is also a growing reliance on bilateral relations between likeminded countries.

While India will continue to partner QUAD and remain a player in the security arrangements for Asia-Pacific, there is a growing urgency to enable peace and stability in the country's own neighbourhood. In this context, given the difficulties and challenges involved in reviving SAARC, building up border trade and active engagement eastwards with formations like BBIN/BIMSTEC and ASEAN could play a very constructive role providing a joint survival strategy in uncertain times. The Indian approach over the last several decades has been based on regional multilateral agreements rather than "shock and awe" tactics based on aggressive unilateral action. This strategy yields results slowly but is far more effective as it recognises mutual interests on the basis of equality. Taken in the form of mutually beneficial, non-threatening cooperation, this would be a far more sustainable. In all these initiatives, to the extent they involve engagement with South East Asia, the NER would have a considerable role to play. The core of the future strategy needs to be to do all that it takes to enable NER to play this role.

Notes to Chapter 12

1. The South Asian Association for Regional Cooperation (SAARC) was established with the signing of the SAARC Charter in Dhaka on 8 December 1985. SAARC comprises of eight Member States: Afghanistan, Bangladesh, Bhutan, India, Maldives, Nepal, Pakistan and Sri Lanka. The Secretariat of the Association was set up in Kathmandu on 17 January 1987. For details see https://www.saarc-sec.org/

2. The Agreement on SAARC Preferential Trading Arrangement (SAPTA) envisaged the creation of a Preferential Trading Area among the seven member states of the SAARC, namely Bangladesh, Bhutan, India, Maldives, Nepal, Pakistan and Sri Lanka and was signed in Dhaka in April 1993. The intention was to promote and sustain mutual trade and economic cooperation within the SAARC region through the exchange of tariff concessions. It was agreed that SAPTA would be a stepping stone to higher levels of trade liberalisation and economic co-operation among the SAARC member countries. For details of the Agreement see https://apeda.gov.in/apedawebsite/COO/SAPTA.pdf

3. For details of the SAFTA agreement see https://commerce.gov.in/wp-content/uploads/2020/05/safta.pdf

4. SAARC has established new institutions such as SAARC Arbitration Council (SARCO), South Asian University (SAU), SAARC Development Fund (SDF) Secretariat and SAARC Regional Standards Organization (SARSO) which have mandates and structures different from the Regional Centres.

5. The BBIN Motor Vehicle Agreement permits member states to ply their vehicles in each other's territory for transportation of cargo and passengers, including third country transport and personal vehicles, on the basis of electronic permits. It was agreed that while border security arrangement between nations' borders would, remain cargo vehicles would be tracked electronically, permits issued online and sent electronically to all land ports. Vehicles would be fitted with an electronic seal that would alert regulators every time the container door is opened.

6   What will it take to connect the Bangladesh, Bhutan, India, Nepal (BBIN) sub-region?; Shomik Mehndiratta, Erik Nora; January 24, 2022; https://blogs.worldbank.org/endpovertyinsouthasia

7. A Boost to Sub-Regionalism in South Asia; Ramaswamy, Sridhar; (on the BBIN Motor Vehicle Agreement); The Diplomat ; 21 June, 2015n 2017-18,

8. BIMSTEC: Bay of Bengal Initiative on Multi Sectoral Cooperation, initially known as BIST-EC (Bangladesh-India-Sri Lanka-Thailand Economic Cooperation), BIMSTEC now comprises seven Member States; namely

Bangladesh, Bhutan, India, Myanmar, Nepal, Sri Lanka, Thailand. For details, https://bimstec.org/

9. Border Trade; Ministry of Development of North Eastern Region; https://mdoner.gov.in/border-trade

10. India and Myanmar signed a border trade agreement in 1994 and have two operational border trade points (Moreh-Tamu and Zowkhatar –Rhi on the 1643 km long border. A third border trade point is proposed to be opened at AvakhungPansat/Somrai. During the 3rd India-Myanmar Joint Trade Committee in October 2008, it was agreed that Border Trade at the existing points would be upgraded to Normal Trade so as to promote bilateral trade between the two countries; India Myanmar Relations, https://www.mea.gov.in/

11. ICRIER: India-Myanmar Border Trade; Working Paper 378; Nisha Taneja et al, June 2019; https://icrier.org/

12. The barter trade that was allowed as a sub-set of border trade between India and Myanmar was abolished by the RBI vide its circular no. RBI/2015-16/230 dated 05 November, 2015. It necessitates trade transactions at the border in permitted currencies in addition to taking recourse to the Asian Clearing Union.

13. As per the DGFT public notice no. 50 issued on 17 December, 2015 it has been decided that Border Trade at Moreh, Manipur would be upgraded to Normal Trade so as to promote bilateral trade between the two countries.

14. Enhancing India-Myanmar Border Trade; Policy and Implementation Measures: Dr. Ram Upendra Das, Department of Commerce Ministry of Commerce and Industry, Government of India.

15. Border Trade; Ministry of Development of North Eastern Region; https: // mdoner.gov.in /border-trade

Chapter 13

Securing the North East

(Over a period of time, due to the continuous interplay of external and internal threats faced in the region, an elaborate security architecture was established in the region which contributed, along with various political initiatives, to bring peace to the region. Going forward, while economic development, good governance and political participation would be essential for the future of the region, this security architecture would hold the key to sustainability of various initiatives to enable economic development of the region and to build it up as a gateway to SE Asia and beyond.)

The troubled legacy of war, armed extremism and insurgency in the North East has required the state administrations and the local police forces to be supported by the Army, Paramilitary Forces and Central Armed Police Forces (CAPFs). In the initial decades following independence, the state administrations were often short of required personnel, weapons and equipment. Police stations were far flung and means of communication poor. In many situations the local police found itself out-gunned by armed extremists who had been given sophisticated weapons and extensive training to use them by their foreign sponsors. Normal policing could hardly cope with the intense, guerrilla tactics involving sudden armed attacks on lightly armed police personnel or on thinly guarded public installations. Initially the Army, and para-military forces such as Assam Rifles had to move in to restore the balance. Gradually the resources and capacities of the local police forces were built supported by an elaborate security structure involving the Army, Central Armed Police Forces including CRPF, BSF etc

As insurgency surfaced in the NER in the 1950s, it was soon realised that mere induction of the Army and Para Military into the region was not enough. The situation was also beyond normal policing and criminal justice administration. Enabling the armed forces to act effectively against armed insurgency also required the enactment of special legislation to empower such forces. This came in the form of the Assam Disturbed Areas Act of 1955. The Armed Forces (Assam and Manipur) Special Powers Act, 1958, followed and was extended to almost all the States of the North East in the following decades. Gradually, with peace returning to the region, the Act is being withdrawn from several areas. However, it remains in force, to be extended over any area if the situation so requires.

Despite these measures, ever since independence, the Northeast has seen long periods of serious armed extremism and conflict. The Indian Army, along with Central Armed Police Forces (CAPFs), had been was called in repeatedly to deal with the situation. Several special army operations were carried out to destroy insurgent/ extremist bases and camps in the region. The 1990s also saw the emergence of special administrative arrangements in the form of Unified Command which brought the State administrations, the Army, paramilitary and CAPFs together. However, when enduring peace seemed within reach, North East erupted again, this time due to ethnic conflict in Manipur.

The Underpinning of Peace and Security

Recognition of the need to participate in governance and providing a political landscape to facilitate this has been the critical element for reconciliation in the region and is necessary for the effective functioning of the security super structure. The road has been long and arduous, stretching over many decades. Mistakes were also made. However, an inclusive approach, commitment to democratic values and dialogue eventually wins over guns and conflict.

The process of assimilation of the peoples of the North Eastern Region began with the establishment of new states from the territories earlier a part of the composite Assam State. Statehood to Nagaland in 1963, Meghalaya in 1972, full statehood to Mizoram and Arunachal Pradesh in 1986 and 1987 respectively (they became Union Territories in 1972) were all a part of this process. This reorganisation was followed by a turbulent phase. However, as the states of the region settled into their new identity, with elected governments changing at regular intervals, the region accepted the electoral route to political power over extremism and insurgency.

Reorganisation also took the reach and access of the state to the remotest corners and vice versa, also opened access of the people to governance structures at different levels. In 1960, the territories comprising Assam (then including the present-day states of Meghalaya, Nagaland and Mizoram) and NEFA had a total of 16 districts, 12 in Assam and 4 in NEFA.

Today, Meghalaya, Nagaland and Mizoram are separate states with 12, 13 and 11 districts respectively. The reorganised Assam state has 35 districts, Arunachal Pradesh (then NEFA) has 25. While the proliferation of states and districts have led to some jurisdictional issues, the administration is much closer to the ground. The local police network has expanded with corresponding increase in police stations. The district being the administrative unit for all development and beneficiary-oriented schemes, public articulation of local needs and access to Government benefits has improved.

The NE states are ruled by governments that are popularly elected through regular elections that are widely participated in. In fact, the voting percentage in state elections in the NE is uniformly high, averaging around 72-75% and going up to 80% in some cases. Elections to Village Panchayats and Urban Bodies are even more enthusiastically participated in. Being relatively small states, the accountability of elected representatives to the people is close and immediate. Inclusive democracy, has proved to be a critical underpinning of any process aimed at bringing peace to the region.

The Security Architecture

Army in the North East

The presence of the Indian Army in the North East[1] is not a recent phenomenon though its involvement in internal security duties became more elaborate post-independence. In 1920, after a number of reforms of the British Indian armed Forces the Eastern Command[2] was formed. The Command's territorial jurisdiction then extended over Delhi, United Provinces, Bengal, Bihar, Orissa and Assam. However, with the outbreak of the WW II, with Japanese invasion of Burma, in April 1942 the Command was designated as the Eastern Army and its Headquarters moved to Barrackpore in erstwhile Bengal province.

The task before the Command was to prosecute war effort during World War II and defend the British Indian territories against Japanese attack. This involved, in the first instance, securing the retreat of the Allied forces across Burma as the Japanese forces advanced and carrying out armed operations behind enemy lines in Burma. This was followed by reorganisation and military engagement to stop the Japanese advance at Imphal and Kohima, which was eventually done after long drawn and fierce battles. This was eventually followed by a campaign for re-conquest of Burma.

From March to August 1947, as a result of impending Partition, the Command formations were split between India and Pakistan. Only two divisions were left with the Indian Eastern Command. Maintenance of law and order became one of its major tasks in the newly independent India. In 1956, the Command was also made responsible for Counter Insurgency Operations against the Naga Insurgents.

The Eastern Command was engaged with defence against external aggression during the India –China War of 1962. This military engagement across the McMahon line, the boundary between India and China, constituted the eastern theatre of the war of the India -China war of 1962 and saw serious military action with the Indian Army facing reverses at high altitudes. The war ended suddenly after three weeks with unilateral ceasefire and withdrawal by the Chinese forces. However, the experience led to significant build-up of the Army and its capacities in the NE Region. This was accompanied by a concerted effort to improve connectivity with the region. So much so, over the decade that followed, Indian armed forces were able to sharply rebuff further attempted Chinese incursions across the Eastern border. This build-up has continued and the Indian Army developing capacities to operate in all terrains and securing country's international borders stretching East of Nepal to Myanmar from further external threats. The international border, with China however, remains unsettled and a potential threat, requiring Army/s deployment and attention at all times.

Again, in 1971, following disturbances and genocide in the then East Pakistan, the Eastern Command spearheaded military operations through a lightening advance through East Pakistan territory which led to the defeat and capitulation of the Pakistani forces located there leading to the surrender of 93000 regular Pakistani Army troops. This led to the independence and emergence of Bangladesh as a new nation in India's eastern neighbourhood.

In addition to external security, Eastern Command, now headquartered at Kolkata, has been tackling the internal security situation through its corps headquartered at Tezpur (Assam) and Dimapur (Nagaland), for the last 65 years in Nagaland, Mizoram, Manipur and Assam[3,4]. This has, of course, been an additional task for the Army over and above their principal task of securing the nation against external aggression. Internal security operations are also complex as they require the troops to operate largely in the grey zone where the action has to be measured and restrained, taking place as it is against Indian citizens. After dealing with insurgency in the Naga and Mizo Hills, during the period 1990-2005, the Army was again called to the aid of civil authorities. Through a series of swift actions described elsewhere in this narrative, the Army destroyed a number of insurgent bases in swift actions described elsewhere in this narrative, that broke the back of insurgent/extremist movements in the North east. As result of these operations the extremist cadres were largely forced to surrender with only a small number able to flee the country.

Army in the North East has operated under trying conditions, in diversion from its prime objective and training, using only a limited and light range of weapons against heavily armed extremists. Many soldiers have laid down their lives so that peace prevails in these troubled states. Yet the Army presence has convinced all elements, external or internal, of the determination of the Indian state to resolutely deal with any threat. Over time, the Indian army presence in the North East has expanded considerably due to continuing external threat with improved infrastructure for mobility, modern weapons and support by the Indian Air force. Obviously, the principal task of the Indian Army in the region is to defend India's borders for which it has to continuously develop its tactics and technology and train its personnel to operate in diverse terrains ranging from high Himalayas to riverine areas and tropical forest covered hills and plains. In fact, with the gradually improving situation in the North East, it is planned to disengage the Army for internal security duties to allow them to concentrate on the external threat. All the same, the Indian Army continues to be on standby to back stop any effort to maintain internal security and provides critically important under-pinning of the security architecture of the NER

The Para Military Forces

Assam Rifles

Assam Rifles is the oldest armed force that has been continuously deployed over nearly 200 years to defend India's North East. Set up shortly after annexation of Assam after the Anglo-Burmese War in 1826, as a paramilitary police force, it was initially called the Cachar Levy[5] and comprised approximately seven hundred and fifty men. Formed as a police unit, its initial task was to protect British Indian settlements against assaults and depredations by local tribes as British presence continued to move deeper into the north eastern parts of their Indian Empire. Over time, this force was expanded and was given wider territorial role as Lushai Hills (present Mizoram) and Manipur came under British control. It was named the Assam Frontier Police in 1883, the Assam Military Police in

1891, renamed Eastern Bengal and Assam Military Police in 1913. Finally, in 1917, after its splendid performance in the First World War, it was given its current name – the Assam Rifles.

The Assam Rifles (and its predecessor units) served in a number of roles, conflicts and theatres including World War I in Europe and the Middle East. In World War II they served with distinction in Burma, fighting a number of rear-guard actions as the Allied forces retreated. It formed the famous Victor Force which carried out strikes behind Japanese lines. The force then joined up in the defence of the country's eastern borders against the Japanese invasion particularly in Naga Hills, fighting fiercely in the defence of Kohima. One of the Assam Rifles battalions (the 4th) even trained as airborne troops and was dropped near the Sittang River behind Japanese lines. Another Battalion, as part of Lushai Brigade was sent ahead into Burma of the rest of the force to organise resistance in the Chin Hills.

Following the end of the war, for some time, the five Assam Rifles battalions became part of the civil police under the Assam Inspector General of Police. After independence, however, the Indian government reorganised Assam Rifles as a paramilitary force with its own Director General.

The role of the Assam Rifles continued to evolve as it was called upon to assist in disaster management when in 1950 a devastating earthquake hit the Assam region. During the 1950s, in the face of growing tribal unrest and insurgency, the task of maintenance of law and order and countering insurgency also fell to the Assam Rifles. In fact, for a long time after independence, Assam Rifles was the first responder to deal with any disturbance in the Northeast beyond the control of local police. Later, when the Army was also called upon to assist in maintenance of Internal Security, the experience and knowledge of the region available with Assam Rifles proved invaluable to the army in conducting internal security tasks. The force was once again called to undertake a combat role when, during the 1962 Sino-Indian War when it was used to delay the advancing Chinese forces so that the Indian Army could re-establish its defence lines.

Prior to 1965, this force was under the Ministry of External Affairs who were looking after North Eastern Frontier Agency (NEFA) affairs. It was transferred to the Ministry of Home Affairs in 1965 when the latter took over this responsibility. Now, it functions under dual command structure - as a border guarding force under the Ministry of Home Affairs (MHA) and when engaged in internal security duties or in times of war, as a paramilitary force under the Indian Army (Ministry of Defence). The number of battalions under Assam Rifles has increased from 5 in 1947 to 46 today, with its own training and logistics centres. The rank of the force commander was also upgraded to that of Lieutenant General.

Since 2002, Assam Rifles has been guarding the Indo–Myanmar border. As mentioned earlier, this is a very complex border with population of same ethnicity living on both sides of the border. In addition, there is a 16 Km wide economic zone providing freedom of movement to people from either side. With political turmoil emerging in that country following the Military Coup, the task before this Force has become increasingly complex. The hold of the Central Government in Myanmar, particularly over the northern region, was tenuous at best. The recent coup that brought military rule in Myanmar has thrown the country into turmoil. Over the last half century or so, several ethnic armed groups and militias have existed in Myanmar but rising ethnic tensions in that country after the Coup seem to have given them a new lease of life. The proliferation of weapons and armed cadres across the border, all beyond the control of the central authority in Myanmar, combined with the die-hard Indian insurgents who have fled NER and taken refuge there, makes the situation extremely volatile. Again, post-coup, with international sanctions being clamped on Myanmar, the Military Junta, despite its reservations about China, has tended to rely heavily on that country for support. The tensions along India-China border, the growing rivalry between India and China in the Indian Ocean region, raises the potential of Myanmar as springboard for a hostile hybrid intervention in the North East.

The role of Assam Rifles in managing the Myanmar border is therefore critical to any economic engagement eastwards. However, given the special circumstances of the NER due to its geographical remoteness and neighbourhood comprising several countries almost completely surrounding it, there may be some merit in developing a special role for Assam Rifles in addition to its border guarding duties. At one level, it should be able to supplant the Army, who should be spared internal security duties to be able to concentrate on national defence imperatives. For this, it could be equipped with a higher level of weaponry and equipment, including an air and water wing, enabling it to deal with all militant situations including counter-insurgency.

Assam Rifles could also develop capability to carry out special operations in a range of situations in urban, rural, remote, riverine, forested, hilly and mountainous areas. For this it may be trained to operate drones and

Unmanned Aerial vehicles (UAVs) and equipped with suitable weaponry, equipment, vehicles, UAVs, helicopters and river craft[6].

The recruitment of personnel into Assam Rifles should reflect a pan-India complexion enabled by a mix drawn from the North East as well as from other parts of the country. The Force should have its recruitment, training and promotion policies with a view to developing its own cadre of officers. It should have its training schools for officers and other personnel. Its officers and staff should also have access to other training schools as well such as the Counter-insurgency School at Vairangte as well as those operated by Army, State Police administrations and CAPFs. Selected personnel may be deputed for training in these institutions so that the Force acquires a multi-disciplinary capability. Assam Rifles personnel should have promotional avenues opened to them to senior positions as in the case off some CAPFs.

For Assam Rifles to develop in the lines suggested, it may be necessary to address the dual control framework[7]. Since jurisdiction and control issues are often difficult to resolve, some innovative solutions would be required. Since its work would span both internal security and national defence functions, one option could be to create a special administrative arrangement under the central Department of Internal Security, with independent budgeting and drawing representation from the relevant ministries and organisations at different levels. The force may be allocated for special roles depending upon the situation (e.g., internal security or external aggression). Other options are also possible. However, a detailed and careful analysis of its future role and the best way of achieving it would help in ensuring that Assam Rifles, with its long and proud history is able to perform its duties in keeping national security to its full potential[8].

Border Security Force

The series of wars with Pakistan and China fought after independence highlighted the need for the Army to modernise its armaments, tactics and training to deal with external aggression over different terrains. A need was felt for a paramilitary force specifically designed to guard and manage international borders so that the Army could be relieved of the continuous attention and commitment of resources and manpower to manage extensive national borders in peacetime[9]. The force so constituted was the Border Security Force (BSF) and guards India's western border with Pakistan and the Indo-Bangla Border in the East. BSF has also played a very important role in Liberation of Bangladesh.

BSF is classed as a CAPF and such may be called upon, on the request of state governments to help in restoration law and order whenever deemed necessary. However, it is a border guarding force with its primary duty being management and continuous protection of the borders. Over time, BSF has grown in strength and capability to carry out supervision of India's borders. In the East these stretch over 4096 km of rivers, hills, paddy fields and forests spanning West Bengal and several NE States[10].

The Indo-Bangla border has been the source of migrations from Bangladesh into NER in India in the past, to the extent that such in-migration, particularly in Assam, sparked off serious Anti-Foreigners Agitation in that state. It was hoped that the Assam Accord of 1985 would put this issue to rest. However, a phase of extremism that morphed into a severe insurgent problem during the 1990s followed. Eventually even though the National Register of Citizens in Assam was updated and recompiled under the supervision of the Supreme Court, it has not been accepted in some quarters and remains an open issue. In this background, the responsibility of preventing further in migration into the North East from Bangladesh continues to fall on BSF.

Today BSF[11] has grown considerably. Currently this force has about 186 battalions with nearly 2,00,000 personnel. It is the only Central Armed Police force to have its own commando units, Water and Air Wings and an artillery regiment to support the BSF Battalions in their operations. In addition, three battalions of the BSF, located at Kolkata, Guwahati, and Patna, are also designated as the National Disaster Response Force (NDRF) which is a multi-disciplinary, multi-skilled, high-tech force for all types of disasters and can deploy to disasters by air, sea, and land. In addition to physical guarding of the border BSF also uses advanced technology for border management.

CRPF

The Central Reserve Police Force (CRPF)[12] is a highly trained central police force that can be deployed by the Central Government on the request of a State Government to assist its local police forces in maintaining law and order[13]. Over time, in addition to crowd control and quelling riots and communal disturbances, CRPF has acquired proficiency in counter insurgency operations and jungle warfare[14].

North Eastern Sector is one of the oldest Sectors of CRPF and came into existence in year 1976 as Sector-IV. It was re-named the North Eastern Sector in 1987. The Sector is well equipped and self-sufficient with its own infrastructure so that it can contribute forces immediately to assist the state police. It can also support rapid mass deployments, if needed, flown in from other parts of the country. The CRPF North Eastern Sector is spread out as three Group Centres located at Guwahati, Khatkhati and Silchar where it also operates its own Arms Workshops. It has its own Training Centre (ATC) at Khatkhati to train newly recruited personnel and its own intelligence wing. While CRPF strength can be augmented by induction from other parts of the country, the NE Sector of the Force has 11 operational Battalions including 1 CoBRA Bn (trained in anti-extremist jungle warfare). The CRPF North Eastern Sector has proved itself continuously in the areas of policing, dealing with extremism and anti-insurgent operations.

The CRPF constitutes a very important additional support to the state police forces and indeed it is now the first to be called in to support state police in any emergency. All the NE State administrations deeply value the presence of CRPF and speak highly of the professional competence of the units deployed in this area.

SSB

The Sashastra Seema Bal (SSB)[15] was established as Special Service Bureau in May 1963, in the aftermath of the Chinese aggression in 1962. Initially raised as a covert and disruptive force to counter any invading army, SSB Seema Bal came under aegis of the Ministry of Home Affairs in 2001. SSB was declared a Lead Intelligence Agency for Indo-Nepal (June 2001) and assigned the Indo-Nepal border. It also has 25 battalions of combat personnel spread out across Group Centres and arms training centres where it imparts training to volunteers for village protection units. It also has specialised training schools such as for High Altitude and Mountaineering. In the NER, the Bureau is now organised as a regular paramilitary force and deployed to guard the Indo Bhutan Border.

The Armed Forces Special Powers Act, 1958

Although the federal division of powers as per the Constitution placed the responsibility for maintaining law and order on the state governments, the difficult situation in the North East immediately following independence compelled Government of India to develop special arrangements. These came in the shape of legislation that allowed special powers to Indian armed forces to deal with armed insurgency in the region. These arrangements have continued till date resulting in long term engagement of the armed forces to maintain peace in the region along with local state governments.

The Assam government imposed the Assam Maintenance of Public Order (Autonomous District) Act in the Naga Hills in 1953 to deal with the growing insurgency in that area. The situation however worsened into a violent armed insurgency. This was followed by the Assam Disturbed Areas Act of 1955, providing a legal framework for the paramilitary forces and the armed state police to combat the rising insurgent violence. The insurgency however kept on spreading and consequently the Armed Forces (Assam and Manipur) Special Powers Ordinance 1958 was promulgated. It was replaced by the Armed Forces (Assam and Manipur) Special Powers Act, 1958 on 11 September 1958, later to be renamed the "Armed Forces (Special Powers) Act, 1958", (the AFSPA)[16].

The "Objects and Reasons'" appended to the Armed Forces (Assam and Manipur) Special Powers Bill stated that "Keeping in view the duty of the Union under Article 355 of the Constitution, interalia, to protect every State against internal disturbance, it is considered desirable that the Central government should also have power to declare areas as 'disturbed', to enable its armed forces to exercise the special powers". The Act, later AFSPA, therefore empowered only the Governors of the States and the Administrators of the Union Territories to declare areas in the concerned State or the Union Territory as 'disturbed'.

The AFSPA Act was amended in 1972 and the powers to declare an area as "disturbed" were conferred concurrently upon the Central government along with the States. Currently, the Union Home Ministry issues periodic "disturbed area" notification to extend AFSPA only for Nagaland and Arunachal Pradesh. The notification for Manipur and Assam is issued by the State governments. However, with passage of time, a convention of informal consultations with the State Government evolved. While the Central Government retains unilateral power to impose or revoke AFSPA in any state, now such a decision by the Centre is generally taken after receiving a recommendation from the state government. The territorial scope of this Act was expanded to cover the then states of Assam (including territories which later became the states of Nagaland, Mizoram and Meghalaya), Manipur and Tripura. In November 2016, Government of India has extended AFSPA to three districts of Arunachal Pradesh- Tirap, Changlang and Longding.

The draconian powers vested in the security forces under this law evoked several protests, particularly in Manipur. Gradually, as the 21st century dawned, a strong public movement emerged against this Act in Manipur and some other NE States, compelling judicial notice being taken of the excesses reported to have occurred in exercise of powers under this Act. Finally, after nearly 60 years, NE states are coming out of the purview of this Act (Tripura in 2015; Meghalaya in 2018, at the behest of the state governments). It has also been revoked in several districts of Assam (23 out of 32), and in some parts of Nagaland and Manipur in 2021. While there is demand in some quarters for repeal of this Act, it remains in force and may be extended to any area if the situation so requires.

The Unified Command

The concept of Unified Command, first tried out in J&K[17] in 1993 where it was set up under the chairmanship of the Chief Minister with Army commanders as advisers, was adapted to Assam in 1997 through a modified, three-tier structure comprising:

i) A Strategy Group to identify, develop consensus on and to coordinate policy responses to deal with a given situation, headed by the Chief Secretary (by the Chief Minister on occasions) and including the Army Corps commander (IV Corps), senior Civil Administration officials from the Home Department or other departments based on need, the State Police, Central and State intelligence agencies, Army and paramilitary and CPO command structure,

ii) An Operational Group[18] headed by the Commander IV Corps (Tezpur) and including the State police, Paramilitary organisations, CPOs and Central and state intelligence agencies;

iii) A District Level Coordination Committee under the chairmanship of the Deputy Commissioner including local police and the senior most army officer in-charge of the army personnel deployed in the district, to enable coordination and oversee implementation at local level.

The Unified Command experience in Assam has been very positive, leading to the state administration and the security forces working in a seamless manner with optimal utilisation of security forces and coordination at all levels. However, the Unified Command experience varies across the region. A Unified Command structure was also set up in Manipur in 2004.

However, with persistent conflict and violent Meitei-Kuki clashes in the state, another parallel structure, this time headed by the security adviser to Govt of Manipur (a retired DG of CRPF) was set up in 2023.

The security structure provided by the Central Government in the North East is very elaborate. Overall, the security architecture described above backstops the state police machinery depending upon need. However, as events in Manipur have shown, the Internal security challenges in the Northeast have not entirely vanished but have changed with time. How the nature of the internal security aspects has changed in the region is examined in more detail in the following chapters.

Notes to Chapter 13

1. Role of the Armed Forces in Internal Security: Time for Review; P K Mallick; Centre for Land Warfare Studies.

2. In 1895, the three Presidency armies of Bengal, Bombay, and Madras were abolished and their elements constituted into the Indian Army, divided into the Bengal, Bombay, Madras and Punjab Commands. Eventually, after some reorganisation, the Bengal Command became the Eastern Command in 1920, then with its summer headquarters in Nainital and winter headquarters in Lucknow. In 1942, during WW II, the command was re-designated as Eastern Army and its headquarters moved to Barrackpore from where it guided operations on the Burma Front. Its HQ was moved to Ranchi in 1947 and then to Lucknow in 1955. However, on 1 May 1963, post Sino-Indian War, Kolkata was made HQ of the Eastern Command. More on Eastern Command at https://indianarmy.nic.in/

3. Internal Security Scenario of North East India; Brig R Borthakur; Indian Defence Review; Issue Vol. 30.1 Jan-Mar 2015

4. Counter-Insurgency Operations in Northeast http://www. indiandefencereview.com

5. From 'Cachar Levy' to Assam Rifles: All You Need to Know About India's Oldest Paramilitary Force; News Desk, News18.com; Last Updated: NOVEMBER 13, 2021

6. For more on Assam Rifles; https://www.assamrifles.gov.in/

7. Tiwary, Deeptiman (7 December 2021). "Explained: Assam Rifles' dual control structure, and its role". The Indian Express.

8. Shakespear, Leslie. (1929). History of the Assam Rifles. Macmillan: London. Reprinted in 1977 by Firma.

9. The Border Security Force (BSF) is India's border guarding organisation at its borders with Pakistan and Bangladesh. It is one of the seven Central Armed Police Forces (CAPF) of India, and was raised in the wake of the Indo-Pakistani War of 1965 "for ensuring the security of the borders of India and for related matters".

10. BSF has been termed the First Line of Defence of Indian territories. Ever since its constitution in 1965, in the wake of Indo-Pak conflict over the Rann of Kutch, it has been engaged in various active roles during wars fought by India. With 192 battalions comprising sanctioned strength of 270,000 personnel, it includes, in addition to its border guarding personnel, an air wing, navy, an artillery regiment and several specialised units. It is currently the world's

largest border security force. under the control of the Ministry of Home Affairs

11. For more on BSF; https://bsf.gov.in/

12. The CRPF was derived from the CRP (Crown Representative's Police) on 27 July 1939 with 2 battalions in Nimach [North Indian Mounted Artillery and Cavalry Headquarter], Madhya Pradesh. Its primary duty at the time was to protect the British residents in sensitive states of India. The CRP was renamed as Central Reserve Police Force under the CRPF Act, 1949. The CRPF's primary role lies in assisting the State/Union Territories in police operations to maintain law and order and counter-insurgency.

13. The Central Reserve Police Force Act, 1949.Ministry of Home Affairs, Govt. of India

14. CRPF also has special units such as the Rapid Action Force (RAF) formed in October 1992, to deal with communal riots and related civil unrest, and the Commando Battalion for Resolute Action (CoBRA), one of the few units of the Central Armed Police Forces specifically trained in guerilla warfare.

15. The Sashastra Seema Bal (SSB) is a border guarding force of India deployed along its borders with Nepal and Bhutan. It is under the administrative control of the Ministry of Home Affairs (MHA). The force was originally set up under the name Special Service Bureau in 1963 in the aftermath of the Sino-Indian War to disrupt enemy operations.

16. The Armed Forces (Special Powers) Act, 1958; Ministry of Home Affairs, Government of India; https://www.mha.gov.in

17. Unified Command HQ in Counter Insurgency and Role of Intelligence in J&K Dr Bhashyam Kasturi* South Asia Terrorism Portal

18. The functions of the Operational Group are:

   a) To synergise the counter insurgency operations conducted by the Army, paramilitary forces and the state Police and to respond to all crisis situations resulting from terrorist/extremist/insurgent action;

   b) To devise action plans, deployments and to define the areas of operation of the Army, paramilitary forces and the State Police; To monitor the inputs from district-level coordination committees; and,

Chapter 14

The Changing Nature of Internal Security Challenges in the North East

(While the Indian State has responded in a very determined manner to separatist and fissiparous tendencies in the NER, using military where necessary, the continuous engagement and dynamic response of the Indian State has also been based on democratic inclusion and integration. The disaffected elements have been engaged in dialogue, with the Indian State accepting the need for economic development of the region and wider participation of the local population in governance. Consequently, over time, most of the insurgent / separatist movements of the region reconciled to coexistence within the Indian Union rather than continuing conflict with the Indian State. This brought comparative peace to the region. However, ethnic and other identity-based fault lines exist, with the potential of erupting violently and causing threats to national security and requiring a dynamic response)

Over time pan-ethnic/regional movements for insurgency and secession in India's Northeast have entered into dialogue and discussion with the Indian State and have, for the most part, favoured solutions within the Indian Constitution. Simultaneously, with better connectivity and economic development increasing proportion of the local population favoured peace and sought opportunities for advancement, economic, social and political, in the vast Indian nation and economy.

In the early decades post-independence, the political option was shunned by more extremist elements who tended to join militant organisations seeking armed struggle. However, resolute response by the State through its security forces showed the futility of such thinking and gradually, as the 21st Century dawned, the ranks of the militants started thinning. Eventually, many erstwhile militant factions came over ground, with their cadres surrendering along with their arms and ammunition to the State authorities. In some cases, friendly relations with neighbouring countries, particularly Bangladesh, resulted in extradition/repatriation of some of the erstwhile dreaded terrorists. The extremist factions progressively lost popular support and, with improving security infrastructure, also found it difficult to operate in the region.

The process of weaning away the general public of the NER from extremist /separatist ideologies has been facilitated greatly by the ability of the Indian State to welcome back many of the elements that strayed away and entering into dialogue with them. This resulted in several Peace Accords, political reorganisation of the region by creation of new states and joining the political process by the erstwhile militants and insurgents. Many such elements contested elections and won them also from time to time, forming governments and sharing political power at all levels. The restoration of the political process, serving as positive outlet for the local aspirations of the people, considerably weakened the separatist urge.

However, the road to lasting peace is not fully traversed yet and securing lasting peace in the region is still a work-in-process. In most parts of NER, including Assam, the surrender and return of armed militants[1,2] to normal civic life has been fraught with new challenges. The rehabilitation of such elements and their re-induction in the society at large has proved to be a complex affair. Access to new sources of illegal arms needs to be totally cut off, the surrendered elements have to be rehabilitated, socially and economically, so that they do not return to extortion and participation in various illegal activities relating to drugs, arms etc.

In some parts of the Northeast, militant underground factions are still numerous, armed and powerful. They not only represent an alternate centre of power to the local people but also occasionally clash violently with the security forces and with each other. There is also a small element of die-hard extremists who have fled into their sanctuaries outside India from where they continue with their separatist agenda. They occasionally combine with each other and launch occasional attacks on Indian security forces. They also extract funds from the public in several areas falling in India and are very likely also aided and supported by foreign powers inimical to India

While separatist extremism tends to attract most attention, it is also essential to recognise that NER is home to ethic/ religious / communal / intra- tribal fault lines. The suspicion of the "other" or the "outsider' still determines the political thinking in the region. This has led to violent conflict erupting along such fault lines over the years of which the most recent is the Meitei-Kuki conflict in Manipur in 2023. This confrontation erupted as a result of an order by the Manipur High Court opening up grant of Scheduled Tribe status to the majority Meitei community, a step that was viewed with great apprehension by the Kuki-Zomi tribals of Manipur, who feared loss of their lands and share of development resources. The resulting conflagration of inter-ethnic violence has taken well over hundred lives, with police armouries looted, with gross violation of human rights and acts of violence against women, and at the time of writing, is continuing sporadically.

While the identity-based claims in North Eastern states have led to a plethora of legal instruments that provide ethnic exclusivity such as Inner Line Permits, autonomous jurisdictions, restrictions on outsiders regarding land ownership, employment and economic activity in several areas all these measures are not proof against the impulse to have exclusive access to state patronage. Development investment is viewed as a zero-sum game with any measure likely to benefit one population group is viewed as a loss by the others.

In addition to the ethnic fault lines, there is the unfinished agenda of identification and deportation of illegal migrants in Assam. The compilation of final, acceptable version of the National Register of Citizens in Assam, the largest of the NE States, intended to identify genuine Indian citizens, has also proved to be a divisive exercise and remains a work-in-process.

As we have seen, NER is no stranger to war. The shadow of 1962 conflict with China still persists. The unsettled international border with China and claims raised by China from time-to-time over Arunachal Pradesh has resulted in ongoing confrontation between India and China across the Line of Actual Control (LAC) along the Arunachal border. There are also several disputed areas which keep the LAC perpetually on the boil. Occasionally local people from the India side, using traditional routes for hunting and cattle grazing, tend to stray into disputed areas and are arrested by the CPLA requiring extensive efforts for their release. In fact, every year, there are several incidents where the Chinese enter disputed land, build structures or leave behind markers in an attempt to show that the land belongs to them.

The external threat so posed to India is exacerbated by a huge military build-up by China across the LAC. China has built many new roads, airports and helipads as part of their defence preparedness ever since their occupation of Tibet. This in any case requires presence of large and diversified Indian military formations across high Himalayas to defend Indian territory. The stand-off has also led to border skirmishes over attempts by China to alter the status quo, particularly in Dokalam, north of Bhutan. The rivalry between the two Asian giants has now spilled over to the Indian Ocean and the Indo-Pacific Region with India joining formations such as the Quad to counter growing Chinese Influence and belligerence across the oceans. This rivalry is already leading to diplomatic spats between the two countries, such as the one following arrival of the Chinese naval surveillance ship in Hambantota port in Sri Lanka. In the past China has supported separatist /insurgent movements in the North East, a scenario that could play out again in the North Eastern Region.

Meanwhile on the far away Western Border, relations with Pakistan have remained hostile, with Pakistan following a strategy of hybrid war against India. In the past, both Chinese and Pakistani agencies, acting clandestinely through Myanmar, Bangladesh and Nepal, were active in fomenting trouble In India's North East. With changes in the political landscape in Nepal and Bangladesh such activities have reduced considerably but it would be idle to presume that they have ceased altogether or may not be resumed in the future. In fact, changes in the political landscape in the immediate Eastern neighbourhood can have immediate, adverse impact on the security situation in the North east.

With the internal situation deteriorating in Myanmar after the military coup and re-emergence of Myanmarese local insurgent groups and "armies", the situation has become all the more volatile along the Indo-Myanmar border. Fighting between the military and armed resistance groups that emerged after the coup has intensified in Myanmar during 2022. There are indications that resistance groups are organising beyond the village level. Alliances are also being formed between the many armed resistance groups and the People's Defence Force (PDF) under the National Unity Government (NUG) opposed to the military rule. Established ethnic resistance groups, including the Karen National Union/Karen National Liberation Army (KNU/KNLA) and the Kachin Independence Organization/Kachin Independence Army (KIO/KIA), have continued to support resistance groups that have emerged after the coup. In Kayin state, the combined forces of the KNU/KNLA, the Karen National Defence Organization (KNDO), and the PDF have engaged in intense fighting with the military.

Elsewhere, in Rakhine state, tensions between the military and the United League of Arakan/Arakan Army (ULA/AA) have been increasing, as the

ULA/AA has consolidated its control over parts of the state. Despite an informal ceasefire in place since shortly after the November 2020 election, clashes have still been reported. Unarmed resistance to the military dictatorship has also persisted through 2022 to 2023. Demonstrations against the coup have continued. The military has cracked down on demonstrations by resorting to mass arrests across cities with the intention of preventing demonstrations. There are reports of more than 1600 pro-democracy protesters being killed by the military while a UN Human Rights Report presents a grim assessment of 1.3 million displaced people; 28,000 destroyed homes; villages burned to the ground; an estimated 13,000 children killed due to violence, involuntary displacement and deprivation; a looming food crisis; and nearly 700, 000 Rohingya in de facto internment camps within Myanmar.

The unsettled conditions in Myanmar, combined with the presence of some extremist elements from India sheltering in that country, the field is again open for elements hostile to India to have easy access to arms and ammunition and trained cadres to carry out hostile hybrid disruptive operations in the NER.

The internal security situation in the NE Region is, therefore, is dynamic and made volatile by both internal issues as well as external variables and threats. The existence of various ethnic/communal/linguistic fault lines, unresolved local political issues resulting from identity politics in the NER itself, political changes in India's Eastern neighbourhood, the dynamics of great power rivalry in the form of the New Cold War or the confrontation between India and China across the borders or in the Indian Ocean, acting singly or in concert can alter the situation in a very short time. In this backdrop, the question remains as to whether periods of comparative calm, such as the current one, signify a permanent transition to lasting peace. The experience of past decades shows that forces disruptive of public peace and order and internal security situation in the NER are dynamic and responsive to both internal and external stimulants.

Therefore, it is critical to ramp up the peace dividend wherever and whenever possible through diversified economic development that results in increased employment and higher incomes for the people of North east. The hope for a better life will help in aligning the balance of interests with peaceful co-existence within the Indian framework. In this context the Act East policy, with increasing economic engagement with SE Asia and India's Eastern Neighbourhood, makes eminent sense. While, the Central Government, the state administrations and the security forces will have to maintain a high level of alertness in the foreseeable future to neutralise various threats as they arise, an opportunity exists for India to counter such tendencies through economic engagement East.

Security for the Future

The Changing Response to Internal Security Challenges

It has to be recognised that the view of the local population towards security forces, though influenced by the legacy of past violent conflict is gradually changing in some parts of the North East. There have been cases of use of excessive force in retaliation to militant attacks. In some cases, innocent civilians became victims of inadequate intelligence or mistaken identity[3] on the part of the security forces. In the early phase of insurgency, the response to militant attacks was directed towards "area punishment" which resulted in grave distress to non-combatant population. Many families lost their members, some due to action by security forces others due to militant violence. The people also generally suffered on account of being trapped in the cross-fire between militants and the security forces, with normal civic life being denied to them for decades, education of children and family incomes badly disrupted.

Over a period of time while there was an urge for peace in the region, the security force, with considerable experience of countering extremism /insurgency and terrorism, maintaining public order and internal security the response of the security forces also became more nuanced in their response and sensitive to ground realities. Despite periodic acts of confrontation with the security forces, the first two decades of this century saw conflict dissipating gradually. In fact, during the second decade there were serious plans of freeing the Indian Army of Internal Security duties to enable them to deal with external threats. Some of the factors guiding this change need a closer scrutiny to evaluate their capacity to build sustainable peace in a changing environment of internal security.

Post North East Reorganisation, the political leadership of different states took time to adjust to the dynamic of electoral democracy. Initially conflicts took place as state government were seen as extensions of the Central Government. However, the rhythm of elections changed such perceptions over time as erstwhile underground leaders stepped into the political arena, contested and won elections and formed local governments distinct from the Centre. Gradually they also learnt to work with the central security forces (whom they were fighting earlier). However, irrespective of Central

Government support, they have to take full responsibility for maintaining peace and order in their respective states.

As for the Security agencies, experience shows that, deeper knowledge and understanding of local issues helps in dealing with separatism and insurgency better. Earlier, in many cases, disruptive outcomes of local issues and conflicts were conveniently blamed on insurgency by the local administrations. With long experience in the region and permanent establishment of physical infrastructure and organisational network in the region, the Army, Para Military and CPAFs developed their own intelligence wings. The Unified Command, where sensibly used, has enabled the sharing of intelligence and information on real time basis, resulting in more accurate identification of real causes and persons behind disruptions of law and order, violent or otherwise. Intelligence based, pin-pointed Identification of anti-national/disruptive elements, their bases and operating areas has also helped in the evolution of tactics that enabled their isolation/neutralisation, with minimal harassment to non-involved local population. To a great extent this has been facilitated by a willingness of the local public, tired of conflict and violence, to come forward with information regarding extremist /insurgent elements. The communication network and surface transport network are vastly improved, enabling quick response. This is a far cry from the earlier policy of penalising the whole village or area for any extremist activity occurring in their area. However, given the possibilities of ethnic/ linguistic/ communal strife in the North East, the security forces will have to build on this experience and calibrate their response, involving use of pin-pointed and minimum force necessary, based on close understanding and information of ground realities.

In recent years social media has emerged as a powerful but double-edged tool in modern times. On the one hand, it can spread inflammatory and hateful content as well as incitement to violence; on the other it brings information about incidents of violence along with lapses and omissions of state administration/ Police forces to the attention of the nation and the world at large. Any event, including any transgression by the security forces is recorded over cell phones and goes viral in minutes resulting in serious political and administrative fallout. The use of social media has created a new dimension for response by the administration and the security forces which cannot be wished away. As of now the administration response to such situations has been to shut down the internet and telecommunication network to allow for public agitation to cool down. This can, however, provide only a temporary solution as suspension of normal means of communication encourages rumours and false narratives to spread and objectionable content can appear once communications are restored, stretching conflict further and ingraining it long term in public psyche. Local administrations and security forces have to address such situation head-on, maintaining open communication with media and the public, countering false information and rumours promptly and regularly.

Civil rights activists have been active in the North East, particularly in Manipur. Their work has helped in exposing human rights violations and excesses by security forces. The resulting judicial oversight has led to a review of AFSPA. In this regard protest against the security forces following Operation Bluebird in the Oinam[4] villages following an attack on Assam Rifles by Manipur militants, the 16 yearlong campaigns by Irom Sharmila[5] against the AFSPA after the Malom[6] incident and the civil protests following the killing of Manorama Devi[7] stand out. The involvement of Meira Paibis[9] in Manipur is another example. During conflict, violence does result in extreme responses on occasions. There has to be continuous corrective action to prevent such cases from recurring. Covering up cases of excesses not only fosters resentments but also encourages more irresponsible behaviour. On the other hand, where the local population is deeply divided along ethnic lines, involvement of civil society is also equally divided and can come in the way of effective action. The Meitei-Kuki divide in Manipur following recent ethnic clashes is a case in point. While it is essential for the security agencies not to adopt adversarial positions insofar as civil society is concerned and to remain neutral, to the extent the local civil society helps in the maintenance /restoration of peace, working with them would help build a bridge to the hearts and minds of the local people. In any case, the security forces have to learn to navigate a delicate course through situations where civil society and social media are highly activated.

Some local force commanders have done sterling work in fostering goodwill amongst the local communities. Local units of various security forces have also rendered help and assistance in rescue and rehabilitation of local communities through disaster relief action. In many cases involving natural disasters or highway accidents, the security forces deployed in the area acted as first responders in launching rescue operations or providing medical aid to the victims. It has been seen that where there has been a closer engagement, participation and support by the security forces in local socially relevant programs aimed at better health, education and youth participation in sports etc, support has been forthcoming from local communities in efforts to keep the peace.

216

Eventually the work of the media, social media, civil rights activists and the political system delivers information about injustice to the public domain. It is then a matter governance on the one hand and firm judicial redressal on the other. Irrespective of the forces deployed and their armaments, in situations where governance fails, either politically, through lack of consensus or through biased or inadequate executive action, antagonisms within the legislature or judicial delays, the sense of grievance will continue to fester. In the past, judicial redressal has been slow and inadequate[8]. Justice delayed, being justice denied, each incident of enters collective memory as an event of repression and continues to foster resentments, deepening fault lines and raising the spectre of future conflict. In addition to ensuring fair, inclusive, responsive and responsible governance, it is essential for judicial oversight to be strengthened and delivery of justice made speedier.

The above multi-pronged approach needs to be built upon and strengthened further. Wherever employed, it has helped resolve many resentments of the past that may have been created through action then taken by the security forces. Today recruitment drives by security organisations, earlier regarded with deep distrust by local public, elicit enthusiastic response from local youth wishing to enlist. To respond well to the internal security challenges of the future, security forces, in addition to maintaining a continuing commitment to values enshrined in the Indian Constitutional and democratic processes, will need to continue with a multi-dimensional, nuanced approach to dealing with such situations.

State Police Forces

The CAPFs and the Army can backstop and support the efforts to maintain peace and public order and provide the wherewithal to balance the asymmetrical force available with insurgent groups vis-à-vis local police where needed. They cannot work effectively in the absence of a clear mandate from the local, elected state governments, who as per the Constitution have the responsibility of maintaining law and order in their jurisdictions. Besides the role of elected, governments is crucial in building consensus by ensuring a political balance and representation of all population groups, thereby allaying resentments and smoothing over differences. The elected governments in the states obviously need a well-functioning administration and a civil police force to carry out their responsibilities. In this context, to enable sustainable peace in the NER it would also be critical to build up the capacity of the state police forces to provide credible and confidence inspiring civil policing and effective participation in the criminal administration system. This requires, first and foremost, the ability of the local police forces to overcome ethnic, religious, linguistic etc loyalties and carry out law enforcement and maintain public order in an impartial manner. This is a serious challenge in the North East where identity can override commitment to impartial policing to the extent that it sometimes it becomes practically impossible for police personnel belonging to one ethnic group to police areas populated by others.

Jurisdictional issues across states in the North East are a major constraint in the effectiveness of the North eastern state police forces in dealing with interstate issues. These constraints do not impede the militant/ insurgent/ criminal elements who easily move and operate across the region. A framework that enables police forces to share information and track criminals and offenders across jurisdictions needs to be developed. A common crime related data base across the region needs to be developed with digital access available at a suitable level to the local police.

The demands of urban policing are not yet adequately recognised in the North East. There is also an excessive emphasis on raising paramilitary battalions, a hangover of the colonial times and the concentration on maintaining law and order across a vast geography. The state police forces need to build capacity to respond to civic situations and effectively carry out criminal investigation including cybercrimes, white collar crime, economic offences in addition to actions disruptive of peace and public order. Special recruitment, training and equipment would be required for constabulary and officers for such urban policing. The gender imbalance in the police needs to be corrected by recruitment of more women. The state police forces will also have to develop special forces trained to deal with urban terrorism and extremism that resorts to violence through guerrilla activities in the countryside.

Significant investment requires to be made in modernisation[10], training and capacity building of the constabulary and officers particularly at Assistant / Sub -inspector level. Police training schools such as the one at Jorhat in Assam and the NE Police Academy at Barapani should be developed to offer a wide variety of courses leading to enhanced qualifications. Promotional policies need to be revamped to encourage capacity and skill building, in addition to performance in the field. Modern policing requires state of the art knowledge in a number of disciplines. Police personnel should be encouraged to pursue advanced studies and specialise in relevant areas.

Police personnel also need to be provided with modern weapons, secure communications and training in use of digital technology in law enforcement work. The growing policing requirement needs to be met with suitable numbers of personnel on the ground. Such requirements need to be calculated providing for reasonable working hours to police personnel, with changes in shifts and duties to prevent fatigue. Secure housing and facilities like schooling and leisure activities would go a long way in raising police morale and, consequently their effectiveness.

Notes to Chapter 14

1. Policy towards surrendered insurgents; Press Information Bureau, Government of India, Ministry of Home Affairs, 07 FEB 2018 4:46PM by PIB Delhi

2. Surrender Cum Rehabilitation of Militants, Press Information Bureau, Government of India, Ministry of Home Affairs, 20-March-2018 16:00 IST

3. Army operation in Nagaland goes awry, 15 civilians dead; December 05, 2021/ Updated December 12, 2021 10:09 am IST - GUWAHATI/ NEW DELHI; https://www.thehindu.com; Dinakar PeriI, Rahul Karmakar.

4. Manipur's horror: When Operation Bluebird struck terror; Hindustan Times, Nov 05, 2014; Rahul Karmakar

5. Irom Chanu Sharmila; https://en.wikipedia.org/;

6. The Massacre in Manipur that Prompted Irom Sharmila's Fast-Unto-Death Sixteen Years Ago; Anubha Bhonsle; 09 January 2016; https://caravanmagazine. in/

7. Thangjam Manorama was a 32-year-old woman from Manipur, who was arrested and later found dead on 11 July 2004. Investigations revealed that she had been tortured and raped before being killed. The incident led to widespread and extended protests in Manipur and Delhi, including a march by naked women in Imphal. In 2012, the Justice Varma Committee recommended measures, partly attributed to the protests following Manorama Devi case, for reviewing AFSPA with a view to reducing violence against women.

8. Following Manorama Devi incident, a commission of inquiry was set up by the Manipur government in 2004, which submitted its report in Nov 2004. The matter also came up before the Guwahati High Court who ruled that since the Assam Rifles, the paramilitary force in whose jurisdiction the incident happened, had been deployed under the Armed Forces (Special Powers) Act, 1958, the state government did not have jurisdiction over them, and the case should be dealt with by the Central Government. Consequently, the Inquiry Report was never put in public domain. In December 2014, in a case filed at Supreme Court of India, the Apex Court directed the government to pay a compensation of Rs. 10 lakhs to Manorama's family. However, the identification of culprits and their punishment remains a pending issue.

9. Meira Paibis (Women torch bearers) is a women's social movement in the Indian state of Manipur. Referred to as the "guardians of civil society", Meira Paibi origin dates back to 1977, in the present Kakching district. Their name refers to the flaming torches they carry during their protest marches. According to A. K. Janaki Leima, one of the movement's leaders, Meira Paibi

has been fighting against drug abuse, crimes against women, and the Armed Forces Special Powers Act (AFSPA).

10. Modernisation of State Police Forces (MPF) Scheme; Ministry of Home Affairs, Government of India

Chapter 15

The Regional Trade Architecture

(Economic engagement is the most sustainable of all routes to building long-lasting relationships. However, for that to happen India's NE Region has to be compatible with demand and supply patterns of the wider SE Asian Region. To a large extent this will depend upon unlocking the productive potential of the NER enabling it to provide a wide range of goods or services and building it up as a trading zone. This will require, in addition to ensuring public safety and security, durable and extensive infrastructure, efficient supply chains and closer integration with the production and business centres in the rest of India, reliable financial arrangements and credible institutions for the conduct of business, including simplified regulatory framework).

Economic Development through Trade

Policies for economic development of the NER have evolved over time but have generally had an inward orientation, perhaps due to practically the entire development support coming through central funding. In the initial decades the region was beset with insurgency and extremism and all external contacts were viewed suspiciously by the Indian state. During this period the adjoining SE Asian Region was also struggling with poverty and was not a significant participant in regional trade. With launch of poverty alleviation and food production programmes launched in India during the 1970's, attention turned towards rural development for a while. However, the Anti-Foreigners Agitation in Assam and continuing insurgency in various NE states kept economic development issues on the back burner. The result was that till the 1990s the region grew very slowly.

There are of course, private businesses operating in the North East. These are generally centred around plantation activity (tea) and domestic trade and associated services. Investments in encouraging industrial development in the region, pushed over last three decades have yielded limited dividends, primarily in food processing. Currently, the region has limited potential for any large-scale manufacturing activity which requires an extensive ancillary eco-system to function. There is a nascent, but steadily growing services sector, whose full potential is yet to be realised due to digital connectivity and broadband access issues.

With the turn of the century, investments in infrastructure in the North East grew at a much faster pace. However, these investments were focused on improving connectivity of the NER with the rest of India rather than positioning NER as a connectivity hub linking the neighbouring countries and the SE Region. Some initiatives like the IMT Trilateral highway were envisaged but the progress on these has been very slow and has now been disrupted due to disturbances in Myanmar. However, road, rail and river-based links with Bangladesh have picked up and shown steady progress.

For the future economic development of the region, re-orientation of policies towards trade, both internal and external would be more effective. It is generally recognised that Trade facilitation allows better access for businesses to production inputs from wherever they can be efficiently and cost-effectively obtained and supporting greater participation in global value chains (GVCs). Further, identifying and reducing unnecessary costs related to trade procedures is essential for firms to take full advantage of new market openings. This is especially true for micro-, small- and medium-sized enterprises (SMEs), for which high costs of trading can be a deterrent. In addition, trade facilitation is critical for perishable agricultural products which are highly sensitive to delays.

This also calls for a greater focus on trade-based connectivity that makes it easier for firms and people to access opportunities, markets, and supply-chains. This requires connectivity, encompassing physical, tele-communication and digital facilities, that facilitates the flow of services, goods and people within and across borders, regardless of their location e.g. hub or feeder or remote. Good connectivity, designed to reduce the average cost to access markets, as a buyer or supplier, would open up trade opportunities and link them to entrepreneurship, resulting in broader area development.

India has made painstaking efforts to set up a better trade eco-system with ASEAN. However geo-political trends in the region, ranging from tensions in the South China Sea and the Taiwan Straits, war in Ukraine, emergence of the New Cold War and re-ordering of the multi-lateral trade arrangements in Asia and Pacific have overtaken such bilateral initiatives requiring fresh policy evaluations and decisions as to how India would engage with its neighbourhood in the changed circumstances.

Meanwhile India's Eastern Neighbourhood and the extensive land borders surrounding the NER can well be an economic opportunity given the potential of border trade with Bangladesh, Nepal and despite the internal disturbance in that country, with Myanmar. This would require a re-evaluation of the local infrastructure requirements in border areas, development of a large number of trading points and a border trade customs framework. In fact, border trade is already taking place in the informal sector. Recognising it and enabling a trade friendly regime with related exchange infrastructure and financing arrangements would go a long way in transforming the extensive border areas. Customs and Border Management

RCEP or not?

Development of ASEAN as an organisation kept pace with the rise of SE Asian economies in the latter half of the last century. India's Look East policy initiated in the 1990s especially emphasised building up trade relations with ASEAN. This happened gradually through a number of agreements such as the ASEAN-India Trade in Goods Agreement (2010), the ASEAN-India Trade in Services Agreement and the ASEAN-India Investment Agreement (both signed in 2014). However, the trading pattern of ASEAN has been altered by China's Belt and Road Initiative (BRI) and the Regional Comprehensive Economic Partnership (RCEP). While BRI is a unilateral initiative by China to push investments in individual SE Asian and other countries, RCEP is a regional trade agreement that came into force on 1 January, 2020 encompassing ASEAN as well as several Pacific Ocean economies (some countries e.g. Republic of Korea and Malaysia joined later). In fact, it is a comprehensive free trade agreement amongst ASEAN countries and Australia, China, Japan, Korea and New Zealand and covers trade in goods, services, investments, economic and technical cooperation. It also creates new rules for electronic commerce, intellectual property, government procurement, competition, and small and medium sized enterprises. Given the size of the participating economies, RCEP is China driven and dominated.

Despite being one of the participants in negotiations for the Agreement ever since they started in 2012, India has not joined the RCEP.

Ministers from 15 countries had signed the Agreement by 15 November 2019 with India indicating (in November 2019) it was not in a position to do so. However, the Ministers' Declaration on India's Participation in the Regional Comprehensive Economic Partnership (RCEP); 15 November 2020 has kept the door open for India to join at a later date. Even without India, RCEP is still the world's largest free trade agreement.

While with US China rivalry and the New Cold War, many developed economies are cautious about expanding trade and technology ties with China. The imperative for ASEAN countries is, however, different as they cannot ignore an economy the size of China. This provides both an opportunity and a challenge for India. On the one hand the global situation is favourable to India developing as a major hub in the high value supply chain encompassing the developed world. On the other there is the issue of subsuming India's economic interests in a regional trade platform. The policy conflict over whether India should stay out of such trade blocks and follow an autonomous line persists. Traditionally India has hesitated to commit to low duties in trade blocs or FTAs as it feels this would restrict its policy options. However, the possibility of joining global value chains, attracting investments and pushing exports eventually gets restricted with this approach. Particularly so as the WTO regime is still struggling to overcome the effects of the Covid Pandemic and is beset with the phenomenon of major economies pursuing national concerns. A new consensus for a common rule based global world trade is yet elusive. Instead, many countries are pursuing FTAs in their immediate neighbourhood.

Now, in addition to trade policy reservations in India, post the border stand-off, the relations between India and China have also deteriorated. A possible alternative to RCEP could be either to pursue bilateral trade or to join a trading block that does not include China, such as the Japan-led Comprehensive and Progressive Agreement for Trans-Pacific Partnership (CPTPP), Indo-Pacific Economic Forum (IPEF) or other free trade agreements in the Asia-Pacific region. These initiatives being new do not as yet have the capacity for trade facilitation comparable to ASEAN/RCEP.

Indo -Pacific Economic Forum (IPEF)

Meanwhile, on 23 May 2022, the Indo -Pacific Economic Forum (IPEF) was launched jointly by the US and partner countries of the Indo-Pacific region in Tokyo. It seeks to strengthen economic partnership among participating countries with the objective of enhancing resilience, sustainability, inclusiveness, economic growth, fairness and competitiveness in the region. IPEF does not involve market access but is built around four "pillars": Trade, Supply Chains, Energy and Infrastructure, Anti-Corruption and

Taxation. IPEF has 14 members, namely, Australia, Brunei, Fiji, India, Indonesia, Japan, Korea, Malaysia, New Zealand, Philippines, Singapore, Thailand, Vietnam and the US.

India has joined three "pillars", but not Trade- which deals primarily with trade and commitments to the environment, labour, digital trade and public procurement.

Supply Chain Resilience Initiative (SCRI)

One fallout of the growing belligerence of China and the disruption caused by the Covid pandemic is that in April 2021, Australia, India and Japan launched the Supply Chain Resilience Initiative (SCRI) in the Indo-Pacific. The SCRI served as a wake-up call to many countries exposed to excessive dependence on China for a wide range of intermediate products and finished goods including electronics, consumer goods and pharmaceuticals. Furthermore, growing tensions between the China and the United States and its "like-minded" Indo-Pacific partners, exacerbated by Beijing's aggressive military and diplomatic tactics over Taiwan, South China Sea and the disputes with Japan over Senkaku islands and with India over Eastern Ladakh only made the imperative of moving value chains away from China a more urgent goal. In this context, the Indo-Pacific centred SCRI challenges China's dominance in trade and is an economic response to its militarised and aggressive foreign policy.

Trade Related Infrastructure

As a part of the Trade oriented development policy investments have to be directed towards trade related infrastructure. As per the World Bank, focus on such infrastructure calls for sustained investment in logistics and transport services, regional trade facilitation and development of trade corridors, transit and multimodal transport, customs and border management, port efficiency (in the case of NER, Dry Ports, River Ports and Inland Container Depots). This has to be backstopped by agreements, bilateral or multilateral, on trade of goods and services and protocols and agreements on movement of vehicles, railways, craft ships/boats and persons, storage, quarantine, disease control and testing and certification facilities for trade in agriculture/ horticulture/ livestock etc. More than anything, it has to be backed by a Trade Facilitating Financial Infrastructure.

For all the intentions of policy pronouncements regarding economic engagement, actual business and trade and the relations such activities engender also require a Trade-facilitating Financial Infrastructure (TFI).

The elements of the TFI to facilitate trade and international business and commerce is substantially available in India but needs be extended to the NER through appropriate institutions and organisations. Since NER is expected to be positioned to economic engagement across borders, this perspective will require the TFI to function across national jurisdictions as well. It is worthwhile to dwell briefly on the nature and requirements of this substantive requirement.

For an engagement that encompasses India's immediate neighbourhood in the East, the NER and SE Asia, the TFI that would power it would require a well-founded, clear, transparent, and enforceable legal basis for each material aspect of its functioning in all relevant jurisdictions. It should be efficient, based on governance arrangements (in this case trans-national governance arrangements) that are clear and transparent, promote the safety and efficiency of the TFI and support the stability of the broader financial systems of participating jurisdictions. It should be able to enable efficient and low-cost exchange management.

Such Infrastructure has to provide a framework for the comprehensive management of legal, credit, liquidity, operational, and other risks of persons, businesses and institutions involved in trade and business across borders. It has to provide a stable framework for settlements, both money settlements and physical deliveries (of instruments and commodities), that provide finality in a time bound manner. It has to provide secure depositories of various kinds (including securities, documents and commodities) that enable collateral management and exchange-of-value settlement systems. It should have rules and procedures that enable the segregation and portability of positions of a participant's customers and the collateral provided with respect to those positions.

The systems of the TFI should be designed to be scalable, ensuring high degree of security and operational reliability with business continuity arrangements in the event of various disruptions. Such risks can arise due to internal disturbance or economic crises in any jurisdiction, collapse or volatility in its currency or disruption of transport, communications or supply chains due to any reason, including natural disasters.

To ensure credibility the TFI should have objective, risk-based, and publicly disclosed criteria for participation, which permit fair and open access. It should use relevant internationally accepted disclosure practices and communication procedures and standards in order to facilitate efficient payment, clearing, settlement, and recording. Finally, it would have to submit to appropriate and effective international regulation, supervision, and oversight by international institutions and specially designed bodies including central banks, market regulators or other relevant authorities of participants.

Needless to say, such TFI applicable across national jurisdictions cannot be developed and established unilaterally by any country but will have to be negotiated multilaterally. India's engagement with ASEAN had been working towards developing such systems. With advent of new arrangements like RCEP, CPTPP etc that involve ASEAN countries with several non-ASEAN economies, the task is more complex, particularly as India is yet to take a position on joining any such arrangement. Currently the option is to ether adopt international rules which may be more suited to developed economies and based on international governance and arbitration. These also may be at variance with those adopted under the regional trade alliances. The other option would be to enter into bi-lateral FTAs, which may lead to frameworks that are restrictive and may lead to costly choices and in the long run, prove in-efficient.

In any case, for the NER to participate in business trade and commerce across borders, it would require all the elements of the TFI extended to it through an efficient, credible statutory and institutional framework. It would be well worth the effort to make the NER a participant in the National Trade Financial Infrastructure, an exercise that will take time, but can be pursued under the Act East Policy.

Removing Internal Barriers to Trade

In addition to providing an outward trade orientation to the NER economy, there is a need to remove internal barriers to trade and movement. Many states in the NER are today closed to free movement of goods and persons on account of regimes such as the Inner Line Permits, restrictions on sale and purchase of property, habitation and commerce etc. The existence of several states in NER with different jurisdictions also makes coordination of economic policies and administration difficult. This has been encountered in dealing with insurgency and terrorism and even in interstate crime relating to drugs and arms trafficking, wildlife poaching and trade in protected birds and animals as also in animal parts.

A good beginning could be made with harmonisation of jurisdictions and legal frameworks. If necessary, regional institutions under the aegis of the NEC and including representation by all the states could be entrusted with this task. NER states also need to undertake reforms in local laws to make them more business friendly including in labour and land regulations.

Looking Ahead

Therefore, a key policy decision that will guide the future of Act East Policy and indeed any economic engagement east with ASEAN and the Pacific relates to how India can keep its trade framework with ASEAN relevant and growth oriented. This would include a decision on whether or on what conditions India should connect to a regional trade agreement such as the RCEP or some other organisation. The issue is still open with India yet to make up its mind.

On the basis of the engagement so decided, the role that the NER can play would have to be determined. In any engagement with Eastern Neighbourhood or ASEAN, this would be substantial. However, this will require addressing the internal barriers to trade in the NER and developing trade related physical, statutory legal and financial infrastructure.

Notes to Chapter 15

1. Brief on Regional Comprehensive Economic Partnership (RCEP); Ministry of Commerce, Government of India

2. ASEAN: The Regional Comprehensive Economic Partnership

3. In Asia, President Biden and a Dozen Indo-Pacific Partners Launch the Indo-Pacific Economic Framework for Prosperity; White House Brief USA; https://www.whitehouse.gov/

4. The Indo-Pacific Economic Framework: What it is — and why it matters; CNBC, 25 May 2022; Su-Lin Tan

5. Australia-India-Japan Trade Ministers' Joint Statement on Launch of Supply Chain Resilience initiative; Ministry of Commerce, 27 APR 2021posted by Press Information

Chapter 16

Co-opting the Neighbourhood

(The Eastern Region of the Indian Subcontinent, including the Indian North East, not very long ago, was interconnected and interdependent. It underwent a partition in 1947 creating international boundaries across a region that had been a single entity for millennia. East Pakistan, now Bangladesh, is the new 20th century nation state interposed between The NER and rest of India, but for a narrow corridor. It shares borders with India, stretching almost 4096 km. 1,880 kms of this border is with north-eastern states of India, namely Assam, Meghalaya, Tripura, and Mizoram and the rest is with West Bengal. The legacy of the Partition in terms of communal, linguistic and ethnic conflict, subsequent wars and sensitivities over migration have resulted in a new reality, with challenging imperatives for international relations across borders. The need now is to look forward and find ways to overcoming the obstacles posed by the legacies of the past to cooperation and shared prosperity.)

Today, in addition to the security architecture built by deployment of a range of security forces in the NER The immediate eastern neighbourhood comprising Bangladesh, Bhutan, Nepal and Myanmar equally holds the key to stability of the Region. India's relations with Bangladesh and Nepal have seen considerable turbulence at times, though finally shared interests enable friendly relations to prevail. Yet the international neighbourhood is critical for building connectivity, ensuring internal security and fostering economic development. Any strategy for economic development of the NER with the objective of enabling an engagement eastward has to bolster internal security efforts with diplomatic initiatives to secure the cooperation of all these countries. To do so, it is important to understand their internal political dynamics.

Bangladesh

Due to its geographical location, deep historical, cultural and economic links, Bangladesh is critical to the future growth of the NE Region. In fact, pre-Partition, the Great North Indian Plain and the Bengal Delta were connected seamlessly to the NER and Burma. The access to North India Eastwards was severely curtailed with East Bengal being reconstituted as East Pakistan, later emerging as the independent nation of Bangladesh.

Bangladesh gained independence in 1971 with support and armed intervention by India. The internal politics in Bangladesh has, in the past, cast its shadow on relations between the two countries. The assassination of the Prime Minister of Bangladesh and the leader of the Awami League, Sheikh Mujibur Rahman on 15 August 1975 and the political turmoil that followed disrupted the close relations between India and Bangladesh. Gen. Zia-ur-Rahman who became the President of the country, founded the Bangla Nationalist Party in 1978 and sought to distance Bangladesh from India and focus on Bangladesh's Islamic identity. However, in 1981 he too was assassinated by a group of Army officers. In 1982, military rule was imposed in the country formally. The emergence of Bangla National Party and the Awami League in the 1990s, led to the two parties forming governments in rotation. However, A period of instability followed with cliques within the military siding with different parties and conspiring and attacking each other.

This period of instability in Bangladesh had its impact on India's NE Region as well. The continued influence of the army and the growing involvement of Pakistani Intelligence services in Bangladesh affairs made dealing with insurgency in the NER all the more difficult. It is no accident that the peak of civic disturbance and insurgency in the NER coincided with political turmoil in Bangladesh for nearly three decades following 1982.

The situation in Bangladesh and relations with India improved gradually after the return of the Awami League in 2008. The cooperation since extended by Bangladesh by denying insurgents sanctuary in Bangladesh and repatriating some of the top insurgent leaders hiding there was a great help in neutralising insurgency and extremism in the Northeast. Currently, a spirit of cooperation prevails between the two countries[1] which both would do well to nurture. Yet the internal developments in both India and Bangladesh have the potential of disrupting this cooperative phase.

The 4096 km long Bangladesh-India border is the fifth-longest in the world. For a very long time, due to migration related issues and support extended by Bangladeshi authorities to insurgency in the NER, Indian approach was to seal of the Border by fencing and intensive patrolling by BSF, with only a few closely monitored transit points. As a result, Indo-Bangla trade was very difficult and limited representing only about 10 percent of Bangladesh's trade and 1 percent of India's trade. These figures compare poorly with East Asian economies, where intraregional trade accounts for 50 percent total trade.

Within the South Asian Region, however, Bangladesh is now India's largest trading partner, accounting for 32.26% of India's trade in the region in 2021[2]. Insofar as NER is concerned, since 2008, trade points across the international border have also been gradually increased. As of now Bangladesh has five land ports with Tripura, Meghalaya and Assam. Another seven are envisaged in these states.

India's northeastern states are connected with the rest of India only through the Siliguri corridor, (the" chicken's neck.") This has led to long and costly routes between northeast India and the rest of India and the world. The opening of new transit routes for Indian trucks travelling to and from northeast India through Bangladesh, operationalisation of the India-Bangladesh-Nepal Motor Vehicles Agreement (MVA) and the removal of border frictions for bilateral trade are critical to enabling significant economic benefits to Bangladesh and India.

Bangladesh is positive to developing as a transit hub in the eastern part of the Indian sub-continent. Connectivity so created would be beneficial to the economic growth of Bangladesh, which would be the preferred transit route for a host of goods meant not only for the NER but also Bhutan and Nepal. For these countries as well as NER, access to the sea would be economically available through Bangladesh. Bangladesh has responded gradually but positively to restoration of connectivity across its territories. Several rail links between India and Bangladesh that existed in pre-Partition times have been restored. Similar progress has been made regarding river routes as well. Bangladesh Ports have been opened up to goods traffic meant for the Indian NER. Further development of river transport systems, in addition to providing a cheaper mode of transport would open the entire region to coastal trade as well. However seamless transit through Bangladesh for North eastern States is yet to be achieved.

Bangladesh, Bhutan, India, Nepal (BBIN) arrangements are well suited for such trans-national infrastructure of all kinds and should be developed as a much larger investment platform. Issues relating to sharing of river waters such as the Ganga, Teesta etc have been bedevilled Indo-Bangla relations in the past with overhang over cooperation in other spheres as well. Therefore, for progress to be made on transit arrangements through Bangladesh, understanding and agreement has to be fostered on sharing of river waters as well. This is a priority area for both India and Bangladesh and past experience indicates that progress on both is to some extent interlinked.

Bangladesh, therefore, has to be viewed as critical for connectivity of the rest of India to NER and beyond as well as for the overall peace and economic development of the NER. The ongoing talks between India and Bangladesh for a Comprehensive Economic Partnership Agreement (CEPA) and the recent accord on sharing of Kushiara River waters are encouraging. However much more needs to be done. As of date, the relations between the two countries are warm and point towards progress on all fronts. This has created a momentum that must not be lost.

Nepal

Over millennia, as close neighbours, India and Nepal have deep-rooted people-to-people contacts of kinship and culture. The two countries have maintained an open border with a long tradition of free movement of people across the Indo- Nepal border stretching over 1868 km and touching five Indian states – Sikkim, West Bengal, Bihar, Uttar Pradesh and Uttarakhand. The India-Nepal Treaty of Peace and Friendship of 1950[3] forms the bedrock of the special relations that exist between India and Nepal. Nepalese citizens avail facilities and opportunities on par with Indian citizens in accordance with the provisions of the Treaty and nearly 8 million Nepalese citizens live and work in India.

However, kinship and cultural affinity apart, the relations between India and Nepal have also seen their ups and downs over the last several decades. The relations dipped after the India annexed the Kingdom of Sikkim in 1975 when Nepal advocated a Zone of Peace in the Himalayas to which India was quite lukewarm. This was followed by disputes on trade and transit resulting in the existing trade and transit treaties with India expiring in 1989 without a fresh treaty being entered into. This led to the economic blockade of Nepal by India in 1989-90 and was followed by delinking of Nepalese Rupee from the Indian Rupee.

Efforts were made in the 1990s to restore relations. The blockade ended and a dialogue was restarted. But Indo-Nepal relations took a turn for the worse with the end of the monarchy in Nepal in 2001 when King Birendra, Queen Aishwarya and their family were assassinated. Also, ever since 1990, Nepal had seen the rise of a strong Maoist opposition to the monarchy and elected form of government. In 2006, King Gyanendra, successor to King Birendra, was also forced to relinquish power. On 21 November, 2006, the then Nepalese Prime Minister Girija Prasad Koirala and chairman of the Maoist movement in Nepal, Pushpa Kamal Dahal (also known as Prachanda), signed a Comprehensive Peace Agreement (CPA) 2006, committing to democracy. A Constituent Assembly was elected in 2008 which on 28 May, 2008 declared Nepal a Federal Democratic Republic, formally abolishing the 240-year-old monarchy.

Nepal today has a President as Head of State and a Prime Minister heading the Government. However, the dynamics of electoral politics and changes in Government in Nepal has been accompanied by ebb and flow of the relations with India. In recent years, the influence of Maoism in Nepal and emergence of the Madhesi movement, (which sought equal rights for Nepal's Madhes region) in Nepal's domestic politics, along with the strengthening economic and political influence of the People's Republic of China has caused the Nepalese government to gradually distance itself in its ties with India. This has also led to voices within Nepal to revise the pact to reflect "new changes and realities". While India has reiterated its commitment and support to Nepal, Nepal has been trying to balance its relations with its two neighbours. However, occasional spats between Nepal and India over boundary claims apart, gradually the relations between the two countries have settled down to a dialogue with a realistic appreciation of each other's interests.

Despite all the swings in Indo-Nepal relations, today, India is Nepal's largest trade partner[4]. Indo-Nepalese trade had been growing steadily, though it suffered a setback during the Covid pandemic. It has bounced back again[5].

Good relations with Nepal are a strategic necessity for India, sitting as Nepal does over the Siliguri Corridor linking India to North-eastern region. Nepal also adjoins Sikkim, a sensitive NE state bordering China. Nepal has also been a hotbed of activities by intelligence agencies of both India and Pakistan, and of late also China. On its part, being landlocked, Nepal's major concern has been its lack of access to the rest of the world, a concern that has deeply influenced Indo Nepal relations in the past. Transport connectivity would remain a major issue in Indo-Nepal relations. Nepal would need access to the sea for its economy to develop. This can be facilitated only through India and economically, via ports in both West Bengal (India) and Bangladesh. Development of transnational road and river systems across Nepal, India and Bangladesh enable vehicles and vessels bearing goods to move to and from Nepal in a more cost-effective manner. Therefore, while there are several areas of bilateral cooperation between India and Nepal, integrating Nepal into the connectivity infrastructure in the Eastern region is critical to building lasting and sustainable relations with that country[6]. The BBIN initiative is a good platform that can enable transnational connectivity in India's immediate neighbourhood, with considerable direct benefit to Nepal and indirect benefits to all the participating countries.

There are several areas where both countries can cooperate bilaterally with each other to mutual benefit of both. Of these water resources management concerning the common rivers is one of the most important. A large number of small and large rivers flow from Nepal to India and constitute an important part of the Ganges River basin. These rivers are major sources of flooding in both Nepal and India, but if tamed, could provide irrigation and power to both countries. A three-tier bilateral mechanism was established in 2008, to discuss issues relating to cooperation in water resources between the two countries but needs to convert dialogue into concrete action on river management, irrigation and flood control.

Electricity exchanges represent yet another area of mutually beneficial cooperation between India and Nepal. While India and Nepal have had a Power Exchange Agreement since 1971, along with transmission interconnections for power exchange in the bordering areas, an agreement on 'Electric Power Trade, Cross-border Transmission Interconnection and Grid Connectivity' between India and Nepal was signed on 21 October 2014 to facilitate and further strengthen cross-border electricity transmission, grid connectivity and power trade between the two countries. Under this initiative For India has funded the first high-capacity 400 kV cross-border power transmission line (completed 2016) followed by two additional 132 kV cross-border transmission lines in 2017. India is currently also supplying about 600 MW of power to Nepal. South Asia's first cross-border petroleum products pipeline, constructed and funded by Indian Oil

Corporation Ltd., connecting Motihari in India to Amlekhgunj in Nepal was inaugurated in September 2019.

For Nepal to unlock its economic potential, it is imperative to transform its transport into economic corridors that have potential for attracting private investments and generate job opportunities. They can result in other benefits such as narrowing down development gaps among the plains and the Kathmandu Valley with its hilly regions by providing them better access to production networks and regional markets.

From sub-regional trade perspective, Nepal's 1,868-km border with India has 20 entry and exit points for trade. In recent years, India has also been assisting Nepal in the development of border infrastructure through upgradation of roads; cross-border rail links and establishment of Integrated Check Posts. However, despite these efforts, traffic congestion, high transportation costs and poor quality of transit regimes make the movement of persons and goods cumbersome and costly.

Post Covid pandemic and with the continuing war in Ukraine, Nepal is faced with a brewing economic crisis. Its foreign exchange reserves have fallen, inflation is high and crop loss due to natural disasters has added to its food-fuel inflation. With food, fuel and commodity prices surging internationally in the wake of the Russia-Ukraine war, rapidly increasing expenditure on imports has contributed to a significant depletion in foreign exchange reserves and ballooning of the balance of payment deficit. It is important to enable economic stabilisation of Nepal through significant ramping up of Indo-Nepal trade facilitation before economic problems snowball into political unrest. As in the past, such unrest is bound to have negative connotations for India.

Myanmar

Looking East beyond the NER, Myanmar (earlier Burma) is an extremely important country in the immediate neighbourhood of the NER. Being the land bridge to South East Asia, the dynamics of the internal situation in that country has an immediate bearing on India's land connectivity and economic relations with SE Asia as well as internal and national security of the NER. A brief review of the political developments in Myanmar is relevant to understanding the challenges associated in engaging with that country.

Myanmar gained its independence on 4 January 1948 from the United Kingdom. After independence an effort was made to establish a constitutional government in Myanmar but due to absence of nationwide administrative framework, poor governance and rising ethnic insurgencies, failed to last. Finally, the military, known in Myanmar as "Tatmadaw" was invited to form a caretaker government in 1958. The military junta announced an election in 1960 which was held and led to a civilian government under U Nu. Political infighting and internal strife fuelled by multiple insurgencies, however continued, leading to a military *coup* on 2 March, 1962 under General Ne Win. After the *coup*, the military government suspended the Constitution, and appointed a Union Revolutionary Council (RC) and governed Myanmar by decree. Thereafter, military rule in Myanmar continued till 2010. Since independence, Myanmar has also been engrossed in rampant ethnic strife ever since with its many ethnic groups engaged in conflict with each other or with the Myanmar Central Government.

During the first period of military rule under General Ne Win, which continued till 1988, the country was shaped into one-party socialist state under the army led party called as Burma Socialist Programme Party (BSPP). Though outwardly stable, the country continued to face violent internal conflict, with the military's hold over several areas in the North being quite tenuous. However, in the 1990s there was another movement for restoration of democracy in Myanmar which resulted in the Military Junta agreeing to a phased return to election-based governance. This movement was spearheaded by the National League for Democracy, founded on 27 September 1988 and led by Aung San Suu Kyi, the daughter of Myanmar's national hero General Aung San who had led the fight for the country's independence in 1940s. The party won a substantial parliamentary majority in the 1990 Myanmar general election. However, the ruling military junta refused to recognise the result.

Eventually, in 2008, a new constitution was prepared, approved by referendum and brought into force. However, under the 2008 constitution, it was ensured that the military would continue to hold predominant position in the country's governance. For instance, the military would appoint the Union Election Commission and have the final say over the election results. Key ministries including justice, defence and the interior would also remain under its control in addition to a large number of seats being reserved for the military. The 224-member House of Nationalities would have 168 elected candidates and 56 nominated by the military chief, while the 440-member House of Representatives would have 330 elected civilians and 110 military representatives. Other laws restricting participation of a several categories of citizens in the political process were also passed.

General elections were held in Myanmar on 7 November 2010, in accordance with the new constitution. However, the National League for Democracy boycotted the elections due to its opposition to the election laws and also because many of its most prominent members were barred from participation. The election was consequently won in a landslide by the military-backed Union Solidarity and Development Party, USDP. In 2011, the military junta was officially dissolved, and a nominally civilian government was installed.

However, the 2011 election came in for a lot of criticism. Eventually the military junta entered into a dialogue with the NLD and made some concessions. Following this, the NLD announced its intention to re-register as a political party. In the 2012 by-elections, the NLD contested 44 of the 45 available seats under the leadership of Aung San Suu Kyi, winning 43. Later, in the 2015 general election, the NLD won a supermajority in both houses of the Assembly, paving the way for the country's first non-military president in 54 years. However, Aung San Suu Kyi could not be appointed President due to a special law passed by the military but was designated State Counsellor. NLD's win was repeated in 2020 by even bigger margins. However, in 2021, another military takeover followed and the elected government was deposed. This sparked off popular protests, a state of affairs that persists in Myanmar even today. Meanwhile, Myanmar faced major criticism in its treatment of the Rohingya minority.

The Rohingya Crisis

The Rohingya are a Muslim ethnic minority group who have lived for centuries in predominantly Buddhist Myanmar. Despite living in Myanmar for many generations, the Rohingya are not recognised as an official ethnic group and have been denied citizenship since 1982, making them the world's largest stateless population. The United Nations has described the Rohingya as "the most persecuted minority in the world."

In August 2017, a wave of ethnic violence broke out in Myanmar's Rakhine State in areas dominated by Rohingyas, reportedly with the participation of the "Rohingiya Arsa', a Rohingya armed group. The Myanmar military retaliated by military operations which the United Nations later described as a "textbook example of ethnic cleansing". Entire villages were burned to the ground, thousands of persons were killed or violently separated from their families, forcing more than 900,000 Rohingyas - half of them children - to seek refuge in the Cox Bazar's region of Bangladesh. The army in Myanmar, however, maintained it was fighting Rohingya militants and denied targeting civilians. Myanmar now faces a lawsuit accusing it of genocide at the International Court of Justice (ICJ), while the International Criminal Court is investigating the country for crimes against humanity. The country's elected government led by Aung San Suu Kyi repeatedly denied allegations of genocide but could not, or did not, do anything to condemn or restrain the army or restore peace.

Return of Tatmadaw

In the 2020 election, Aung San Suu Kyi led NLD once again won a landslide majority, getting even more votes than in the 2015 vote. Having faced considerable international criticism over handling of the Rohingya issue it was expected that the Government of Myanmar would take steps to deal with the plight of the Rohingyas. The still powerful military however disputed the results, claiming election fraud. On the day new parliament was to a sit for the first time, the Tatmadaw detained State Counsellor Aung San Suu Kyi, President Win Myint, and other government leaders. They then proceeded to take control of the government, and instituted a state of emergency, with Burma's Commander-in-chief of the armed forces, Min Aung Hlaing, as the Leader of the country.

Protests for Restoration of Democracy

The military coup d'etat evoked immediate mass protests in Myanmar which were attempted to be brutally suppressed by the army, with more than thousands[7a] of protesters being killed and several thousand more imprisoned under extremely harsh conditions. However, despite its harsh response and use of force, the military has not been able to quell popular protests, which are gradually turning more violent. The struggle for restoration of democracy in Myanmar has turned bloody but is continuing. After the 2021 coup d'etat, the National Unity Government, in forefront of the resistance against the Myanmar military government, has formed an armed wing, named the People Defence Force estimated to be numbering nearly 50000, consisting of several local resistance groups and other newly-formed anti-junta ethnic militias, such as the Karenni People's Defence Force and the Chinland Defence Force.

The internal situation in Myanmar, which in any case remains disturbed due to the presence of a large number (over 30) of armed insurgent groups and armies, some of them having cadres numbering thousands, has been made worse by the *coup d'etat*. Many of them have been in conflict with the Myanmar military over half a century are violently opposed to the military junta. They control vast areas where reach and influence of the Myanmar government is quite limited. The situation post 2021 military takeover has thrown the country into turmoil and its economy into shambles, a situation made worse by international sanctions imposed by western countries.

Engaging Myanmar

The disturbed conditions in Myanmar make India's border with that country very volatile. There is little likelihood of direct armed conflict between India and Myanmar. However, the porous border is now more susceptible to movement of insurgents, extremists, on the one hand and of illegal arms, drugs etc. on the other. Movement of involuntarily displaced persons, many belonging to ethnic groups populating both sides of India-Myanmar border lays the bordering states open to illegal immigration also. Currently many of the hard-line factions of the NE insurgents, driven out of NER, have taken shelter there. Some of them are attempting to form a coalition centered around Western South East Asia.

Myanmar, during the decade 2010-20, was the focus of several initiatives taken up by India to improve connectivity with SE Asia[7]. The chaotic law and order situation in Myanmar has, however, put paid to any near term hopes of using Myanmar as a land bridge connecting NER to SE Asia. However, the disturbed conditions in that country post Military coup and activities of such armed groups and factions in that country have resulted in disruptions in completion of infrastructural projects taken up in Myanmar through Indian assistance such as the Kaladan Multi Modal Connectivity project. In fact, many road and rail connectivity initiatives across Myanmar stalled as Myanmar withdrew from some and was unable to perform its obligations in others.

The relations between Myanmar and Bangladesh, post the Rohingiya Crisis, also remain a cause for concern, with their overhang on initiatives such as BIMSTEC. Cut off from international trade by sanctions, the military rulers of Myanmar turned more towards China who strongly supported crushing of pro-democracy protests and promised all types of aid to Junta. India has also been treading a careful line by keeping its diplomatic channels open but without actively supporting the repressive military regime. Therefore, India is faced with a very difficult phase of economic and diplomatic engagement with Myanmar. As things stand today securing any kind of Myanmar economic cooperation to regional international initiatives is difficult. Given the internal conditions in Myanmar, absent any radical change in the governance of that country, this appears to be quite a challenging task in the foreseeable future as well.

Bhutan

Ties between Bhutan and the great Indian culture and civilisation are ages old. Guru Padmasambhava, a Buddhist saint from the region falling within present-day Bihar in India played an influential role in spreading Buddhism and cementing traditional ties between people in both nations.

In modern times the engagement formally dates back to 1910 when Bhutan became a protectorate of British India, allowing the British to "guide" its foreign affairs and defence. When India declared independence in 1947, Bhutan was among the first nations to recognise it. Since then, the relationship between the countries has become stronger, especially because Bhutan also has a historically tense relationship with China, particularly after the Chinese annexation of Tibet, and in recent times due to Chinese occupation and militarisation of the of the Doklam plateau, a disputed strip of land between Bhutan and China.

The basis for bilateral relations between India and Bhutan was formed by the Indo-Bhutan Treaty of Perpetual Peace and Friendship of 1949[8]. However, Article 2 of the treaty critically gave India a role in guiding Bhutan's foreign policy. Some changes in the treaty were made in 2007[9] recognising the sovereign status of Bhutan and allowing Bhutan to import arms as long as Indian interests are not harmed and there was no re-export of the weapons. In addition, the current treaty provides for 'national treatment' and equal privileges for citizens on each other's soil.

India opened an office of a Special Representative in Thimphu in 1968, Bhutan reciprocated in 1971. The two offices of special representatives were upgraded to full-fledged embassies in 1978.

During the 1990s many Assam extremists and insurgents set up bases in Bhutan from where they carried out their activities in India. Eventually, with cooperation of Bhutan, the Indian army, in collaboration with the Royal Bhutan Army launched special operations killing or capturing most of the insurgents hiding there and destroying extremist camps.

India is Bhutan's largest trading partner[10]. In 2018, total bilateral trade between the two countries stood at Rs. 9227.7 crores. Over last two-three decades, India has also made considerable investment in Bhutan to tap its hydro -electric potential by construction of dams along with power generation. The electricity generated is purchased by India thereby enabling revenues to the Bhutan exchequer. Four hydro-electric projects (HEPs) totalling 2136 MW are already operational in Bhutan and are supplying electricity to India. This hydropower cooperation comes under 2006 Agreement on Cooperation in Hydropower. India is also the most popular educational destination for Bhutanese students -almost 4000 Bhutanese students are enrolled in Indian Universities at any time, many of whom are also provided scholarship by Govt. of India.

Today Bhutan continues with its special relationship with India and forms an important pillar of the BBIN partnership.

Building Local Engagement: Border Trade

As mentioned earlier, India has generally adopted a very restrictive border-trade policy framework, particularly with Myanmar, with trade being permitted only in a limited number of locally produced items through barter. Border trade with Bangladesh, however, has been receiving support from both countries. In December 2015, however, there was a shift from "Barter Trade" to "Normal Trade" along Indo-Myanmar border with a greater emphasis on Normal Trade.

Even though a small start, the recognition of the value of border trade and efforts for its resumption are a welcome development. However, lack of agreement between the designated banks on both sides (e.g. on availing the Letter of Credit (LoC) facilities and allowing currency conversion), several restrictions on exports as well as on the number of items in barter trade inhibit border trade. There is a need to liberalise this regime further. The movement along each of these issues is likely to be slow considering the cross-border nature of insurgency on either side and in case of Myanmar, restrictions imposed by the Military Junta in that country.

However, the emphasis on agriculture and border trade should be maintained along both Bangladesh and Myanmar. There is also a need to put into place appropriate infrastructure that provides access from both sides, basic amenities including shelter, gender sensitive toilets and clean drinking water as well as arrangements for shelter and storage of commodities. Both countries need to enter into protocols that allow movement of their respective nationals in each other's territory while enabling the BSF/ Assam Rifles and corresponding border guards on Bangladesh (Bangladesh Rifles) and Myanmar to better monitor safety and security to participants along the border. India may also consider a Special Economic Zone at Moreh.

Building Engagement: Disaster Management in the Neighbourhood

All the countries in the South Asian region—Bangladesh, Bhutan, India, Nepal, Pakistan, and Sri Lanka—are prone to extreme weather and geological events- floods, landslides, droughts, cyclones, earthquakes, and tsunamis etc. As population and urban/semi-urban centres have grown, the estimated total population affected as also estimated damage resulting from such events has increased over time. With changing climatic conditions, natural disasters are likely to increase further in frequency as well as intensity across the region.

The NER Region and its immediate neighbourhood comprising Bangladesh, Bhutan, Nepal is even more vulnerable. Being located in the Himalayan/ sub-Himalayan region, it is subject to high level of seismic activity and catastrophic flood. Despite the common challenges faced by the South Asian countries, regional cooperation for disaster management has been limited.

While South Asian countries have their respective disaster management agencies, there is little disaster anticipation, planning or preparedness. For one, the hostile relations between India and Pakistan have resulted in SAARC being rendered ineffective- so much so that two countries have refused to even participate in SAARC meetings in each other's territory. Further, the emergency response to natural disasters is dominated by the national armed forces as they possess training in human resources, equipment, and capabilities not available to other agencies and nonstate actors. This is often one of the key challenges in regional cooperation, or in planning for and building disaster resilience, as each country is wary of inviting neighbouring armed forces into their territory. Armed forces from other countries may be used, if at all, to handle post-disaster emergency operations. Consequently, bilateral and multilateral agreements for disaster management, which require patient cooperation over a longer period of time, have had limited success.

The devastating earthquakes that ravaged Nepal in the spring of 2015 demonstrated the risk of disaster that affects all of South Asia. They also demonstrated the real limits to a regional disaster management and response. According to The Kathmandu Post, almost 4175 troops from 18 countries were deployed for rescue and relief operations. However, SAARC had no plan for this response mode of transporting relief materials. The lack of a pre-coordinated plan or resource management created tensions even in the capital Kathmandu. The situation in remote areas, where the road links were damaged and helicopters were the only mode of transporting relief materials, was even worse.

Recently, in 2022, the severe floods that ravaged Pakistan, killing nearly 1500 deaths and rendering millions homeless also highlighted the inability of SAARC or any regional mechanism to help in disaster management and render humanitarian aid. To some extent this is an outcome much of Pakistan's own making. Yet SAARC's inability to overcome strained relations between two of its members and focus on areas of mutual interest reveals its weakness.

In this respect the ASEAN experience is worth a closer scrutiny. In 2003, just before the tsunami, the ASEAN established the ASEAN Committee of Disaster Management (ACDM) which formulated its Comprehensive Agreement on Disaster Management and Emergency Response in 2005, followed by a Framework for Work Program. This Framework enables cooperation, coordination, and technical assistance for disaster management in the ASEAN region; A Coordinating Centre for Humanitarian Assistance on disaster management was also set up in Jakarta in 2011 to coordinate emergency operations. This Centre, in addition to developing a common vision among the member states with respect to disaster management, encouraged members to develop professionalism with various exercises in different countries, stockpile relief goods, and maintain consistent and adequate budget and staffing.

While the abiding hostility between India and Pakistan combined with the presence of China through its BRI initiative has rendered SAARC or any South Asian regional grouping unlikely in the foreseeable future, it may be worthwhile to restart some regional initiative in the BBIN or BIMSTEC region. India is in a unique position, with its scientific and technical manpower and Disaster management organisations at the central and state level to build up a framework similar to the ASEAN in say, the BBIN region with a reservoir of expertise on the subject to be shared through civilian channels. It can contribute significantly towards capacity building in all aspects of disaster management. This involves building on shared empathy toward regional neighbours and facilitating public cooperation and partnerships across the national borders. However, establishing networks for disaster management that would foster cooperation at

Government, institutional and individual level would help in augmenting local preparedness, mitigation, response, and recovery efforts. Besides it would build lasting ties between people that would transcend beyond political changes in respective countries.

Notes to Chapter 16

1. Indo-Bangladesh trade has been increasing steadily since 2008 when it was just US$ 3.6 billion, to reach US$ 15.83 Bn in 2021. It has been heavily skewed towards exports from India, with US$ 14.07 Bn Exports; US$ 1.76 Bn Imports- an issue likely to figure in future Indo-Bangla Trade talks.

2. Despite ups and downs in the past, Indo-Bangla relations are currently friendly and based on mutual cooperation. The land boundary agreement between India and Bangladesh, signed on 6 June 2015, settled decades old border disputes. However, negotiations over the sharing of water of the transboundary rivers are still ongoing.

3. Treaty of Peace and Friendship Between The Government Of India And The Government Of Nepal; Ministry of External Affairs, Government of India; https://mea.gov.in/bilateral-documents. Treaty of Peace and Friendship

4. India is the largest trading partner of Nepal. Total bilateral trade in 2018-19 reached INR 57,858 cr. (US$ 8.27 bn) in 2019-20. While Nepal's exports to India stood at INR 3558 cr. (US$ 508 mn), India's exports to Nepal were INR 54,300 cr. (US$ 7.76 bn). Indian firms are among the largest investors in Nepal, accounting for more than 30% of the total approved foreign direct investments in that country. Nepal is India's 11th largest export destination, up from 28th position in 2014. In FY 2021-22, it constituted 2.34% of India's exports. (Ministry of External Affairs, Government of India)

5. Indo-Nepal bilateral trade reached over US$ 7.66 billion during the last eleven months of the fiscal year 2020-21, with Imports from India amounting to US$6.95 billion and exports to India over US$0.07Bn.

6. There is potential for developing four economic corridors in Nepal, all culminating at some major production/consumption centres in India. In turn, they could get connected with the national highway networks of India. Out of them, the construction of the Western (Karnali) Corridor is in progress, and a major part has already been completed. The success of this corridor can serve as a good example of how economic corridors can contribute to inclusive growth and reduce transportation costs.

7a. Since the coup in February 2021, the military and its allies have killed at least 3,452 people, according to the U.N.

7. India-Myanmar bilateral trade grew from US$ 994.45 million in 2007-08 to US$ 1.6 billion in 2017-18, an approximate increase of 61 per cent. However, in 2017-18, there was a significant decline of 26 per cent in India Myanmar trade from the previous year with India banning lentil imports from Myanmar. Trade slowly recovered in 2020, growing to about $1.61 Bn again. The Military coup of 2021 has disrupted trade again in 2021 with estimates pitching the bilateral trade level at about $1.3-$1.4 Bn.

8. Treaty of Perpetual Peace and Friendship Between the Government of India and The Government of Bhutan, Darjeeling, 8 August 1949; Ministry of External Affairs, Government of India.

9. India re-negotiated the 1949 treaty with Bhutan and signed a new treaty of friendship in 2007. Whereas The 1949 Treaty provided that " The Government of India undertakes to exercise no interference in the internal administration of Bhutan. On its part the Government of Bhutan agrees to be guided by the advice of the Government of India in regard to its external relations." The new treaty provides that " In keeping with the abiding ties of close friendship and cooperation between Bhutan and India, the Government of the Kingdom of Bhutan and the Government of the Republic of India shall cooperate closely with each other on issues relating to their national interests. Neither Government shall allow the use of its territory for activities harmful to the national security and interest of the other"

10. India has been the largest and the most important trading partner for Bhutan since 1961, when Bhutan's development Plans were launched. In 2020, overall trade with India was recorded at Nu. 94.89 billion (including electricity), which accounted for 82% of Bhutan's total external trade and the figure without including electricity was recorded at Nu. 67.18 billion, which accounted for 77% of Bhutan's total trade. The overall import from India accounted for 87% of the total import value with or without taking into account trade in electricity. Exports to India accounts for 90% of total exports including electricity and 77% without electricity.

Chapter 17

Strategic Interplay- India's Comprehensive National Power and Engagement East

The Indian economy has grown steadily over the last several decades so that it is now world's fifth-largest economy. Meanwhile, the rapid development of ASEAN countries South East Asia, emergence of China as a world economic and military super-power, the enduring economic might of Japan and South Korea have resulted in greater attention being paid by India to East Asia, as a means of expanding its economic space beyond its formerly wholly westward orientation. The Look East Policy of the 1990s was a recognition of the potential of engaging within Asia and has been further strengthened and carried forward through the current Act East Policy.

Over millennia, the SE Asian Region, earlier known as Indo-China, has been a confluence of Indian and Chinese trade flows and cultural influences. India has had historic links with each of the ASEAN countries. The positive role played by India during the de-colonisation phase in Southeast Asia has built considerable goodwill for India. The economic engagement with ASEAN was a logical re-establishment of mutually benefit trade ties with the SE Asian region that had been disrupted by the exploitative links during the colonial period that affected both India and ASEAN equally. Ever since the 1990s India has engaged systematically with ASEAN across a wide range of economic and trade related arrangements. This engagement needs to be strengthened further.

The spread of ASEAN countries deep into the Pacific Ocean makes this region critical for access by India to the Pacific and beyond to the US, Japan and the Americas. Therefore, even though the task has made all the more complex by the emergence of new trade arrangements such as the RCEP, maintaining a systematically expanding economic engagement with ASEAN has to be an abiding feature of the Act East Policy. To continue the momentum of economic engagement with SE Asia, India would have to take a few decisions regarding the nature of its participation in the new trade arrangements in the region.

However, the growing economic might of China, its strained relations with India due to the border stand-off, its aggressive stance in the South China Sea and its looming presence in South East Asia is perceived as creating a hegemony that could be detrimental to India's economic and security interests in SE Asia. From focus upon an increasing economic engagement with ASEAN, India is looking at a greater trade and security framework that goes beyond ASEAN and encompasses the Indo-Pacific region. This has resulted in India's participation in groupings such as the QUAD. However, irrespective of various geo-political perceptions or Indo-Pacific aspirations, India can ill afford to neglect the SE Asian Region. In fact, strategically, it is critical for India to maintain and strengthen its security and cultural engagement with this region.

Acting East, it would be prudent to build upon its Neighbourhood First approach and integrate it in the Act East Policy. In India's Eastern and NE Region, this combination translates into close relations with the countries adjoining its Borders in the East and North East. India's participation in various regional groupings such as BBIN, BIMSTEC etc. in addition to a deepening relation with ASEAN would provide strong leverage to a growing and sustainable arrangement. This approach is relevant in a global environment badly disrupted by the Covid Pandemic, the war in Ukraine, international shortages and price volatility in petroleum products, fertilisers and food. The global trade order and flows are also affected by the New Cold War between the Western World on one side and China and Russia on the other. The growing nationalistic sentiment, seen even in developed countries, which seeks self-sufficiency rather than economic inter-connectivity, is, however not conducive to smooth operation of the global trade system, disrupted as it is due to the recent pandemic. There is now a tendency to form regional trading blocs and zones. For India, in so far as Asia is concerned, give difficulties of access to West and Central Asia, Acting East is a natural choice.

While the growing economic engagement eastwards will require full involvement of Indian economic strengths and capacities, the North Eastern Region holds the key to a deeper engagement with the countries located in India's immediate eastern neighbourhood as well as ASEAN. However, all the constituent units of the NER have unique identities and histories stretching back several centuries, if not millennia. Effort would be required to enable all the NE states to contribute their unique strengths to enable a growing, diversified but comprehensive economy in the region that can meaningfully engage with the neighbourhood as well as with SE Asia.

Given the turbulent past of India's North East, the work in process of assimilation into the modern Indian state and the undercurrent of conflict powered by clashing ethnic identities, there is a need to change the narrative from confrontation to cooperation. Economic Development of NER has to be based on a new narrative that builds upon trust and cooperation, encourages innovation to facilitate technology-based production systems, trade and commerce, enables widespread gainful employment, rising incomes and standards of living of the people at large is a key lever to bring about the confluence of the economic growth, internal security, international engagement and national defence. Most important, for such engagement to be sustainable, the NER has to develop in a manner that enables it to participate in the business networks and supply chains across the SE Region and add value to them.

The NER has unique and intense problems of external and internal security. However, over the last half century or so, the NER has overcome several phases of internal disturbance. India has been successful in resolving such conflicts and despite challenges, will continue to do so in future. Public safety, law and order, Internal security and national defence have to improve to provide the bedrock for economic activity. Today India has a well-developed security architecture in the North East that can meet any internal and external threat. It will need to be maintained for the foreseeable future to build confidence and ensure that the region continues on a positive developmental path and help India build credible relationships with the ASEAN region.

While good governance, institution building, internal and external security are critical to opening up the path of development and modernising the economy of the NER, in addition to the engagement with ASEAN, a strong economic engagement with India's immediate neighbourhood in the East comprising Bangladesh, Bhutan and Nepal (the BBIN Region) and Myanmar is equally important for the region's stability and progress. For a harmonious relationship to be achieved, India's international borders with Bangladesh Bhutan, Nepal and Myanmar have to be managed through trained personnel, both civil and paramilitary, with use of communications and technology that allows movement of legitimate personnel and goods

251

efficiently while addressing concerns relating to illegal immigration and smuggling.

The historical development of each country located around NER has been complex and unique. The relations of these countries with India have also followed a convoluted path alternating between friendship and outright hostility. Therefore, engagement with them would require a major diplomatic effort and considerable patience. It would, however, be well worth the effort for India to stay invested in the countries adjoining NER.

Time and again, events across the Globe have highlighted the importance of land connectivity in building a deep and abiding security and economic engagement across geographies. India's North Eastern Region is an extensive land bridge to SE Asia with age old cultural links. It can and should play the role of a platform and a bridge for India's strategic interests East in the times to come as well. For this to happen the requirements of intra-regional and international connectivity have to be met, institutional arrangements to meet the complexities of regional trade and economic exchanges created and the region plugged into the exchanges and supply chains for both the ASEAN as well as the BBIN region. By building upon the cultural connect and economic interdependence between various ASEAN countries as well its international neighbours the cycle of positive economic growth would not only contribute to internal security but also build India's Comprehensive National Power in the East in a sustainable manner.

To participate meaningfully in international trade flows, NER has first to be "brought up to speed" to match the imperatives and capacities of engagement with ASEAN countries who have, over the last half century, achieved tremendous economic progress and human development. This would require a comprehensive investment in human development through investments in health education and capacity building, efficient intra-regional connectivity, harmonisation of laws and resolution of jurisdictional issues and an environment encouraging entrepreneurship and business activity.

India's Comprehensive National Power (CNP) needs to be oriented towards building international partnerships and creating win-win situations amongst nations. While military strength and the ability to project it are essential elements of CNP, the purpose of CNP is best served by a strong military not as a tool to create regional hegemony or as an instrument of aggression, but to resolutely defend and protect its interests if diplomacy fails. Strength of a nation, however, lies in not only possessing CNP but in a nation's ability to deploy it in pursuit of its strategic aims. While India, due its size and strength has eventually to play a global role, given the emerging Asian and Geo-political scenario, India has to view its Engagement East as one of its strategic aims, critical to its national security and reinforcing its Indo-Pacific and global aspirations. A critical facilitator of this strategic aim is comprehensive development of the North East, with stable and credible business and trade institutions, enabling deeper international trade relations Eastwards. In that sense, the Act East Policy and the NER are inextricably tied together.